♡ For our BELOVED
Soul brother
Gary
We love you!
Sandra & Daniel ♡

CODEBREAKER

DISCOVER THE PASSWORD TO UNLOCK
THE BEST VERSION OF YOU

SANDRA AND DANIEL BISKIND

©2018, HEARTPOWER, LLC

MARINA DEL REY, CALIFORNIA

Published by HEARTPOWER, LLC

Cover and Book Design: Brooks Cole / HoloAgency

CODEBREAKER / SANDRA & DANIEL BISKIND
First Edition

ISBN: 978-1-54394-620-8

CAUTION: SPIRITUALLY INTOXICATING!
Do not drive or operate heavy machinery
while under the influence of this book.

PRAISE FOR SANDRA & DANIEL BISKIND

Sandra and Daniel are profound healers, trainers, speakers, and authors who do some exceptional transformational work. I've experienced their work and found it truly life changing— so much so that I had them work with my entire staff, with magical results. They have an amazing ability to shift energy and remove blocks on very deep levels.

From the first time I sat down with them, I knew something special and profound was about to happen. Their unconditional love, joy, and radiance filled the room. An hour later, I left more calm, more centered, more my true self, and more creative than I can remember. They are the real deal, and I highly recommend them and their work. It is transformational wizardry at its best.

~ JACK CANFIELD

Co-author of the *Chicken Soup for the Soul* series, *The Success Principles*, and a featured teacher in the film *The Secret*

By any measure, this book is destined to make contributions unmatched in such areas as love's importance, power, jump-starting the process, rating your state of love, and how to become the best version of yourself...And more good news: the book flows like a beautiful poem. It is at the same time impactive, instructive, surprising at times, profound, and yet easy to read and fun. My advice is to bask in the sun and LOVE that flows from the book into your heart, and learn how to let it flow from your heart into other hearts. You will love the experience.

~ WILLIAM BRYANT

Former Chairman of the Board, American Chamber of Commerce Executives

As a chiropractor, I've been aware of the importance of mind body connection, and I've experienced first hand what the mind can do to the body. But this book is like a fine art masterpiece in demonstrating the connection. "Intense emotional experiences often result in controlling programs that imprint DNA." And it's not just one generation.

Sandra and Daniel perfectly and clearly explain the difference between the ego mind code and the divine mind code. And, I'm here to tell you, Sandra and Daniel are living examples of the divine mind code where enlightened forgiveness is the anchor, the key to the code to live a PLATINUM life to the fullest.

Now, Sandra warned me that just holding the book would change my vibration. But when I read page 33, "A parent or sibling says things like, 'Who do you think you are?'" I had to put the book down. I looked around the room. It was like the book was speaking to me. You see, my mother always said those words, and asked, "Do you think the world is waiting for you?" I was hooked from that page on and had to learn how to break the code!! This book speaks to each and every one of us personally and profoundly.

Then the meditations were life-changing! The Four Questions were asked first on page 87: What am I feeling? What am I focused on? How do I want to feel? What focus will serve that? Well, by the time I saw them again on page 315, I was completely changed, and it was as though a different person had inhabited my body. And, that new person is here to stay.

My favorite was the Quantum Neutrality Process. While going through it, I actually felt my physical balance return and knew emotional balance was restored even more dramatically.

In summary, you must not only read this book, but live it!

~ DR. CAROL SOLOWAY

*CODEBREAKER comes straight from the heart and is written
so deceptively simply. I am sure that people reading it will
absorb the words on a very deep level without even realizing
the changes the words will be making in their lives!
Thank you both for your dedication to humanity and
for your ever-present, loving connection.*

~ ALISON QUEDLEY

Former publisher and editor *In Touch* magazine

*I've worked with a lot of healers, but rarely do I meet one who is as
quick to the heart of the matter as Sandra. In a matter of minutes,
she was tuned into the core issues I was dealing with and the root
causes. A few minutes later, I could feel a tangible shift, like a
weight had been lifted and a new level of energy had been opened.
Something was palpably different about me—and all of this in
minutes, not months! I look forward to what's possible with her
incredible work, and encourage anyone struggling with issues
(especially the seemingly unsolvable ones) to experience this
for themselves.*

~ DEREK RYDALL

Transformational coach, best-selling author of *Emergence*
and *The Abundance Project*

For all my life I have been uncomfortable expressing love to the people closest to me. There has always been this resistance to express the one emotion that is the essence of our existence. As a result, there has always been this hole in my life that I ignored and that has denied me the depth and richness of life I deserve. Sandra, in just three sessions, nailed what had happened in my past and knew what was preventing me from being the person I so desperately wanted to be.

She has a rare gift and talent to pick up what the blocks are and how to resolve them. As a coach for Tony Robbins and with many mentors in personal development, I know for a fact that very few have this ability. After working with her, I feel more at peace with myself and know that I am now on track to express and experience more love in my life.

~ GARY RUSH

Anthony Robbins business and success coach

As a private mentor, Sandra masterfully pinpointed the dynamics in my life that were blocking my joy, undermining my love relationships and curbing my financial success. With precision, she energetically disrupted the programs that were unconsciously running me. The root of all challenge is vibrational blockages and once she integrated them, my vibration and frequency were dramatically up-leveled. Today my life flows with ease, I'm healthier, happier and I feel fully in charge of my own destiny. Sandra embodies a gift that truly changes everything!

~ JAN DESAI

Soulspring.org

*Thank you both for developing the
PLATINUM life transformation program.*

*Our weekly show has been on the air for three years. That means
about 150 shows and therefore 150 guests. We've seen the content bar
get higher and higher every year. You proved that to be true on July
27th when you appeared on the show as our featured guests.*

*For starters, both of you blended and supported each other in what
turned out to be not only an informative conversation, but also an
enjoyable one. That's not easy to do unless that demeanor is already
part of your DNA. This was proof that you not only talk the (living
the PLATINUM life) talk but WALK it too.*

*So now for the reason why you were here, the content! The content
that you developed is way more than meets the eye but if we had to
say it in one word it would be...HOPE. You tell us through your own
life's example as well as through complicated research that if or
when we go through your program we will be transformed into a
peaceful and grounded force! One able to make a difference even
by just being present! Say what you want, but if you can find one
person that would not be interested in that transformation, we'll
gladly interview that person to find out why!*

*To say this program is needed right now in the workplace at all levels
is an understatement. I know we're grateful for meeting you both
and learning about your PLATINUM life program. Thank you!*

~ CHARLIE AND EVA

"Corporate Talk with Charlie and Eva"

Your book made my jaw drop. It was the most unbelievable feeling that came over me while I was reading it and since then. And I have searched for that feeling in every program, therapist, book, journal, coping skill on the planet. So to have found that feeling for the first time is the most incredible gift God has ever given me. And he worked through you to show me. I NEED to keep reading. Thank you both so much. I am truly grateful.

~ MOLLY COCHRAN

Sandra and Daniel Biskind are world leaders in teaching us to neutralize our emotional triggers...allowing us to discover the hidden triggers that rule our lives—and to disconnect their powerful impact! These extraordinary spiritual/personal growth leaders have nailed the formula that allows us to remove all the stressors that stand in the way of great peacefulness and resourcefulness. Once firmly established in "neutrality," then everything else is attainable—financial success, vibrant relationships, health, a life of purposeful meaning, and more. They guide us there with their love and their gift of wisdom.

~ JACKIE LAPIN

Best-selling author of *Practical Conscious Creation:
Daily Techniques to Manifest Your Desires*

Sandra has a direct connection to deep spiritual wisdom, and an uncanny ability to uncover the blind spots and help clear the blockages that keep you from living your best life. I highly recommend the powerful transformational work and books that the Biskinds are bestowing on the world.

~ DONNA STONEHAM, PHD

Author, *The Thriver's Edge*

To sift through my thoughts and find a completely different person than two days ago has brought me to a place of great appreciation, and Sandra, I need to thank you for this. For me, the amazement of your work is that my life's structure is still there; people didn't disappear. But, my deep emotions have changed. The shift that has taken place within me is unbelievable.

~ ALISON HORA

Professional diving instructor

One of the most important decisions I have ever made in my life was to work on a personal level with Sandra and Daniel. I have worked with them for more than eight years because doing this work shifts me from crisis point to a place of absolute relief and neutrality in a matter of minutes. It has transformed my life on every level and in every part of my life dramatically, and continues to do so. Thank you, Sandra and Daniel.

~ AMBER BRECH-HOLLINS

Mother of Gracie and Noah, and photographer

To say I am passionate about the new and improved direction in my life would be an understatement. Nothing I have ever done can compare to the breakthrough technology that I have been lucky enough to experience through Sandra and Daniel and their PLATINUM Life System programs.

~ ROBERT HURST

Business owner and entrepreneur

WOW! Words almost can't do justice to the incredible work that Sandra and Daniel do. To be able to go from totally on edge, stressed, depressed, angry, and "over life," to feeling happy, content, aligned, powerful, strong, and "in love" with life again, all in the space of a 30-minute session—truly amazing! I really appreciate being me again.

~ JAMES HOLLINS

Business owner and entrepreneur

"The timing for this work is perfect. From just one session with Sandra, a tremendous weight was lifted off my shoulders to move forward with my most important work in the world. And that same energy is contained within the pages of this work on many different levels...awaiting the aligned leaders, change makers and mischief makers ready to step forward in a bigger way."

~ YANIK SILVER

Author, *Evolved Enterprise*

Sandra and Daniel's work and the PLATINUM System presented in CODEBREAKER are superb! Experience more love, joy, peace, prosperity and make a greater contribution to others.

I am forever grateful for this work. I encourage busy CEO's, leaders & professionals to do this work and take your business to a place of more alignment, prosperity and greater contribution.

Magnificent!

~ DORIA (DC) CORDOVA

CEO/Owner, Excellerated Business Schools® / Money & You® Program

As President of the Canfield Training Group and past President of Chicken Soup for the Soul I have published 230 books in my day and I'm telling you this book is awesome! Sandra and Daniel are the secret sauce to my success. If you feel stuck or scattered or you're just totally frustrated and you're just not getting to the place you want to be - buy this book! It's going to change your game completely.

Jack and I work with them regularly — they are our personal confidantes. They coach us all the time and they have given us more information, and helped us with more breakthroughs than anyone we have worked with. So make sure you don't miss out and get Sandra and Daniel's book. You will absolutely love it.

~ PATTY AUBREY

7X's New York Times Best-selling Author
and the Woman Behind the World's First
Billion Dollar Book Series

CONTENTS

Chapter 2: LOVE:
Ignite the Secret to Your Success   92

FOREWORD

There are essentially two things that will make you wise— the books you read and the people you meet.

~ JACK CANFIELD

I still remember my first meeting with Sandra and Daniel at a mastermind in my home in Santa Barbara. I instantly felt the frequency of love they talk about in this book. I felt calm, clear and creative—more myself than I had felt in a long time—just from being in their presence. They walk their talk and fulfill on their promise of profound transformation. The frequency of love and stillness is transmitted in this book and, now that you have it in your hands, you can access it whenever you choose.

As a young man I was mentored by W. Clement Stone who introduced me to the field of personal transformation. In the years since, I've been privileged to know and work with many thought leaders from around the world. Personal transformation is my passion; it's in my blood and my DNA. My devotion to it in my own life, and my desire to help others transform their lives, was the motivation behind the *Chicken Soup for the Soul* series and *The Success Principles*, recently re-released in the 10th anniversary edition. In addition to my books, I've created numerous training programs; and our Train The Trainer program has become an industry standard. My involvement in the hit movie, *The Secret*, filmed at a meeting of the Transformational Leadership Council that I co-founded, was also spurred by my lifelong passion for personal transformation.

Both in my role as a teacher and in my private life, I've worked with the Law of Attraction and have decades of experience in the arena of overcoming limiting beliefs. I am keenly aware of the tenacity of certain beliefs that continue to impact people's lives, even after dozens of transformational workshops and years of therapy and coaching. So when Sandra and Daniel described their approach as a mind training system that truly sets people free, my interest was piqued. Their approach to solving the unsolvable is to address unconscious limiting beliefs—what they refer to as dysfunctional codes—in a fresh and utterly unique way.

I've experienced their work firsthand and can attest to the effectiveness of their system. In a single session, Sandra and Daniel helped me and my business partner achieve a huge breakthrough on an issue we'd been struggling with for two decades. That breakthrough took our relationship to a whole new level and led to a quantum leap in our business when we created a new and inspiring vision that is exciting to us and to our team.

Sandra and Daniel's gifts were also evident when they worked with members of our staff and facilitated a huge transformation in their interpersonal relationships. Our company culture was transformed into one that has an unusual degree of emotional freedom, which fosters creativity and brought about a notable breakthrough in productivity.

I've also witnessed the impact Sandra and Daniel have had at our private mastermind retreats. Their unique contribution amplifies the effectiveness of the sessions delivered by me and our other coaches by identifying and neutralizing unconscious programs that would otherwise sabotage their best plans and aspirations. This optimizes our participants' ability to achieve their goals and dreams. Even my peers who are already at the top of their game have reported remarkable breakthroughs as a result of their work with the Biskinds.

CODEBREAKER is positively overflowing with valuable information, and yet the authors place great emphasis on your experience and underscore the fact that true change isn't a matter of learning more information. Sandra and Daniel even go so far as to point out that most people already possess the tools, techniques, and mindset needed to be successful, and yet have been unable to fully utilize their inner (and often outer) resources due to blind spots that conceal counterproductive programs in the unconscious.

CODEBREAKER presents their system in a way that allows you, the reader, to absorb and enjoy it in multiple ways and on many levels. While the system is accessible to beginners, it is also highly relevant and effective for advanced students. The provocative stories throughout the book demonstrate the impact of their approach and actually initiate a transformative process in the reader. Delightful in and of themselves, these stories serve to ground the teaching and, in turn, help you achieve tangible results.

The Biskinds' goal with this book is to empower you to embody this new thought system, to make it "bio-available." To paraphrase what we say in *The Success Principles*, if you work the system, the system works. *CODEBREAKER* beautifully complements those principles and can enhance your ability to apply them effectively by neutralizing the friction caused by unconscious programs that run beneath the level of awareness.

While casual and inconsistent application of the Law of Attraction is the most common way people undermine their success, the self-sabotaging thoughts and ideas they harbor in the unconscious are the most insidious cause of failure. This system can instantly shift those unconscious programs and make the shifts sustainable.

This book is spirituality made practical. Like many readers of body-mind-spirit books, I enjoy the esoteric and the mystical. I am especially impressed when esoteric information can have a profound effect in real life. That is what Sandra and Daniel have achieved in *CODEBREAKER*. What's more, they tackle the challenging subject of nondualism in an original way that not only makes it understandable but useful in everyday life.

I was also impressed by the fact that, even though the content in *CODEBREAKER* is very deep, the authors never lose their sense of humor. It's an inspiring adventure expressed in the authentic voice of contemporary spiritual masters.

I encourage you to apply what you find in this book. If you already apply *The Success Principles: How to Get from Where You Are to Where You Want to Be*, this book will help you do so with maximum grace and ease. Warm and user-friendly, *CODEBREAKER* offers a comprehensive set of tools, techniques and support resources. You can immediately begin to optimize the return on what you've already invested in your own growth and transformation.

Learn to identify and neutralize your dysfunctional codes, and YOU become a Codebreaker. The result is freedom, like karma washing off your body. This puts you in a unique position to change not only your life, but the lives of those around you. As a Codebreaker, you will be empowered to manifest not only your heart's desire, but to contribute to the awakening of all sentient life. You will, in essence, have the "secret password" to enlightenment.

JACK CANFIELD
Santa Barbara, July 2018

A Personal Message and an Important Request for You from the Authors

Life requires a code. Activate the right code and you can have the success you want— you can experience the life of your dreams.

After decades of research and development we have deciphered the code to living as high frequency beings. We have created a system we are excited to share with you so that you too can experience the life of your dreams. Our life purpose is to set people free from the unconscious programs that sabotage their capacity for happiness and success.

How do you define success? What does success mean to you?

In a seminar attended by highly accomplished people, the participants paired off and asked each other this question. *"What do you really want?"* After listening to the response, the questioner then asked, *"And what will that get you?"* After listening to that response, each questioner then repeated the question, *"And what will that get you?"* Within two to at most four more rounds, everyone came to the same answer. Everyone answered with some variation of peace, love, and/or joy. In other words, everyone wants to be happy.

Ironically, the critical variable in whether or not we experience happiness is not our external circumstances but our internal state—our state of mind. That is what determines whether we respond creatively to externals or whether we react in sub-optimal, habitual patterns. As energetic beings we are constantly vibrating at various frequencies. Our frequency determines our state and our state determines our frequency.

So to be happy—to experience peace, love, and joy— we ask, *"How can we influence our energy, our frequency, and our state?"* And since it is ultimately not dependent on externals, what are the internals that control it?

The simplest answer to this question is to look at your code, as it is your mind that controls your state. Without exception, everyone operates by codes. The almost eight billion human codes in operation on the planet today all ultimately reduce down to only two: the divine mind code, based in love; and the ego mind code, based in fear. When you operate in the divine mind code, you embody the best version of you and you experience happiness. When you operate in the ego mind code, you experience suffering.

CODEBREAKER presents a comprehensive system to train the mind and empower you to master your codes. This allows you to experience happiness as your natural state as it amplifies the frequency of success—however you define success.

We have found through personal experience and the experience of thousands around the world that this new thought system is powerful and effective. We are sharing this with you so you can transform your thoughts, your life, and your world. When you follow and implement the system, it works!

The effects of energy leakage—ultimately caused by corrupt codes—simply cannot be isolated to one limited compartment of our lives. True success is wholistic; it involves the balance not only of our inner and outer life, but the different areas of life. It depends upon our code, which shows up in our mindset, attitude, and frequency.

To paraphrase Oscar Wilde, success is a science; if you use the code, you get the result.

We are dedicated to your personal transformation, to empowering you to master your codes so you have the success you desire, in your work; your relationships; your health; in your sense of meaning and purpose; and especially in your basic moment-by-moment experience of life.

As you delve into *CODEBREAKER* we invite you to think seriously about what success means to you.

Please use the inquiry process described above, alone or with a partner, and dig deep to find your answers. Once you have the answer, ask yourself, *"Who do I have to be to naturally achieve my goals?"* Then ask yourself where your life will be if you don't take the steps needed to realize your answers?

The next step is in your hands.

Your thoughts, both conscious and unconscious, are the only things stopping you from experiencing the life you want.

~ SANDRA & DANIEL BISKIND

Imagine if we could eradicate the war between the ego mind's unconscious priorities and the soul's desire to be whole—to be the best version of who we are.

How natural would it be to accelerate the soul's evolution into enlightenment if that were possible?

It is possible, and now is the time to embody all that we are—the three-dimensional human being and the multidimensional divine, mystical, energetic being that is our True Self.

We are all spiritual beings with physical form on a quest to become whole. With the right keys, code, and mindset we can easily course-correct back to this overarching purpose. **Ultimate transformation only happens when we're fully present in both the physical world and the spiritual world.** Here we can create deep and meaningful relationships, achieve higher levels of awareness, maximize our contribution and impact, and lead a life of meaning and purpose.

Welcome to this step in the evolution of your soul! *CODEBREAKER* is dedicated to empowering your transformation, to supporting your rapid change and profound inner growth. Collectively, the evolution of the soul is accelerating the realization of the new human: awakened, enlightened, self-actualized, and whole.

More than at any other time in history, the potential is emerging to make huge shifts in consciousness that can take us, both individually and globally, into a whole new dimension, living in the high frequency of peace, love, awareness, trust, integrity, neutrality, unity, and mindfulness...PLATINUM.

As an adolescent, Daniel realized what scientists and philosophers alike had known, that everyone is always operating by codes. It is our code that determines our frequency and our frequency determines our level of joy and wellbeing. We choose our codes by default or by design. Our choice of code empowers and uplifts us, or it deepens the rut we find ourselves seeking to escape. *CODEBREAKER* has been designed to empower you to use the high frequency PLATINUM master password to unlock the code to become the best version of you.

In the nineteenth century there was a powerful transformational movement in the United States known as the Great Awakening. Now, in the twenty-first century, an even greater awakening has emerged. Unlike its nineteenth-century predecessor, which was religious in nature, this broader, deeper movement is global and is based in spirituality rather than religion.

Homo sapiens is giving birth to a new species, *homo spiritus.* This is the transformation from thinking humanity to spiritual humanity; from the head to the heart; from the ego mind to the divine mind.

Spirituality, to paraphrase Deepak Chopra, is the domain of awareness where we experience values like truth, goodness, beauty, love, and compassion, and also intuition, creativity, insight, and focused attention.

When one represses emotion, one's body hurts; when one represses consciousness, one's mind aches; when one represses spirituality, one's soul suffers.

~ VALERIE V. HUNT, PHD

Similar to the holographic nature of the universe, and the mind, this book presents a wholistic thought system in which every part is not only consistent with the whole but contains the essence of the whole. We call this thought system a True Self Hologram. Each key word in the PLATINUM master password is a symbol for a high frequency aspect of our True Self, which can be examined from different angles to focus on specific attributes.

CODEBREAKER presents the tools, techniques, and practices of the PLATINUM Life System™ to change our frequency via mind training—not just education. To get full benefit, they need to be practiced. Mastery always involves repetition and practice. As Bob Proctor said, *"Repetition is the first law of learning."* Changing our frequency and mastering our mind—the prerequisites to experiencing the life we want— is no different.

Bruce Lipton, PhD, writes, *"The character of our life is based upon how we perceive it...Our beliefs control our bodies, our minds, and thus our lives... We can control our lives by controlling our perceptions."* And, since all of our perceptions are projections, the sixty-four-thousand-dollar question is, how do we control them?

It is the code we are using in any given moment that controls our projections and perceptions. With or without awareness, we each choose our own code, and our choice of code is frequently triggered by an unconscious program that blocks or limits success.

Not only our state, but our entire experience of life can change instantly with the removal of these unconscious blocks that are obstacles to living in wholeness.

One example is an extremely successful 62-year-old career woman who had never been married and lived alone with her cat. She was desperate to find resolution around an ongoing, emotionally incapacitating issue.

She had spent 40 years and hundreds of thousands of dollars trying to find peace. In her teens she had experienced an incestuous relationship with her father, and ever since then its impact tormented and sabotaged her personal life. During a private session, we identified the core programs stopping her from ever having the kind of intimate relationship she longed for.

We neutralized her programs and deleted their effects using the Quantum Neutrality Process.™ This "power tool set" is explained in Part III, Chapter 6. The emotional charge around the events and decisions dissipated as we transformed the negative programs that were sabotaging her life. She visibly shifted from someone who was a traumatized victim afraid of never having a fulfilling and meaningful relationship to feeling peaceful and optimistic about her future. In a word, she was finally happy.

Both of us have had to overcome our share of debilitating life challenges. To thrive in adversity, we had to find inner strength and personal power. We did that by using the inner work presented in this book.

To really experience the richness of life, real love, and authentic forgiveness, we had to master our frequency and train our minds in order to come to that place of peace and love. The PLATINUM Life System has been invaluable in helping us through the tough times by bringing us back into resonance with our True Self.

Having reached that place inside ourselves, and having assisted thousands of people around the world to do likewise, our next step in living our life purpose was to write this book and share the PLATINUM Life System. It has transformed our lives, and can help you do the same.

CODEBREAKER is a guide and mentor to support liberation from unconscious programs on our hero's journey from the head to the heart. For some, this book will provide stimulating new ideas. For others, it will provide valuable confirmation that they are on the right track.

There's no need to change religious or spiritual beliefs for this work to weave miracles into our lives. In various ways we all face the same challenges. Depending on the software programs and code running in our unique human computers, we may experience various emotional adjustments while dealing with these challenges.

No matter how daunting or overwhelming circumstances may seem, like us and countless others, you can turn your life around.

Operating in the right code will accelerate the soul's evolution into enlightenment and wholeness as we experience greater levels of inner peace, joy, happiness, success, and optimal wellbeing—and a closer connection to the divine within.

With infinite love and gratitude,

SANDRA & DANIEL

PART ONE

PART

I:

LIVING IN WHOLENESS

— UNLOCK YOUR PLATINUM LIFE

We are what we think.
All that we are arises from our thoughts.
With our thoughts, we make the world.

~ BUDDHA

Have you ever felt like invisible barriers are holding you back, keeping you in a loop of negative mind chatter and life patterns that do not serve your highest good? You are not alone. Most people are only functioning at between 5 and 15 percent of their potential. It is the programs in our minds that are holding us back. Even our private clients—highly successful people who are committed to getting to the next level—experience blockages not because of a deficiency in their skill set, tool set, or rational mind set, but because of unconscious programs that prevent them from making optimum use of their resources.

Reprogramming Your DNA for Success

Our programs create habit fields in the mind, and these show up in neural pathways in our brain and encoded patterns in our DNA. When an event and subsequent decision is surrounded by an emotional charge, it can become an unconscious program that controls your behavior. These controlling programs can be inherited or environmentally acquired, as well as resulting from past lives and first-hand experience. Humans are hard-wired for stories, and we find controlling programs often appear like mythological or archetypal stories that are recorded in your genetic memory and stored in your DNA.

Russian scientists, led by biophysicist and molecular biologist Pjotr Garjajev, have made impressive discoveries about the mutability of DNA. They found that words and frequencies can be used to reprogram animal and human DNA. Their work helps to explain the critical role that your frequency and intention (i.e., your code) have in DNA's response to language.

Parallel examples can be seen in the work of the late Masaru Emoto, who has extensively documented the effects of distant prayer and language on the structure of water crystals. Only recently have we gained understanding into the previously inexplicable, miraculous transformations effected by prayer and affirmations. Fascinating insights into their mechanics and that of other important phenomena, including hypercommunication and intuition, are being discovered at an increasing rate in the twenty-first century.

The insights, empirical research, and modern transformational technology and tools in this book will expand your understanding of how to change your everyday experience of life. Our mission is to equip you with the skills to unlock and retrain your mind to free yourself from the thoughts, habit fields, brain patterns, and encoded DNA that hold the programs, beliefs, and ideas preventing you from having the inspiration, income, and impact you are destined for.

Your passwords access corrupted or inspirational encoding depending on where you are in the evolution of your soul. As your level of awareness changes, you develop more gratitude, kindness, generosity, compassion, and the ability to forgive and love unconditionally.

Your aware soul is making the conscious choice to bring in the divine mind as its new programmer, taking the time to neutralize and delete the programs developed in the ego mind's world and to forgive the painful results of those programs. If left unforgiven, they would only continue to corrupt the system.

Delving into your conscious and unconscious programs and getting to the core beliefs around any feelings of fear, negativity, and pain is the ultimate way to avoid illness. Don't be afraid. This will turbocharge your evolutionary expedition into wholeness, and the more you become whole, the less room there is for the ego mind to buck, both at having its stories undone and at having to forgive—even if in its enlightened self-interest.

THE MASTER PASSWORD: PLATINUM

The PLATINUM Life System is based on timeless spiritual principles and gives us the resources to change our thoughts so we can change our life and solve what seem to be seemingly unsolvable problems. It offers the master password to unlocking our codes to personal empowerment and an inspirational life.

The eight high frequency beingness states unlocked by the PLATINUM master password are:

Peace, Love, Awareness, Trust, Integrity, Neutrality, Unity, and **Mindfulness**

The PLATINUM Life System incorporates proven tools, techniques, and practices that help us upgrade our operating code and master our minds to live as the phenomenal beings we are. We can stop the madness—the dysfunctional mind chatter, negative self-talk, repetitive self-sabotage—and master our minds so we can reshape our thoughts, feelings, and behavior. It starts with the commitment to do what it takes to experience a better life.

We need to understand that thoughts are tools. Are we using them as productively as we can? Are our thoughts serving us well, or are we their victims? It's up to us.

~ DR. TOM MORRIS

EVERYONE LIVES BY CODES

Living by a code is not optional. However, you have the choice to mindfully select your code by design or mindlessly let it run by default.

Selecting a low or high frequency code is not about working less or working harder or setting a lower or higher bar for your life. It is all about who you are being while you are doing whatever you are doing.

How much happiness are you experiencing? How much joy? Only when experienced can these states be shared with others. Have you ever noticed how charismatic someone is who is happy? They walk into a room with a genuine smile and instantly the space is filled with magnetic energy. Peace, love, joy, and happiness have very high frequencies, and those frequencies are so irresistible that everyone can sense them.

They come from a place of wholeness and are expressions of your True Self. If you are not regularly and consistently experiencing peace, love, and happiness, you need to ask yourself, *"What code is blocking my way?"*

In order to master the PLATINUM high frequency beingness states, we also have to master the core blocking frequencies that subvert them. These guilty culprits are constants in the ego mind code.

THE PLATINUM
HIGH FREQUENCY ATTRIBUTES OF
YOUR TRUE SELF AND THEIR
CORE BLOCKING FREQUENCIES

PLATINUM	BLOCKERS
PEACE	Unforgiveness
LOVE	Fear
AWARENESS	Obliviousness
TRUST	Worry
INTEGRITY	Fragmentation
NEUTRALITY	Attachment
UNITY	Judgment
MINDFULNESS	Asleep

When a poem appears, please take a deep breath and relax. Do not rush through it, but savor it.

Each one has been deliberately chosen to catapult you into your heart and illuminate your soul, flicking the switch on the light within. Through Daniel Ladinsky's high frequency translations we invite you to join with Hafiz as they bare their God-drenched souls through these poems as often as you can.

FOR A WHILE

We have all come to the right place.

We all sit in God's classroom.

Now,

The only thing left for us to do, my dear,

Is to stop

Throwing spitballs for a while.

~HAFIZ

From *I Heard God Laughing: Poems of Hope and Joy*,
Copyright 1996 & 2006 by Daniel Ladinsky
and used with his permission.

Our objective is to empower you to become your own codebreaker and upgrade your life on every level—not only spiritually but also on the levels of wealth, health, relationship success, and happiness.

There is an experience of life we are all longing for. Recoding facilitates new levels of spiritual freedom that lead to a whole new way of being. The aim of this system is for you to experience the ultimate mind shift. We are inviting you to shift from the head to the heart, from the ego mind code to the divine mind code, from fear to love. PLATINUM is the key that unlocks your mind to awaken your consciousness and liberate you from your unconscious personality programs.

You are so much more than what your physical senses reveal. You are far more than the mere sum of your automated programs, conditioned thinking, and mindless self-talk. PLATINUM acknowledges that the real you is already perfect, that you are a PLATINUM being. This is your True Self. Most people never realize this because their soul is asleep. How often do you sleepwalk through life?

We are like the dreamer who dreams and then lives in the dream. This is true for the entire universe.

~ THE UPANISHADS

Activating the PLATINUM password awakens your soul to choose wholeness. As you learn to use the master password to decode your life you automatically break through to great loving relationships, real strength, and the success you aspire to. We invite you to make the commitment to be your own codebreaker and start living your PLATINUM life today.

You might be asking yourself, *"What do I have to give up to live a PLATINUM life?"* Well...let's see. Sex, wine, shopping, credit cards...just kidding! Seriously, you will only be giving up your illusions and stories. You won't miss any of the things you have to give up to live a PLATINUM life, but you will naturally feel better, your light will shine brighter, and you will attract more love in your life. And you will have loads more happiness—which is joy without suffering.

No doubt you have learned that you can think positively about what you desire until you are blue in the face but that does not mean those positive thoughts will manifest as changes in your life. Ultimately, your unconscious programs and patterns will have the last word. Until those are corrected, your ability to manifest your best intentions will continue to be sabotaged by your unconscious thoughts. The information-processing capacity of the unconscious mind is 500,000 times greater than that of the conscious mind, so when they're in conflict, guess which one prevails?

Your life is a masterpiece in the making. Your soul is here to evolve, become whole, and have fun. Let us help you fulfill your purpose by changing the inner landscape of your mind so that the outer landscape of your home, your work, and your relationships reflect the changes you want.

Before we go any further, let's travel back in time for a quick visit with our not-so-distant ancestor, primitive humans.

Primitive Humans

As a matter of survival, our primitive forebears had to continually face the question "kill or be killed?" Having mastered the art of killing, combined with the ego mind's commitment to separation, humanity has evolved in this world of duality into such an alien species that we have become unrecognizable, even to ourselves. The ego mind's campaign for dominance, not to mention its fight for its own survival, never rests. It attacks anything outside its own paradigm and it will not hesitate to harm anyone it sees as a threat, including you!

On the spiritual level, this dualistic system keeps the soul confused and off balance, as it oscillates uncertainly between its two choices, the ego mind and the divine mind. The ego mind code emphasizes use of the two oldest parts of the triune human brain: the reptilian brain and the limbic system. The divine mind code operates predominantly through the newest part: the prefrontal cortex.

We all know our history. The depths of darkness and depravity of the ego mind knows no boundaries. Master of war and politics, it presents a convincing case to the soul to keep choosing it.

Even though the ego mind undermines and tries to pervert love's power to wake us up, a growing number of souls are ready to leave the confines of their illusory coma and move back into the safe haven of the divine mind. If you are feeling the pull to the divinity within you, that means it is time to attend to your soul's evolution.

At first a tentative move by the soul to change direction by changing its choices, it has now taken on the quality of a landslide into wakefulness. The only danger this landslide poses is to the part of the illusion that refuses to get out of the way. The ego mind puts up a great fight, and most souls are not yet ready to make the choice to leave their dream world.

However, help is on its way. All is never lost. Your True Self sits patiently at the foot of the bed you have made for yourself. It never gives up on you and your return to sanity and to wakefulness. It is always poised to gently reassure you when you stir from your sleep that you are in the safe haven of the divine heart, which you have never really left.

When we quit thinking primarily about ourselves and our own self-preservation, we undergo a truly heroic transformation of consciousness.

~ JOSEPH CAMPBELL

It's Time to Change Codes

Have you ever felt unworthy, unwanted, lacking in self-confidence? Have you experienced feelings of depression, sadness, anxiety, or intolerance? The ego mind code has literally corrupted your DNA with codes that inhibit your connection to your True Self, which is your spiritual core and infinite supply of power.

When this happens, confidence goes out the door, replaced by feelings of unworthiness and low self-esteem that result in the body, mind, and soul all suffering. These insidious codes easily have us playing dangerous games that often result in things like unfulfilled relationships, depression, and mindless addiction.

Guilt, shame, and blame join the mix and diminish our ability to shine in the world. The ego mind is the ultimate terrorist. Microcosmically, it terrorizes us; and macrocosmically, it is the secret agent responsible for every act of terrorism on the planet.

Intense emotional experiences often result in controlling programs that imprint DNA. These programs are routinely passed on from one generation to the next. Whether imprinted from childhood or inherited from seven generations back, whenever we're in the wrong code, we automatically become their victim.

That's when we've lost our connection to the light of our True Self. We all know what that feels like. We no longer feel happy or grateful to be alive, but rather experience feelings like compulsiveness, entitlement, and self-righteousness.

Have you ever felt a sense of desperation and sought out people, places, or events that might alleviate your pain and recapture some of the joy of your original state? Searching for love in all the wrong places, have you felt the need to cling to others? Or to entertain yourself with ideas that distract you from the fact that you feel lost? The ego mind's promise to keep us safe and in control is especially seductive when we feel unsafe, inadequate, or out of control. In its world, true forgiveness does not compute. Instead, revenge and separation are honored as though they were noble elements of our human nature.

Like a broken record, lifetime after lifetime, deep down we know there is something missing. At some stage we all ask the basic questions about our existence: Why am I here? Where did I come from? What is the point? Where do I belong in this world? Is there a God? Why is there so much misery, pain, and suffering?

The ego mind's dominance is threatened by the truth, and so it asks unanswerable questions to keep us distracted by its delusions. Separation is the fundamental ego mind strategy—we know it as dualism. It keeps us looking outside, where answers to questions of meaning and purpose are never found, instead of inside, where the answers live and wait for us. If we are prepared for the truth, the answers are simple. Our journey into our own inner world of light and personal power guides us like a ship by a lighthouse. It's time to find our way back home, to change codes and leave behind the illusory world of our ego mind's sad and lonely fabrication where real peace, love, forgiveness, and joy are only fleetingly experienced at best.

Once tasted, our natural curiosity takes us on the magical mystical tour into the world of the heart where we will never be satisfied with less. When we get to the truth and neutralize the core programs and beliefs preventing us from accessing our personal power, we realize we are destined to be our own codebreakers. This awareness leads us to begin the process of shifting mental habit fields, changing neural pathways, and reprogramming DNA. By training the mind correctly we can restore our soul's ability to automatically choose the divine mind code and move into progressively higher states of consciousness.

Mind mastery is the soul's unavoidable journey.

~ VALERIE V. HUNT, PHD

The following images represent what the ego mind code and the divine mind code can look like. Want to have some fun discovering what your codes look like?

🝒 1. **DOWNLOAD:** Go to CodeBreakerBook.com/resources and download your code charts. (Password: PLATINUM)

🝒 2. **OVERVIEW:** Fill them out to see how your ego mind and divine mind codes are influencing your life.

🝒 3. **RECODE:** Finish reading *CODEBREAKER*, and go back to your charts to see how you can revise your codes.

Ego Mind Code

Leads to Suffering and Separation

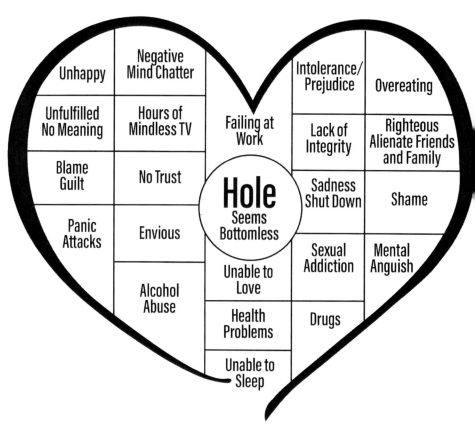

©2018 Sandra and Daniel Biskind

DIVINE MIND CODE

Leads to Living a PLATINUM Life

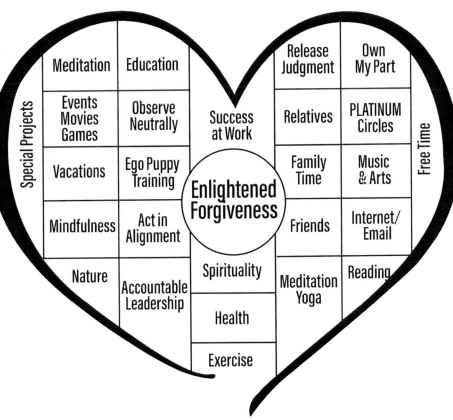

©2018 Sandra and Daniel Biskind

How to Use CODEBREAKER

Assess your state. Take the PLATINUM Self Assessment as soon as possible...definitely before starting Part III. To monitor and record your shifts, take it again when you've finished *CODEBREAKER*.

> ☤ **SELF ASSESSMENT:** Go to
> CodeBreakerBook.com/selfassessment
> and get started. (Password: PLATINUM)

Once you've digested Parts I and II, we recommend spending a week per chapter in Part III, fully experiencing each successive frequency unlocked by the PLATINUM master password. Ideally, follow the system's structure, which has been proven to optimize transformation in both our Live Events and the Activate Enlightenment Online Mastery Program.

There are many ways you can enrich your journey with us. The most obvious is to read from beginning to end.

Focus your intention on receiving the guidance you need, open the book randomly, and the chapter or page you see will be what you need to read in that moment. You can also go directly to the Contents pages and allow your intuition to select the appropriate section to help you feel better instantly.

Make this journey a personal one that best suits you. We do recommend that wherever you start, you circle back to all the chapters, as the book is designed to be experienced as a whole. Each section, like each high frequency beingness quality, works together in a process of integration and realization. In any case, be kind and gentle with yourself. The ego mind will find unexpected ways to sabotage this undertaking, so remain alert for its tricks!

It is invaluable to keep a journal or diary as you read and practice using the tools in *CODEBREAKER*. We have created a *CODEBREAKER Journal* to support you.

Write down insights as soon as they occur. Referring back as you explore and discover new revelations will enrich this process. Track your progress, your changes, and your shifts using the Self Assessment.

Your experience is the key. Stories and teachings are especially valuable in helping the mind to relax around new concepts and to accept new experiences open-mindedly.

Allow yourself total immersion with a beginner's mind. Remember, this is about a whole new thought system—not just minor tweaks and refinements!

As you begin your exploration of the simple yet effective PLATINUM Life System, you will discover multiple uses for each concept. We invite you to take your time, as we did. People who have read this book three and four times have said *CODEBREAKER* became even more useful, insightful, and life-changing the more they read it.

 Sharing this transformational journey with peers on harmonious paths provides unique and powerful rewards.

Here are some of the results you can expect as you move through *CODEBREAKER* and use the PLATINUM Life System:

- A quantum leap in your mental, emotional, and spiritual intelligence.

- Improved behavior, attitude, and effectiveness.

- Feeling loved and understood regardless of conditions in your external world.

- More balance between work, play, and quiet time.

- New patterns and habits that support better health, wellbeing, relationships, and happiness.

- The ability to instantly recognize when an emotional reaction has been triggered and constructively change your response.

- Increased energetic and magnetic attractiveness.

- A greater sense of meaning, purpose, and love.

- More creativity and heightened intuition.

- Greater confidence, power, and strength.

- Reduced negative mind chatter.

- Improved communication and problem-solving.

- More flexibility and inner peace.

- A growing level of happiness and success that will astonish and delight you.

Remember, results often come when least expected. Be open and expect miracles.

Shifts happen as you implement the PLATINUM Life System. Participating in live or online events and VIP Private Coaching Sessions are ways to accelerate your progress.

☌ Go to **http://www.TheBiskinds.com** to learn other ways we can support your expansion into enlightenment and wholeness.

PART TWO

PART

II:

THE AGE OF
TRANSFORMATION:
CULTIVATING YOUR CONNECTION
TO YOUR TRUE SELF

When you are connected to your True Self,
you feel an ocean of peace, love,
and joy moving in you.

~ SANDRA & DANIEL BISKIND

Traditional history calls the first stage of human evolution the age of hunter-gatherers. We then evolved into the agricultural age, the industrial age, and the information age. We have now entered the Age of Transformation.

The amount of change one needed to master in order to live successfully fifty years ago was easily managed. Today the amount of change we all must navigate to live successfully is at least an order of magnitude larger. Charles Darwin, father of the modern theory of evolution, said, *"It is not the strongest or the most intelligent who will survive but those who can best manage change."* This requires new skills, new mindsets, new paradigms, and it requires the tools of rapid change—of transformation, which literally means going beyond form.

Developing these tools requires inner work; it requires mastering your inner game. With accelerating speed have come growing impatience and decreased attention spans, yet more than ever it is vital to be able to maintain focus. This is not simply about learning more information; it's about enhancing your ability to learn and master change. The ability to ask powerful questions is more important than ever. Developing these tools is experiential and requires training and practice.

Ironically, to master adjusting to this accelerating velocity of change so you can thrive requires connecting with the changeless attributes of the True Self—your inner self that is timeless and eternal. From ancient to contemporary times, this has been recognized as the ultimate prerequisite to deep transformation.

The True Self is our essence, our perfection, and our power. It has always existed and always will. It is our beingness that has no needs, because everything we could ever need already exists within.

If we could only be, just be, we could see our infinity. We could see that we are the all.

~ LESTER LEVENSON

What stops us from experiencing our beingness, from tapping into the power source of the True Self? It is our false self, the author of the ego mind code that is based on the mistaken belief that we are separate from our divine source, from the God of our understanding. This belief began the journey into a world very much like the one into which the heroic Alice fell in Lewis Carroll's *Alice in Wonderland.*

Down the rabbit hole we go, becoming smaller and smaller, our connection to our True Self instantly forgotten. Like Alice, we find ourselves in a world so alien and frightening, so distant from the world of the divine, that we think we will never find our way back home.

Along with the belief in our separation and God's abandonment, the mind is hijacked by unconscious guilt and shame as we mistakenly become convinced that we are homeless, which completes the underpinnings of the ego mind code.

Not only does Source await our return with open arms, but in reality we have never left home, except in a dream.

CODEBREAKER is designed to facilitate a deeper, more sustainable connection to the True Self, to guide our journey home. No matter what race, creed, religion, or spiritual path, it is time to consistently reconnect to our divine essence and embody our personal power.

By shifting into the divine mind code, we experience the gift of grace and naturally love who we are. It is from here that we creatively manifest and experience the life of our dreams.

You are what you have been looking for. This you is your True Self. Our goal is to empower you to build a permanent connection with it, which is the most reliable path to enlightenment and wholeness. Embodying the True Self is the ultimate goal of the great spiritual and mystical traditions.

Looking outside is hit or miss. Looking inside is ultimately the only place where reliable guidance can always be found. Cultivating our relationship with the True Self is a lifelong process of learning, discovery, creativity, and growth. Nothing is more important. Nothing is even a close second in value, meaning, and usefulness. This is the foundation that supports success in all areas of life.

Yesterday I was clever,
so I wanted to change the world.
Today I am wise,
so I am changing myself.

~ RUMI

TRAINING TOOLS: INQUIRY AND ATTUNEMENT

There are two foundational training modalities that facilitate creating new habit fields and neural pathways, recoding and up-leveling DNA, and mastering life. The PLATINUM Life System incorporates both Inquiry and Attunement, because used in combination they provide a powerful, proven way to quickly and sustainably change our frequency—that is, our code.

In Inquiry we ask ourselves powerful questions; it focuses on our code and programs. In Attunement we harmonize our practices with the frequency of our choice. Inquiry and Attunement are two sides of the same coin. Used together in a mutually complementary and reinforcing way, they optimize personal transformation. Practicing these two training modalities together is integral to our approach to inner work. Throughout the book—and in our live events and private and group coaching sessions—we teach and train ways to cultivate, develop, and embody them so they become natural.

Important tools we use to facilitate attunement to the divine mind code include meditation, various forms of visualization, and activations. They each retrain the mind, facilitating the creation of new habit fields, new neural pathways in the brain, and new expressions of genetic activation in our DNA. These not only lead to better health and vitality but are prerequisites to optimizing higher awareness. Meditation, visualization, and other techniques that attune us to higher frequencies have been used for thousands of years as rungs on the ladder out of the darkness of the rabbit hole back into the light of the divine mind.

Many years ago, Sandra was asked by a group of nuns to come to their retirement home and teach them meditation. She had no idea that nuns retired, but of course they only retired from professionally helping people, not from their calling to know God. It was a very special experience. Here is her story:

"There they were, all in their mid-sixties and older, still wearing their black and white habits. I couldn't help myself. I felt like Whoopi Goldberg in the movie *Sister Act.* Luckily for everyone and especially me, I wasn't there to teach them to sing!

In unison, they closed their eyes and began to breathe deeply and relax as they followed my voice. What an incredible sight. Have you ever looked at your beloved or child when they were sleeping? Remember how your heart expanded and their loveliness almost took your breath away? That is exactly how I felt in that moment, looking at these incredible women who wanted to learn, grow, and deepen their connection to God.

After the first session, I asked them why they wanted to learn to meditate. The answer was, '*To get closer to God; to know the peace of God better.*'

The unsaid implication from their tone of voice and facial expressions was: Well, why else would we want to meditate? Without ever having formally meditated, they instinctively knew that meditation is a way into the peace of the divine mind."

Meditation is also a proven way to alleviate stress and tension, which cause distress, dysfunction, and disease. A growing number of companies around the world make time for their employees to take meditation breaks. Airline pilots on British Airways have long been taking mandatory ten-minute meditation breaks for revitalization before landing. Research and medicine continue to document that meditation is a proven practice to increase both physical and mental wellness and support a healthier, longer life. Meditation is an effective antidote to stress and supports our natural self-healing capabilities.

Like meditation, visualization relaxes the body to change our state of being, and uses the imagination to bring about intended outcomes. Both the military and sports worlds use the power of visualization to create efficiency, effectiveness, and confidence. Having visualized and achieved something in the mind regularly contributes to success in the field. Visualization can open doors into the unconscious mind where we can delve into our inner world and create new habits and associations that serve us. Repeating the desired new habits creates new neural pathways in our malleable brains that make it easier to maintain our desired new behaviors.

Both meditation and guided visualization can take the physical brain waves down into the frequencies below alpha, known as theta and delta. That's where, just like babies and young children, we access, learn, and absorb information more easily. Theta, 4 to 8 cycles per second, is just above the lowest frequency of delta, 0.5 to 4 cycles per second.

Babies are in almost constant meditative-like states as their brains predominately operate in the delta range until about age two. A child's brain begins to oscillate at the higher theta frequency between two and six. This is the time they learn and process the enormous amount of information that will set them up to live in the physical world.

The senses of babies and children constantly send messages into a brain oscillating at what could be called the programming frequency or, in the case of mind-training, we might call it the reprogramming frequency.

Typically our beliefs are 50% formed by age five, 80% by age eight, and by age fifteen they are 90% to 95% in place. As studies in psychoneuroimmunology have discovered, our beliefs can make us sick or they can keep us well, and can be even more potent variables than our genetic inheritance.

What we see, hear, feel, taste, touch, and learn from our parents, extended family, and environment is absorbed directly by the unconscious mind, where these observations become programs, beliefs, and ideas that literally have the power to change our biological structure.

Have you ever experienced an unaware teacher, parent, or sibling say things like *"Stupid child!"* or *"Children should be seen and not heard"* or *"Who do you think you are?"* These powerful words plant seeds that our unconscious minds process as truth. The untrained minds of babies and children have neither the wisdom nor the capacity to sort truth from fiction.

Even unintentionally, these abusive seeds produce the weeds of corrupted programs that can drastically impact our destiny. The good news is that inquiry, especially when used with meditation and visualization, can help us discover and rehabilitate the damaged plants that grew from the corrupted seeds of our childhood. By neutralizing debilitating beliefs, the PLATINUM Life System ends the suffering they cause once and for all.

To paraphrase Bruce Lipton, PhD, we are no longer victims of mom and dad's double helix; we are no longer just biological machines; and our health is no longer beyond our control—meditation and inquiry is the way.

We have created eight powerful, guided meditations that activate the high frequency attributes of PLATINUM. The *CODEBREAKER PLATINUM Meditation Series* will raise your frequency and reprogram your thoughts and DNA for wholeness, happiness, and success. They can be found at:

 http://www.thebiskinds.com/meditation

CODEBREAKER SUCCESS PRINCIPLES

Breaking the ego mind code enables the soul to awaken, facilitates retraining the mind, and frees us to access the True Self. Here are some key *CODEBREAKER* success principles:

1. **Surrender to not knowing.** Cultivate a beginner's mind. Surrender to the fact that in subjective matters, the ego mind does not know the truth. Even when we are certain we know something, remember that it is only an opinion colored by the perspective of our programs. A belief is simply an opinion we've habitually thought and become attached to.

2. **Ask effective questions.** Discover what is stopping you from changing the way you think. It is either an unconscious or conscious program that stops us from becoming neutral and changing our thinking. Remember, it's just another story.

3. **Make forgiveness your highest priority.** Move on to the next adventure without allowing the pain of the past to be the suffering of the future. We call this enlightened self-interest at its best. Give yourself a break and activate the forgiveness code: Always forgive.

4. **Take radical personal responsibility.** Own your role as the screenwriter, director, producer, casting director, cinematographer, and star of the film that is your life. Remember, perception is projection.

5. **Master your thoughts and you master your whole world.** Without attachment or judgment, become the mindful observer of your inner world.

6. **Speak mindfully and constructively.** When we master our mouth, we only have ourselves to forgive for misthinking rather than needing to ask forgiveness of others for misspeaking.

7. **Neutralize your programs.** They are just stories and beliefs—conscious and unconscious—that block us from accessing our personal power. All will be revealed in Chapter 6, "Neutrality."

As we progress in actualizing these success principles, our experience of life transforms in astonishing ways.

Important Terms

Some foundational concepts in the PLATINUM Life System include the following:

- **Divine mind code:** The operating system of ever-expanding love, joy, and divinity that expresses itself deep within us as our True Self. It is the code of true reality and is based on love where we are free to grow, change, and experience peace and presence.

- **Ego mind code:** The operating system of the self-image that the ego mind has fabricated, where we are held hostage, imprisoned by beliefs. It is the code of false reality, which is based on fear, which is the absence of love.

    In the ego mind code we may have an unconscious program that says we are not worthy of love. That program will influence our operating code, which will inevitably attract situations that prove it. We can't help but sabotage our career, our relationships, and our health when we believe we can never experience love. In this code, corruption is applied to all the high frequency beingness states of the True Self; the ego mind code always tries to pervert them, ultimately distorting and diminishing us.

- **Ego puppy training:** Think of your ego as a puppy. Imagine everyone is born with an ego puppy, and we are each responsible for its training. An ego puppy lesson is given in each chapter.

- **Human mind field:** This is an aspect of what quantum physics sometimes calls the unified field of information and energy, also known as the zero point field. It is a manifestation of the oneness and interconnectedness of all that is and that can be tapped into from a human perspective.

- **Nonduality:** It is the natural foundational state of awareness of the unity of subject and object. It is where we understand we are all connected, not only to each other but also to our divine source and to all that is. As Deepak Chopra said, *"The movement of life is from duality to unity."*

- **Neutrality:** A state in which we are free of belief and attachment. Neutrality's open-mindedness enables us to objectively access higher awareness. The state of empowered neutrality is where the ego mind's thoughts and emotions no longer control us; where it is impossible to push our buttons. Neutrality is essential to peace, love, and real freedom; it is the prerequisite to enlightenment.

- **True Self:** This is the perfection of who we really are. Love is the eternal essence of the True Self, which is whole, complete, and infinite—beyond time and space. It is our expression of the divine mind and is our connection to source, to the God of our understanding.

- **Ultimate mind shift:** The reorientation from the head to the heart is the ultimate mind shift—a total paradigm shift from operating in the ego mind code to operating in the divine mind code.

Integrated Wholeness Scale:
The Evolution of the Soul

The problem of restoring the world to its original and eternal beauty is solved by the redemption of the soul.

~ Ralph Waldo Emerson

The chart below illustrates the concept of Integrated Wholeness. It graphically represents one of the distinctive features of the PLATINUM Life System, which is designed to both awaken us and to liberate us from our unconscious programs.

Our state is a function of the interaction between our level of consciousness and the programs that still possess force in the mind. Consciousness is most easily shifted through attunement, while programs are most easily shifted through inquiry. In this system the two are continuously used in mutually complementary, reinforcing ways.

The inspiration for this concept originally came from contemplating the scale of consciousness in the book *Power vs. Force* by David Hawkins, MD, PhD. His scale is two-dimensional, measuring consciousness in a vertical line going from 0 to 1,000, with 0 being the lowest state of consciousness. The consciousness of the majority of people is negative, at 200 or below. They are firmly entrenched in ego mind thinking. Hawkins calibrated Einstein's consciousness at 499, which he considered the pinnacle of intellect. At 500, the heart opens and we begin to operate out of love.

Unconditional love begins at 540.

Enlightened states calibrate from 600 to 1,000, the theoretical maximum sustainable in a human body. Humanity's most well-known enlightened masters, including Buddha and Jesus, calibrated at 1,000.

The Integrated Wholeness Scale is three-dimensional and logarithmic. It adds a horizontal axis that measures personality programs—issues that need to be resolved to move from one level of awareness up to the next.

Life challenges can trigger negative emotional responses and an infinite range of associated issues. As we move along both the consciousness and personality axes of the scale together, the way we deal with them becomes more efficient and effective. Unpacking personality programs from the level of consciousness helps us to understand how otherwise high-consciousness people can do inexplicably low consciousness deeds.

What does living in wholeness look like? It looks like applied wisdom.

Wisdom is your perspective on life, your sense of balance, your understanding of how the various parts and principles apply and relate to each other.

It embraces judgment, discernment and comprehension. It is a gestalt or oneness, an integrated wholeness.

~ STEPHEN COVEY

INTEGRATED WHOLENESS CHART
EVOLUTION OF THE SOUL

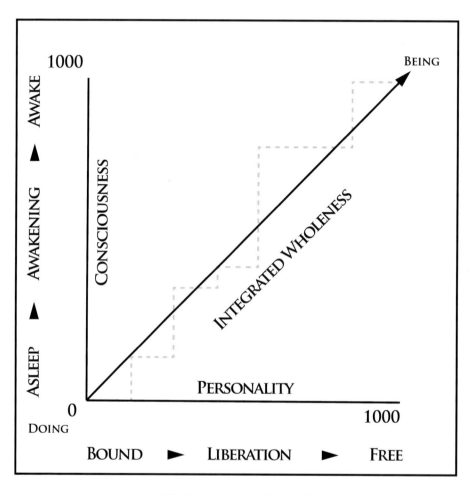

LIVING AN ENLIGHTENED LIFE

Enlightenment is the state in which we are fully connected to the True Self, often characterized by causeless love and limitless joy. It is the state where we directly experience the world without projection. It is the peaceful, confident experience of life, unfiltered by the programs of the ego mind.

Enlightenment empowers us to accept the perfection in everyone, and love without reservation or agenda.

As you read, absorb, and apply the PLATINUM Life System, you will begin to retrain your mind, which transforms your emotions, your physiology, and your experience of life. By reconnecting with the love that you are, you accelerate your soul's evolution into enlightenment and wholeness.

Like many people, have you ever thought, I don't want to be enlightened and live alone high on a mountaintop? After a lifetime's desire to understand and live an enlightened life, we have discovered that is not what enlightenment is all about. No stranger to her own enlightenment experiences, Sandra spent many years working with an enlightened spiritual teacher who visited Australia a few times a year. Here's a story that illustrates how extraordinary enlightenment experiences can be:

"I had just taken a seat when I realized that the whole auditorium was full of an intense, iridescent purple light. Where was it coming from? I had been putting on fashion shows for many years and had often used lighting technicians for special effects. No matter where I looked, I could not find the banks of lights that would have been needed to fill the whole room with this gorgeous wash of colored light.

I asked the person sitting beside me if he knew why our teacher was using purple light, and if could he see where the light was coming from? He looked at me quizzically and said in an are-you-for-real voice, "What purple light? There's no purple light on the stage, or in the room." Well, there was purple light in the room I was sitting in! In exasperation, I closed my eyes. The same purple light was flooding my internal world.

So that's where it was coming from—inside me! I was the source of light. When I asked my spiritual teacher, he told me the purple light I was seeing was my own spirit. Obviously, I could see this light with my physical eyes, but who was seeing it when my eyes were closed? It was my soul—the observer—that part of me that is eternal and capable of fully connecting to my True Self. Like my physical eyes, my spiritual eyes were observing and relaying messages to the brain to process.

I had been working with this spiritual master for over six years, and in that time, I had changed the way I lived my life. I was meditating on a daily basis and working with other amazing healers and teachers to hone my own ability to be the best version of myself.

I realized that I now coped with life challenges with more ease and less drama, and I was capable of being even more creative, more loving, and more forgiving than ever. And, I was totally addicted to the high of enlightenment. Feelings of joy and love would overwhelm me for no reason at all. I would see total strangers and be in love with all of them—no matter what they looked like. If this was an enlightened state, I wanted more.

While driving to Melbourne to see another divine being from India, I asked myself, *"What would I give up to be a fully enlightened being?"* The answer that came up in less than a nanosecond was, *"Everything!"*

During that public session, the speaker invited the few hundred people present to come to the front of the room for a hug. I waited in line for over half an hour. (I would have waited even if I had been the last person in line—and it was a very long line.) When she held me in her arms close to her chest, she just said, "More. More. More." That became my mantra. More love, more joy, more wonder and fulfillment. If this was an enlightenment state, connected to the divine mind, I was on the right path."

From an enlightened perspective, we understand the great mysteries of life, including that humanity has been hoodwinked into believing what the ego mind has told us— that we are separate from our source and from everyone and everything else and need to look outside ourselves to find love, happiness, and fulfillment.

It isn't by getting out of the world that we become enlightened, but by getting into the world...
by getting so tuned in that we can ride the waves of our existence and never get tossed because we become the waves.

~ KEN KESEY

Would you like to know the secret to enlightenment? The great Sufi poet Hafiz reveals it in this poem, in which he refers to an enlightened being as a saint.

When a poem appears, take a deep breath and relax. Rather than rushing through it, savor it deeply.

Each one has been deliberately chosen to catapult you into your heart and illuminate your soul, flicking the switch on the light within. Join with these high frequency beings as they bare their God-drenched souls through their poems as often as you can.

Tripping Over Joy

What is the difference
Between your experience of Existence
And that of a saint?

The saint knows
That the spiritual path
Is a sublime chess game with God

And that the Beloved
Has just made such a Fantastic Move

That the saint is now continually
Tripping over Joy
And bursting out in Laughter
And saying, "I Surrender!"

Whereas, my dear,
I am afraid you still think
You have a thousand serious moves.

~Hafiz

From *I Heard God Laughing: Poems of Hope and Joy,*
Copyright 1996 & 2006 by Daniel Ladinsky
and used with his permission.

Yes, the secret to enlightenment is to lighten up!

The immense power and timeless beauty of the True Self is constantly waiting to be revealed. The soul's journey into enlightenment and wholeness takes us into the mystical world of the divine mind—the guide that frees hostages bound in the illusory world of the ego mind. We are honored to accompany you on your inner voyage into the real world of nonduality facilitated by the True Self.

Use the PLATINUM Life System to crack the ego mind code, become proficient in the divine mind code, and free yourself to live consciously—to be the architect of your own spiritual journey and the master of your PLATINUM state of mind. Create your own version of the extravagantly rich and beautiful PLATINUM life presented to you in this process of everyday enlightenment.

Let's move on now with Part III: The Eight High Frequency Beingness States of PLATINUM.

Peace is the experiential state of your enlightened consciousness.

~ PANACHE DESAI

PART THREE

PART

III:

THE EIGHT HIGH FREQUENCY BEINGNESS STATES OF PLATINUM

CHAPTER ONE

PEACE:
POWER UP YOUR LIFE

*Inner Peace can be reached
only when we practice forgiveness.*

*Forgiveness is letting go of the past,
and is therefore the means for
correcting our misperceptions.*

– GERALD JAMPOLSKY

This is a story about a man called Matthew who came to work with Sandra. It is the perfect example of how our entire life can spiral out of control when we are not connected to our True Self and our natural state of peace. It also demonstrates how awesome life can be when we discover the truth, get neutral, and stop listening to the stories of the ego mind.

CHICKEN NECK

Matthew was in his mid-50s, somewhat overweight, and about 5' 10" tall. He was married with one child and had grown up in Melbourne, Australia. I learned very quickly that he was seeing me after suffering from a severe and painful outbreak of shingles for over eighteen months. After the third doctor he visited had bluntly said that they had exhausted all they could do for him, the doctor told Matthew he should try some form of relaxation. *"After all," the doctor said, "it can't hurt."*

Matthew was a businessman working in a high executive position in a huge Australian company who normally would never consider any alternative form of healing. His tolerance for the excruciating pain, however, was at an all-time low. The torturous pain had worn him down enough that he agreed to try anything, just so long as he could reduce the pain and regain some level of peace—even if that meant trying something as "wacky" as meditating.

I had come highly recommended, and he agreed to a private session, but only after I told him I couldn't help him with the pain if he only wanted to learn meditation. Matthew would have to let me work with him on a deeper level.

He responded by telling me he did not believe in anything like this and did not want any crystals, candles, or that new-age music. Here was another challenge. He lived over an hour away from my home, so I suggested he find someone closer to where he lived. He insisted that I was the one who had been recommended and I was the one he was going to work with. He was a man who was used to getting what he wanted.

The next day Matthew travelled from Melbourne to the seaside town of Geelong to have his first private session. He sat in his car for more than an hour trying to get calm before he mustered up the courage to come in to learn how to get calm. When he walked into the main room, he immediately became agitated.

Without a word of greeting, the first thing out of his mouth was, *"I thought I told you I did not want any crystals, candles, or new age music!"*

In a quiet voice I said, *"Look Mattie, this is my home, not an office, and people give me crystals as gifts. I think they're quite beautiful. The candles are not lit and the music is one of the essential tools we will be using to get you well. I was not prepared to run around rearranging my home for this session, and eventually you will understand the need for the music."*

His only response was, *"The name is Matthew."*

It was a rough start, but a real eye opener for him—and for me. He realized he had to accept the session the way it came or go somewhere else, and I was given a glimpse of the anger and intolerance that had brought this man to me.

After tapping into him, I could feel how completely out of balance he was, with no level of peace in his life. I opened the session by asking what had changed in his life a little over eighteen months previously before being plagued by shingles. Predictably, he said *"Nothing! Absolutely nothing!"* He looked at me quizzically as though I were asking him if he had been to Mars lately.

An unconscious block had been triggered by something, and the ego mind was rocking his world hard enough to send him spiraling into anger and sickness. I asked him to think again, as I knew there was a cause to all his pain and suffering.

He just said, *"Okay,"* looking at me as though I had just teleported myself into my own living room from another planet and was speaking a language he did not understand. At this point he was not able to comprehend the significance or the destructive preconditioned power of his thoughts and his unconscious ego mind programs that were ruining his life and blocking his success and wellbeing.

After looking around the room with its elegant white walls, black granite floors, simple Italian furniture, and its gorgeous blue sea view, and declaring my home looked like a high-class bordello, he promptly sat down and said I could start. Stunned, it was my turn to pause and say, *"Okay."*

I told him we would be using the same music for every session because he would be creating new neural networks that would help trigger a relaxation response from his brain every time he heard the same music. We went through a complete relaxation technique, and to his surprise, he took to meditation like a duck to water. The first session was a success as far as Matthew was concerned, and so he came back a week later. In the second session he had thought of an answer to my question from the week before. Matthew confessed the only thing that had changed was that a new man had been put on at work around that time.

When I asked him how he felt about that, the floodgates opened. It was like I had just opened one of his software programs that he did not even know existed but was holding him hostage nevertheless. With a mixture of extreme anxiety and aggression, Matthew said he thought the man had been put on to replace him.

We had just met part of the guilty program responsible for taking him out of peace and into declaring war on this new employee—and on himself. Shingles is an autoimmune disease in which the body attacks itself. Matthew was running an ego mind code and was on the attack. He continued to tell me his story. He was fifty-four years old, and if he was let go he was afraid of not being able to get another job. To make matters worse, Matthew's immediate boss had asked him to help train the new man.

The ego mind jumped right in and created a fantastic story with devastating results. The program ran something like this: I'm too old to get another job! Why should I train him to take my job? Who does he think he is, coming in here thinking he can ruin my life? Then every night, as though he had left his computer screen on in his head, the ego mind ran an endless loop of these questions and statements. Matthew couldn't sleep, and with anxiety levels at an all-time high, he lost equilibrium in every aspect of his life.

He then proudly continued to tell me no one at work liked this man either. Matthew had effectively enrolled everyone else into believing his story and had created a rift between the newcomer and all the other employees as well. *"We all call him Chicken Neck behind his back,"* Matthew declared with pride. When I asked him how his nemesis had earned the name Chicken Neck, my client replied, *"Because he had some kind of cancer and had to have almost half his neck cut away."* Wow, the plot thickens and the games become even more painful— for everyone.

Having told his story, Matthew was now calm enough to be able to hear some truths. During the coaching session, I asked him had he ever talked to Chicken Neck about what his dreams were for his career. Once again, Matthew looked at me as though I had just come down from the last cloud, and he wanted to know, *"What has that got to do with anything?"*

I pointed out that Chicken Neck was still there and that he still had his job. It seemed he was not going to be replaced; otherwise it probably would have happened by now. There was reluctant agreement on that point. I asked him if he would consider taking Chicken Neck out to lunch to talk to him about his life and his dreams. *"If Chicken Neck has had cancer and lives with this disfiguration, he also has some pretty big programs to deal with."*

This way of thinking was a revelation to him. There is no way Matthew could have connected all the fears and apprehension he was feeling about his work situation with how much he had suffered physically, emotionally, and mentally for nearly two years.

Our hero was learning his lessons the hard way. They come thick and fast when we live in the dualistic world of our illusory tales that the ego mind has conditioned us to believe, and we then perpetuate as the truth. This was a classic example of what happens when we run our stories that we believe are true but are, in fact, pure fantasy.

LESSONS LEARNED THE HARD WAY

His fear and the subsequent anxiety around losing his job and not being able to find another executive position with the same pay grade was followed by anger at finding himself in this vulnerable position. Constant frustration resulted from not knowing he was held hostage by a ruthless set of programs, beliefs, and ideas that had nothing to do with reality.

The truth completely eluded him, as his ego mind kept feeding him a make-believe story that he did not question.

If you don't question your stories, you will never know the truth. They are only stories and they are not reality.

The real cause of the problem is seldom what you think it is. Neither peace nor truth will ever be found in the stories of the ego mind.

The only person he needed to forgive was himself for believing his stories.

Believing your perceptions without questions results in projections not based in reality, which creates the context for mistaken judgments, anxiety, depression, sickness, and even death.

THE TRUTH REVEALED

Matthew promised he would take Chicken Neck out to lunch that week.

At the next session, he was a different man. *"Well, I took Chicken Neck to lunch like you suggested and guess what? He doesn't want my job and never has! He just wanted to be left alone to do his job. You were right. He has really suffered, and we weren't helping things by making his work life a little difficult."*

Silently, my ego mind went straight into judgment. *"A little difficult?"* I thought.

"I've changed that now," said Matthew, *"and we're all getting along just fine. Roger and his wife are coming for dinner next week."*

Oh! At last Chicken Neck finally had a name.

Exactly six weeks after Matthew had bravely ventured outside his comfort zone and into my so called high-class spiritual bordello, he rang to tell me the news. Not only was he promoted at work for demonstrating exemplary relationship skills, but he was no longer angry and in pain and could actually sleep with his wife again. She was back in love with our hero, whom she had been on the verge of leaving if his ogre-like behavior was not curbed.

Sleep was no longer a problem, and Matthew now meditated every day at home to the music he initially did not want to know about. During our sessions, I would also put my hands on his head and give him a transmission of the divine white light energy I had been working with for as long as I could remember. This "hands on" attunement had him melting with bliss while it worked its way through his entire system. He was now more of a marshmallow than a hard nut to crack.

In order for Matthew to get the full benefit of our sessions, I recommended he continue to visualize my hands on his head and this white light coursing through his body as often as he could. This continued to attune him to the light of his own True Self, which accelerated the regeneration and rejuvenation of his skin and the cells in his body.

Once his corrupt ego mind programs were revealed and his mistaken perceptions corrected, our hero was now neutral and free to change his relationship with Roger and to regain peace of mind. Doing what he loved to do again without sabotaging himself with his illusory programs, beliefs, and ideas, Matthew was no longer a captive of his ego mind and its deadly stories.

Oh, and he no longer suffered from shingles.

"But," Matthew said with a smirk on his face, remembering the first time we met, *"that had nothing to do with our sessions."*

I laughed, *"At least you are still true to form."*

THE "SO WHAT?" CULTURE LIVES ON

Matthew called me soon after our last appointment in a state of panic. His wife had made plans to bring their eight-year-old grandchild on their annual vacation without talking to him about it first. "I'm not going to cope with this. After all I've been through these past two years, I need a real break."

"Hang on a minute," I said, *"have you forgotten your new mantra?"*

I had taught Matthew to breathe deeply and say, *"So what? It's okay. It's not real,"* every time his ego mind began running another story. This deep breathing and self-talk instantly takes the edge off anxiety when we lose the feeling of peace around anything. Because the ego mind reacts with total predictability, we can never trust its perceptions and judgments. They will always be based in the illusory world that we have tried to make real lifetime after lifetime.

Matthew was happy to be reminded how easy life can be when he remembered, *"It's okay, it's not real, it's only a story, a program to be corrected so I can realign with peace."* Our hero sent me a postcard from his tropical paradise holiday spot.

Sandra,
Having a great time!
The kid is running amuck and all I can
say is, the "So What?" culture lives on.
Love, Mattie

Mattie wasn't prepared to stop having private sessions, so we agreed to continue over the phone rather than him spending hours in the car. His life was back on track in a way he never thought possible. His tango with shingles and subsequent change of mind had changed his life forever.

Our hero had discovered PEACE, the first high frequency beingness state in the PLATINUM Life System. This enabled him to exchange his ego mind code for the enlightened divine mind code. To complete the healing process there was just one person Mattie had to forgive: himself for not questioning the stories of his ego mind. With diligence, he mastered the shift from blame and unforgiveness—the core low frequency blocker to Peace.

Mattie loved his new life and was excited about cultivating this newfound peace and connection to his perfect point of power. His executive position was secure. He was held in high esteem by everyone in the company as his wisdom continued to bring about fruitful initiatives.

Matthew had learned these life-changing lessons and knew without a doubt that he could no longer blindly trust the ego mind to give him guidance and wise counsel. Taking radical personal responsibility for his thoughts and being able to forgive himself and others was a real game changer. Believing something to be true did not make it so. Just because his perceptions were capable of projecting his judgments no longer meant he would automatically believe them.

WHAT IS PEACE?

- Fully connected to the light of your True Self, peace is your natural state.

- Peace is the state of harmony and balance, tranquility and quiet in which the highest good for all is naturally sought. In this state of serenity, we are free from unsettling thoughts and emotions.

- Inner peace is the bedrock upon which the development of a PLATINUM life rests.

- By connecting to our natural state of peace, we close the door to mental, emotional, and physical distress of all kinds.

- In the state of peace we are fully present. We live in the moment and can relax into the acceptance of what is.

- The core low frequency blocker to peace is unforgiveness.

WHEN THE VIOLIN

When the violin can forgive the past,

It starts singing.

When the violin can stop worrying about the future

You will become such a drunk, laughing nuisance

That God will lean down

And start combing you through His hair.

When the violin can forgive

Every wound caused by others

The heart starts singing.

~HAFIZ

From *The Gift: Poems by Hafiz,*
Copyright 1996 & 2006 by Daniel Ladinsky
and used with his permission.

Your Best Friend, Jo

At live events we often tell a favorite story we heard many years ago about an imaginary friend called Jo. We ask the audience, as we are asking you now, to use your imagination and pretend you have just left your body. (It could be a near-death experience if you prefer.)

You find yourself in heaven. Phewww! You are given the opportunity to look down over the cloud you just landed on and review your life. This is a prerequisite before you are eligible to return to Earth. You become captivated by the life you have just left. *"Look at that!"* you say with enthusiasm.

But wait. *"Oh no! Look at that."* You realize you have to go back. You were given many opportunities to forgive and, for many so-called valid reasons, you did not take them. You can see your own light growing dimmer every time you were challenged and did not rise to the occasion. If you are ever to have real peace, you realize you need the experience of being able to do it better, of being able to forgive.

You are really excited now because you realize you have the opportunity to undo the damage you caused to your own growth and the growth of others. You want to feel better about who you are becoming, and for that to happen, you need to take the high road and practice forgiveness. (And from the looks of the lifetime you are reviewing, you are lucky to have ended up on a cloud at all.)

You jump onto the next cloud that floats by and excitedly address a group of people. *"Hey, I feel so lucky. I get to go back and do things differently. Would anyone be prepared to go back with me and help me?"*

"You've got to be kidding. Why would we want to ruin our next lifetime to help you?"

All day long and into the night, you go from one group of people to the next, always getting the same answers. Totally dejected, you finally lift your head.

There, on the furthest cloud, you see your best friend, Jo. Excitement builds once again as you race over to Jo. With an expectant look on your face, you say, *"Jo, I just have to go back and fix things. You know I can't do it on my own. Will you come back with me? Will you help me? Please?"*

Jo looks into your eyes with deep love and says to you, *"Yes, because I love you so much, I will go back with you, but I have one condition."*

"Anything Jo, anything you want."

Jo says, *"I will go back with you, but only if when I hurt you — because for you to grow and learn the necessary lessons that come from being able to forgive, I will need to hurt you— you remember who set this up in the first place."*

Most people don't speak at this stage. We can literally see the war taking shape in their heads between their ego minds and the wisdom of their hearts.

The head does not want to admit that they could have shattered the peace of the people they have loved and that they are in need of forgiveness. They don't want to admit they had anything to do with the movie that had played out so convincingly.

Without unconditional love, forgiveness is still judgment. And, forgiveness is easier when we accept we are all the same. Forgiveness brings us into the peace of the real world of the heart and unconditional love. Practiced consistently, it ultimately brings us to a place where forgiveness is unnecessary because we understand in reality there is nothing to forgive.

In reality there has only ever been unconditional love, and that is who we are. The heart wins every time when we realize we are actually all one big family and that we have all experienced everything in our soul's epic journey on our way out of the ego mind's world. And on this journey, our heart understands we have to forgive in order to be forgiven—because as we judge another, so our unconscious mind judges us.

SLEEPWALKING

Forgiveness enables us to feel compassion for ourselves as well as for others. It mercifully stops the flow of mindless accusations and recriminations that can lead to World War III with anyone anytime we feel hurt. Remember, when living in the ego mind world, we are all asleep. What we do when we are sleepwalking is not real. Despite the ego mind's best efforts to make it real, it is still only a dream.

The ego mind is determined for us to hang on to our anger, resentment, and stories. These things keep us small and preoccupied in the past rather than being present. They perpetuate misery, sickness, and suffering. If you truly desire happiness and optimal success in your relationships, your work and financial life, and the ongoing health and vitality of your body, you must break the ego mind's hold over your life.

To reclaim the enlightened state of the True Self, we must transcend the ego mind code with its inherent desire to hang on to resentment.

Human nature has become an unconscious minefield that can blow up at any time. Like Matthew, our executive hero who was not aware of the relationship between his mistaken perceptions, judgments, resentment, and anger to the excruciating pain of shingles, we walk through these minefields holding on to our stories and subsequent pain at our own peril.

Would you rather be right or be happy?

PLATINUM SUCCESS PRINCIPLE: PEACE

- Commit to regular meditation.

- Always forgive yourself and others.

- Question your stories and beliefs and don't take things personally.

- Use deep breathing, regular exercise, and seek out natural and peaceful environments to support your peaceful state.

- Use inquiry and attunement tools to restore and maintain Peace.

- Raise your state of Integrated Wholeness to where your buttons are no longer pushed by external forces and peace is your natural state.

- Assimilate the ABCs of enlightenment: Always Be Cool (i.e., don't take it personally).

- Personify the peace you want to experience in the world.

THE FORGIVENESS FACTOR

Forgiveness, peace, love, and joy are inextricably linked. It is only when we've experienced true inner peace that we understand there is another world that exists beyond the ego mind's comprehension. It is an awesome world of wonder and the bliss of pure love. To forgive is the soul's choice that enables us to find peace in a most uncertain world

Pure love is different from the love we feel when the ego mind projects the need to be loved with all its associated programs. In fact, the human mind has always struggled to grasp the enormity of what pure love truly is. Humanity has quite literally buried the light of pure love underneath countless layers of programs and beliefs within the unconscious mind.

People take drugs for many reasons. One is the desire to recapture the experience of pure love, which the ego mind cannot deliver in its make-believe world. When the mind is overtaken by pure love, we realize there is far more to our existence than what we thought. This is the place peace will take us without the need for anything outside of us.

Unlike drugs, many of which will eventually drag us into a living hell or even death, peace will have us gracefully dispense with the illusions that we have clung to, killed for, and been killed for, over and over again.

Peace is that place within us where we have given up the attachment to being right. Not about our engineering calculations, our ability to land a plane, or to be a wise counsel, but as one who needs to have his or her personal beliefs accepted no matter what, right or wrong!

Often, when people first start working with us they tell us they want to find peace in their lives. However, they make it clear that no matter what we say or do, they will never forgive their mother, father, or friend who has hurt them. They have their story of pain and suffering and are determined not to let it go. No way, Jose!

They state very clearly that they are not prepared to forgive and forget the person who has hurt them so much. It's more important for them to be right than to move on and be free from the suffering of the past. They were the injured party and they are stuck in their story. Yet here they are, sitting in a room with two people who were teaching them about enlightenment and love and they thought they could separate forgiveness from the mix.

Use this "Playground" guided visualization to help you find that place of peace through forgiveness.

PLAYGROUND VISUALIZATION

Is there anyone in your life who you have not come to peace with? Do your ego mind programs use these memories to torture you with maddening mind chatter and recriminations of guilt, shame, and of course, blame? Do you feel that you can never forgive them, or yourself, for what was or was not said or done? Odds are there is. The average person responding to this question can name at least three people who still cause inner conflict and feelings of despair and unhappiness.

It's not surprising that one of these people is often a spouse, one or more parents, other family members, or friends.

How do you deal with the lingering, heavy anchor of sorrow and regret that you can't quite shake? The ego mind tells most people it's a hopeless situation and they will never, ever find comfortable closure and inner peace with that person.

Your heart knows what your ego mind will never tell you. You can make peace with this situation and all other stressful issues, including making peace with yourself and those who are still alive yet are clearly candidates to be added to your list, should they expire before you do.

Why not try this creative visualization for yourself? After you read this, close your eyes, breathe deeply, drop your shoulders, take your tongue off the roof of your mouth, and become the observer. Now use your imagination and take yourself into a children's playground. This is not the colorful, plastic play areas of today. You are in a park that is full of weeds. The grass is sparse, and it only has a small sand pit, an old wooden seesaw, a slide, and a swing. There are two small children sitting side by side on the old swing set. They don't notice the heavy, rusting link chains; they are just grateful for the blue sky and to be able to play in the sun with their hair flying freely around their faces as they try to soar higher and higher.

At this moment, in this place, these little children finally feel free. They do not have to think about their alcoholic mum or drug-addicted father or the drama or abuse from any family member who awaits them at home.

In this one magical moment in your imaginary playground, whatever mistreatment those small children are suffering is totally forgotten. But wait! Do these little ones look familiar? Ah ha! Of course. It is your mother and your father from their childhood. You realize that when these children—your parents—go home, they are conditioned and programmed to become the people you knew or know today—just like you have been.

During this visualization, walk over to the swing set and sit on the swing. Allow that little girl or little boy to jump up onto your lap. Hold them the way you would hold any precious small child. Look into the eyes of that child—your mother or your father—as they ask the question they so desperately want to ask you. *"Please, can you forgive me for ever hurting you in any way? I was only doing what I learned to do and what my parents had learned to do before me."*

Now it is up to you. Take a deep breath and focus your attention into your heart. Ask your soul to choose the divine mind code, love them unconditionally, and truly forgive.

*Holding on to anger
is just like grasping a hot coal
with the intent of throwing it at someone else;
you are the one who gets burned.*

~ BUDDHA

THE UNIVERSAL NEED FOR FORGIVENESS

The words and events that trigger pain and suffering are only the outward manifestations of the unconscious programs coming into play between the people involved. We are all the star and the writer, director, producer, casting manager, stagehand, lighting technician, composer, and camera operator of the movie of our illusory lives. When we say "Action," anything is possible. Just like in "The Bold and The Beautiful," we've mastered Hollywood's art of immersing ourselves in feelings of jealousy, anger, frustration, grief, and despair.

Our ongoing TV series entertains us in so many ways, dramatizing our personal programs, past lives, and karma. The ego mind will always script injustice, intolerance, rage, revenge, selfishness, and of course, the need for constant gratification.

How ego mind programs create suffering is endless, and that's only our TV series. Everyone has been trained by the ego mind to become equally creative in their series. The people in our lives often play the roles we have given them in award-winning style. Unlike the joy of receiving a Nobel Peace Prize for excellence in helping humanity, there are no kudos in the awards given each other for how well we can perpetuate suffering—just battle scars.

Redefining and using forgiveness is critically important to our overall quality of life, health, and happiness. "Holding a grudge can kill you," says Jay D. Roberts, MD, citing a Harvard Medical study that discovered that unforgiveness can cause symptoms and diseases of life and death importance, including:

- Inflammation
- Increased cortisol
- Autoimmune problems
- Heart disease
- Cancer
- Severe headaches
- Stomach and abdominal problems
- Increased stress
- Insomnia

The study goes on to show five major benefits of forgiveness:

- Reduced stress
- Better heart health
- Stronger relationships
- Reduced pain
- Greater happiness

To this impressive list we add that forgiveness is paramount in bringing you closer to the God of your understanding and is the prerequisite to getting off the wheel of karma.

SHOCK TREATMENT

Have you ever written a scene for yourself where you had the experience of saying or doing something that you thought was the right thing, only to have it flung back in your face in a way that leaves you speechless? In a state of shock it is often impossible to know what to say.

Equilibrium is lost only to be replaced by suffering. Our programs kick into gear and feelings of self-righteousness surface. Left to its own devices, the ego mind will drive us crazy with an all-consuming litany of not only what we should have said, but how rotten the person was who started this roller-coaster ride into hell.

A friend was at a party where she sincerely congratulated a man on his upcoming award. He had put together a team of people to help fundraise for cancer research. She went into a state of shock when he said, *"I didn't think you would congratulate me."* Completely nonplussed, she rallied enough to ask why he would say that.

He told her that because he had left his dying brother in her and his sister's care to go on vacation, he assumed she wouldn't think he deserved it. This was only one of the many incidents at that party that pushed her buttons and would have had her in tears had she not gone into a silent rage. She could not leave quickly enough.

People often laugh when we say it is easier to be enlightened and to live a happy, peaceful life when you stay at home alone with your cat. My friend was no exception. She is a wise, deeply spiritual woman who walks through life with an air of peace and calm. When she came to me to talk about the events of that night, she knew she needed help to navigate her way into forgiveness and out of the self-perpetuating shock, anger, and confusion of her ego mind.

She was able to laugh when I said it had nothing to do with her. *"It's not about you; it's about the script he has written for himself. You are only an extra, and you have obviously forgotten to memorize your lines."*

Because the ego mind had the upper hand, it continued to protest, *"But what did I do wrong?"* Through the clamor of it shouting she had not considered the fact that he was projecting onto her what he thought about himself. A number of his beliefs were being played out in this one conversation, including:

1. He had not forgiven himself for leaving his cancer-riddled brother to die just so he could have a holiday.

2. He would not have forgiven her if the reverse had been true.

A level of peace was restored as the wisdom of her True Self emerged through her understanding heart. The confusion of *"What did I do to deserve that?"* dissolved when the suffering of her supposed tormentor was exposed. She was then able to rewrite her script so the dramatic storm and choppy waters of unforgiveness gave way to the peace and calm that only true forgiveness brings.

It's not always only about you. You are not the central character in other people's ego mind games. They are. As we diligently train the ego mind to defer to the wisdom of the divine mind, we move into that rarefied air shared by many spiritual masters. With increasingly higher states of awareness, understanding the big picture and deciphering the codes of others becomes automatic. We can discern when it is not about us, as well as how to help others who cannot see what we see. This happens for effective teachers who become a safe haven for others in need.

Two principles essential to implement and embody in order to successfully cultivate a PLATINUM state of mind and live a PLATINUM life are forgiveness and radical personal responsibility. They are inextricably interwoven; in fact, they are two sides of the same PLATINUM coin. True forgiveness ultimately requires and is based on taking radical personal responsibility for being the author of our experiences, perceptions, and life. And that is why forgiveness begins with forgiving ourselves.

Steps to Forgiveness

1. **Catch yourself operating in the ego mind code.**

   Acknowledge there are ego mind programs at work in the situation. And not only someone else's programs and perceptions, but yours.

2. **Select the divine mind code.**

   Take ownership. Reinterpret the situation through your heart. Breathe deeply. Visualize white light filling you with unconditional love. Feel the feelings you would feel if you knew the highest and best for all concerned is being realized.

3. **With unconditional love, forgive yourself and others for choosing ego mind programs.**

   Forgiveness invites grace, and without its unconditional love, forgiveness is still only judgment.

4. **Surrender the situation to your True Self.**

   Peace is restored when forgiveness ends the ego mind's dream of conflict and separation.

ATTUNEMENT:
Meditation on Peace

Center yourself by taking a few deep breaths. Harmonize with the high frequency of peace. Observe your breath and let your body relax. Let go of all judgments. Allow your thoughts to simply come and go.

Say to yourself, *"Peace is my natural state. My True Self is the perfect expression of peace, love, and joy."*

Continue to breathe deeply as your whole being makes the shift to this powerful vibrational frequency of peace. Just as darkness is displaced by light, with every breath you take your feelings are transformed: fear, anxiety, and being overwhelmed are displaced by peace.

Using your imagination, see, feel, or know yourself experiencing the feelings that peace brings to your body, mind, and soul. Continue to imagine, feel, see, and know this peace. Bask in the calm and wonder of the peace that resides within you as you. It has no conditions. There is nothing you need to get, give, or do.

This is your time.

Allow yourself to go deeper and deeper to be more and more relaxed. Invite the True Self to take the stage as you sit centered in your heart, basking in the light of the divine mind code.

With the awareness that your soul is choosing to live the peace that you are, say, *"I am in perfect alignment with my natural state of peace."*

Now imagine a column of white light pouring into your head and filling your body all the way to the tips of your toes. This is the light of your True Self that you have activated by changing your thoughts to peace. Allow this white light to flow freely through you, as you, soothing your entire being, and your body relaxing even more.

With every breath you take, your body, mind, and soul are being regenerated, rejuvenated, strengthened, and renewed. In this state of peace your creativity and wisdom flow naturally.

You have now powered up your life onto the frequency of success.

Stay in this expansive place, relaxing in the peace that you are for as long as you can. Aligned with this unfathomably rich place of unity with your True Self and the cosmos, you can go deeper and deeper into everyday enlightened states.

Engage your imagination and take a moment to bring into your meditation someone who has hurt you. Feel the other person relax, breathing easily and matching up their vibration of peace to yours. Now say, *"I forgive all my programs that have separated us and I forgive all your programs that have hurt me."*

The whole world has just taken a deep breath!

Real forgiveness is the natural expression of peace and love, of the divine mind.

When you are ready, take a few more deep breaths and slowly open your eyes. You are now in tune with the high vibrational frequency of peace. Congratulations. You have just activated the best version of you.

Share it with the world. Stay on this frequency for as long as you can.

If you feel yourself slipping into fear, negativity, or pain, reignite the high frequency of peace with this meditation and imagine yourself as the person you forgive and love.

Keys to Peace

To be in a state of peace, we need to be in harmony with the energy frequency of peace. To attune to this frequency consistently, it is essential to train the mind and create new habits. It is also helpful to set the stage in our homes and workplace. Some simple steps to accomplish this include the following:

- **Use mindfulness meditation daily on your inner journey into peace.** Become the observer of your thoughts and feelings without comment or judgment—odds are you will discover emotional triggers that will need to be corrected so you can be the neutral observer from a place of peace.

- **Make your home and workspace as harmonious as possible.** Use your creativity and intuition to create a stable, peaceful environment in which to work, play, and love. Spirit loves beauty in all forms. That is why the more you create beautiful spaces around you, the more peaceful, uplifted, and content you will feel.

- **As often as possible, visit a place in nature where you can enjoy the beauty and serenity of your surroundings.** Take in the splendor of a sunset or sunrise and allow yourself to feel the joy of being alive in the moment.

- **Get your blood flowing and oxygenate your entire system.** Develop the habit of deep diaphragmatic breathing. Exercise as often as you can: walk, run, dance, lift weights, or just tense and relax. Center yourself and connect with your core essence, perhaps by practicing yoga, tai chi, or any of the martial arts that train you to center yourself to find fluidity, balance, and strength through a state of inner peace.

- **Continually use self-inquiry to stay balanced and mindful and to heighten your level of awareness.** (The Four Questions and Rate Your State below are great practices for this.)

- **To experience inner peace it is essential to forgive.** Remember, you are only ever forgiving ego mind programs—both your own and others'—that have been accumulated since conception, or even before.

- **Creatively use the Playground visualization.** Go back in time and truly forgive anyone, including yourself, who has hurt you.

- **True inner peace is not dependent on external circumstances.** Paradoxically, it is the state in which you can exert the most constructive influence on external circumstances.

Ego Puppy Training 1: Peace

Now, just for fun, imagine your ego mind is your new puppy. Its name, of course, is Ego Puppy! It has already learned some terrible tricks from the rest of the litter, the untrained mother, and the mostly absent father. When you discover Ego Puppy, you are convinced that this feral creature has been roaming wild for centuries.

It is hard to believe it could have learned such obnoxious behavior in only a few months. It's already ruining the carpet; chewing slippers, sneakers, and your most cherished items; stealing food; and regularly keeping the whole neighborhood up all night with its whining and barking. Like the puppy Marley in the movie Marley and Me, it brings chaos and one crisis after another into your life.

It is overwhelming to contemplate how much there is to do in order to undo little Ego Puppy's attachment to trouble. Deep down inside, you know no one else can do it for you. (After all, it really is your ego mind we are talking about.) So you simply must make a start. Take one step at a time, as Ego Puppy would eat Marley for breakfast when it comes to mischief and mayhem.

Per usual, the ego mind has the audacity to complain to its master—you. What did I do to deserve this? Why isn't there someone else to handle the job?

When the complaining finally ceases, you discover the answer. Everyone got a member of Ego Puppy's litter at the same time! And, if you've ever been in a dog-training class, you understand who is really being trained—it's you, the master!

To realize your puppy's full potential will require you to be diligent in the process of undoing little Ego's well-known habitual behavior. Never lose sight of your goal: The ultimate reward is getting off the wheel of karma.

While Ego Puppy is the bad news, there's good news too!

As luck would have it, you also got a baby kitten at the same time. Called Kosmic Kitten, it has four eyes: one physical pair and a spiritual pair that are the source of your intuition. You will learn more about Kosmic Kitten later in the book.

As training finally begins to progress, the stress and suffering caused by Ego Puppy begins to ease off. The body, mind, and soul relax enough to find new vitality and strength as your inner world starts to return to peace. And, you can start to love yourself for who you really are rather than who you seemed to be when Ego Puppy first trotted into existence. When Ego Puppy graduates with honors as a summa cum laude service dog, there will be cosmic fireworks as you celebrate true inner peace.

There are proven ways to help yourself experience peace in this dualistic world of endless drama. Breaking the hold of the ego mind code requires training the mind to practice new ways of thinking. When you train Ego Puppy to sit and stay, you are free to move into higher levels of awareness. Repetition builds a habit field that facilitates the creation of new, increasingly dominant neural pathways. We want to be operating through the prefrontal cortex more and depending on the limbic system and the reptilian brain less. The old pathways reflect programming from lifetimes of conditioning—not to mention eons of genetic inheritance. They habitually force you back into the same thought system—the ego mind code—responsible for the conviction that your programs are the truth.

Okay, so now you know your ego mind is like a new puppy. We don't want to crush it or destroy it. We know resistance breeds persistence. It came into your life as a baby and has all the same needs of any baby. As science has discovered, we all need constant love and attention to reach our full potential as loyal, loving, well-adjusted members of any family. Out of love and enlightened self-interest, you begin to ensure ongoing peace in your life when you take responsibility for training the newest member of the family—your newly recognized ego mind.

The rewards are huge. They go beyond the healing effects this training has on you emotionally and mentally. Even your overall health and wellbeing on a physical level are also positively impacted. A great service dog could easily save your life.

As Ego Puppy experiences your consistency, it becomes more trainable. Through repetition and reward, Ego Puppy learns appropriate behavior from the games you play together. As it earns rewards, peace in your world expands.

INQUIRY—
THE FOUR QUESTIONS: PEACE

This inquiry technique utilizes your internal GPS. It is intentional self-awareness and is based on the use of mindfulness, which is simply observing yourself without judgment. This simple but powerful tool cultivates emotional intelligence.

Use your feelings as a readout on your internal GPS. The more negative you are feeling, the more off course you are. The better you feel, the more on course you are. Making ongoing course corrections is an easy and effective way to manage your state. Use it to connect with your true north, your True Self.

Use this simple set of questions to change the way you feel from one moment to the next. As you practice and become proficient, this technique will become second nature and you will use it like an aircraft's autopilot to course-correct automatically. Use it whenever you feel yourself moving away from your natural state of peace and love and recognize that it is only untrained ego mind mischief at play.

Answer the questions truthfully and spontaneously. Stay focused on the answer to question number four as long as you can. The answers we provide are examples only. Use your own words and the wisdom of your own heart to answer the questions.

1. **What am I feeling?** I feel angry and frustrated.

2. **What am I focused on?** They are wrong and they should do what I think is right.

3. **How do I want to feel?** Peaceful and balanced.

4. **What focus will serve that?** Letting go of the need to be right, noting what we share in common, and accepting responsibility for my feelings.

As you breathe deeply, stay focused in your heart, and with love, immediately forgive anything that pushes your buttons and brings up a program to be corrected and neutralized. Be grateful for the opportunity to become more whole by clearing out yet another unwanted belief or idea that takes you away from peace.

INQUIRY—
RATE YOUR STATE: PEACE

Use these three questions as a guide to rate your state and discover which code you are operating in.

1. **Is there someone in your life you have not forgiven?** Odds are, when we have not forgiven someone, this takes up a lot of rent-free space in the mind. Ego mind makes us into a martyr and often drives us crazy by rerunning the same scenario over and over again. This is low on the Integrated Wholeness Scale.

2. **Have you forgiven yourself for hurting someone else?** The ego mind is quick to make us wrong and punish us for any slip in our magnificence. Become aware of how our words and thoughts are capable of creating pain for others and ultimately for ourselves. Train the ego mind to sit on the sidelines as we bring the True Self back into play where real forgiveness always wins the day. We rate high on the Integrated Wholeness Scale when we forgive ego mind programs and empower ourselves to adjust our thinking.

3. **When was the last time you stopped yourself from judging someone else?** Every time we judge someone else, we have given ego mind the free rein it wants. We cannot know what someone else is going through until we walk in their shoes. Judgments and all forms of separation (including gossip!) keep us low on the Integrated Wholeness Scale.

Using your new PLATINUM password activates your personal power and facilitates tolerance, acceptance, and forgiveness—which is the way to peace. You are now moving higher on the Integrated Wholeness Scale.

An Overview: Peace

- Peace is the state of harmony and balance, tranquility and quiet, in which the highest good for all is naturally sought. In this state of serenity we are free from unsettling thoughts and emotions. Inner peace is the power source that enables our journey into enlightenment and wholeness, into a PLATINUM life.

- When the soul chooses to live by the ego mind code instead of the divine mind code, we are out of alignment with our True Self, which always results in a lack of balance, wholeness, and inner peace. Typically this results in a range of feelings such as despair, grief, panic, aggression, and separation that overpower our lives with devastating results.

- If we do not question our stories, we will never know the truth. They are only stories and have no meaning in the real world.

- The truth is never what the ego mind thinks it is.

- Peace, love, joy, and forgiveness are inextricably linked.

- Peace is found in that place within us where we have given up our need to be right and the compulsion to fight for our fear-based beliefs.

- As we step into our personal power we naturally understand that true forgiveness is the only way to peace. With true forgiveness for ourselves and others, the love, compassion, and joy that result are all the reward we will ever need.

- Peace prompts us to delve into the unconditional love of the divine mind and take every opportunity provided by friends, family, co-workers, lovers, and life to forgive.

- Only when we are at peace can we be fully present— not numb or asleep, but fully awake—and experience life directly.

- Unforgiveness is the core blocking frequency to peace.

When the power of love overcomes the love of power, the world will know peace.

~ Jimi Hendrix

Jimi's inspiring insight applies to each of us: When the power of love of the divine mind code overcomes the love of power of the ego mind code, we will know peace.

Remember, as our hero Matthew learned the hard way, *"It's okay. It's not real. It's just a story."*

As you move forward on life's greatest adventure and build upon the high frequency of Peace as your foundation, it is time to take the next step in connecting with who you really are—which is Love. Are you ready to move on to the next high frequency beingness state in the PLATINUM Life System?

YES!!!! Love: Your purpose is to grow, evolve, and have fun expressing the love that you are.

CHAPTER TWO

LOVE:
IGNITE THE SECRET TO YOUR SUCCESS

Love is a magician.
Everything it touches turns into itself.

~ PAMELA WILSON

You Are What You Have Been Looking For

In virtually every spiritual and religious tradition, there is an archetypal story or myth about what is often called "the pearl of great price." Let's imagine it's time for God to give us the most precious gift of all—to give us the pearl of great price. It is the gift of unconditional love. In truth, it is the love that we are.

In this story, God knows we will place greater value on this gift if we think it is precious and something to be treasured. He wanted to hide this gift in the last place we would look to ensure that when we finally found it, we would value it and not throw it back from whence it came.

As God pondered this, He had the idea to hide it in the ocean at the bottom of the deepest abyss. Oh no, that would not work; the Russians would go there and find it. Then He thought to place this gift on top of the highest mountain peak. But that would not work either; the English would go there. Hmmm, what if it was placed on the moon? No, that still wouldn't work; the Americans would go there.

At last God realized He could place this invaluable gift in the one place humanity would never think to look—right in the center of our hearts.

Well, we are looking into our hearts now and are surprised to find that all the cosmos and more lives there with us. It is the longest expedition all of humanity will have ever undertaken, this journey from the head into the heart—and the most rewarding.

There is no mistaking love.

You feel it in your heart.

It is the common fibre of life,

the flame that heats our soul,

energizes our spirit and supplies passion to our lives.

It is our connection to God and to each other.

~ ELIZABETH KUBLER-ROSS

We have long lived by divine guidance. Although most people find it astonishing, it was not surprising to us that just after dinner on our second date, we agreed we were married as of that moment. Obviously, there was something very powerful going on for two people who had only met moments before to be that certain of such a huge commitment.

We had spent our lives diligently exploring the human potential movement and pursuing the mystical in the same headlong fashion we had pursued our business goals: tuned into our divine guidance, 100 percent commitment, and full-speed ahead. We both had many indescribable experiences outside the understanding of the ego mind and institutional science.

Fortunately, mainstream scientists are now moving closer to the wisdom of the formerly inexplicable spiritual world that mystics have known for eons of time. Our relationship triggered off so many "other worldly" events that it would take a whole book to tell them but, as we are in Love, one of Sandra's enlightenment stories demands to be told.

LOVE IN THE SHOWER

One morning I was in the shower in the front bathroom when a tidal wave of unconditional love filled the whole of my being. I was aware my body was crying and there was no distinction between the shower water and myself. Not only had the water become me and I the water, but in that moment I was connected to everything. I was one with the divine. There was no separation between who I was and the air, the room, the house, the whole of the universe. I was one with all that is. The True Self had completely eclipsed the ego mind's elaborate construct of subject and object, of duality and separation.

I had the vague awareness that my body was still in existence. I was totally detached from it other than to know that it too was only a tiny particle in the divine mind code. I was a sublime, drunken puddle of unconditional love merged into God's grace. Unconditional love courses through the divine mind, which had enveloped my mind. so nothing else existed. Everything finally disappeared into love. I was not frightened because fear simply cannot exist in this state, and I had already had similar experiences of being in this state of awe, oneness, and love.

Somehow I had turned off the water and was stepping out of the shower when Daniel walked from his office at the other end of the house into the bathroom. Radiant with joy, he dropped to his knees, tears flowing, overwhelmed by the waves of energy filling the entire apartment emanating from the center of what used to be my being.

He wrapped his arms around my waist, and leaning his head into my wet stomach, he said, *"I just tracked down the source of the waves of energy that enveloped me in the most beautiful, unconditional love, and total acceptance."*

We weren't drunk or on drugs, but we were both drunk and high in the real world of unconditional love where the heart sings with unbridled joy. In this world, forgiveness accomplishes the impossible. All life is unified in all of its beauty and splendor. And this is who we are; it is our true nature. When you reenter the real world of God, you are perfect beyond the ego mind's ability to comprehend.

When Buddha said, *"I am awake,"* he meant he realized he was awake to the illusory world of the ego mind. This is from one who had become whole in his essence. He woke up to the truth that the world we live in is solely the creation of the ego mind running wild in its dreamlike state.

The love in the shower experience took Daniel and me beyond the realm of our ego minds, and reality moved in on us. When it finally subsided, we were awake to the fact that if it's not divine love, then it is not real.

After the Loss

We were having lunch with our friends, Bill and Sandy, who had each both lost their beloved partners to cancer more than four years previously. In their early eighties, they both looked healthy and vital with a strong, happy life force. There was an air of peace about them that had not come easily after such tragic losses. Bill and Sandy had known each other for two years, and the pace of their inter-town travels to see each other had not slowed down.

They both had full and exciting lives and were still curious, interested, and eager to learn. You know that makes them incredibly attractive, right? Even before they met each other, they could both have taught us a thing or two about the sexiest trait on the planet. Together, they were dynamic. Their new love and joy was contagious. The "geezers" (as they liked to call themselves) were a lot of fun and a pleasure to be around!

Sandy candidly explained that she had been in such despair after the loss of her husband that she had used antidepressants right up until she met her new love. We had seen and felt the despair of our friend, and knew Bill also had a hole in his heart from losing his beloved wife. They had both been through the zombie-like state that makes the world lose all its color, food become tasteless, and the happiness of others seem unfathomable.

Although both Bill and Sandy knew they would never stop loving the ones they had lost, they were smart enough to know there was plenty of room in their huge hearts. Without love, we all feel bereft. Life has no meaning. It feels like a cruel and empty place.

When trauma strikes, such as the death of someone very close to us, a major illness, a divorce, or loss of a job, the pain is great. If the ego mind convinces us that we have a legitimate reason to believe someone else has contributed to our pain, it then becomes excruciating. A common response is to ask, *"Why me?"* and then to become angry and perhaps throw ourselves into other areas and activities.

If the trauma and resentment or guilt is severe enough, there is still a major wound that must be healed before peace and love can be restored. This is often referred to as *"a hole in the heart."* The ego mind is quick to take advantage of all this suffering. Programs surface like, *"What's the point?" "I'm all alone in the world; no one understands what I'm going through!" "I've lost everything, life is not worth living." "No one cares about me, I may as well give up and die!"*

Have you ever met anyone who has felt that way? You might have even asked yourself those questions in times of despair. Frequently, the person suffering from this feels that nothing can fill the hole in their heart and continues on a downward spiral, battling what is an invisible foe. The ego mind's unconscious stories are the invisible enemy.

In other words, our programs are the problem. And even if we do not sink into depression, experience other mental and/ or physical problems, or resort to drugs, alcohol, sex, or food addictions and abuse, with the help from the ego mind the hole in the heart remains. Peace has not been attained and love has not been restored.

The most effective way of closing the hole is to eliminate it entirely. Clearly, enlightened forgiveness is the surest and most effective way to restore peace and create a new foundation of Love.

Peace and love are the bedrock of being able to live a PLATINUM life. When the soul chooses the divine mind code, we evolve into the best version of who we are, moving up and across on the Integrated Wholeness Scale. Life often feels not worth living when below 200 x 200 on this model of the evolution of the soul. It's only when we attain at least 500 x 500—at love or above —that the ego mind's diversionary questions settle down and life becomes that crazy good experience we all want it to be.

WHAT IS LOVE?

Pure love is your essence. Your purpose is to grow, evolve, and have fun expressing the love that you are.

- Love is a state and energy, not an emotion. As energy, it is the most powerful energy of the cosmos.
- Love is the catalyst of creation and is infinitely powerful.
- Love is the fuel of miracles.
- At our very core, love is who we are. It is an expression of the perfection of the True Self when unimpeded by ego mind programs.
- Without love it is impossible to successfully live a PLATINUM life because more than anything else, love facilitates transformation.
- The divine mind code fully incorporates love. It is filled with authenticity, openness, transparency, acceptance, empathy, and respect.
- Love supports the development and growth of real success and happiness.
- When we have not yet awakened to the love of the True Self, it is easy for the ego mind to fool us into believing true love is somewhere "out there." No wonder every person at some stage has been looking for love in all the wrong places.
- The core low frequency blocker to love is fear.

Your task is not to seek for love,
but merely to seek and find all the barriers
within yourself that you have built against it.

~ RUMI

I Know the Way You Can Get

I know the way you can get
When you have not had a drink of Love:

Your face hardens,
Your sweet muscles cramp.
Children become concerned
About a strange look that appears in your eyes
Which even begins to worry your own mirror
And nose.

Squirrels and birds sense your sadness
And call an important conference in a tall tree.
They decide which secret code to chant
To help your mind and soul.

Even angels fear that brand of madness
That arrays itself against the world
And throws sharp stones and spears into
The innocent
And into one's self.

O I know the way you can get
If you have not been drinking Love:

You might rip apart
Every sentence your friends and teachers say,
Looking for hidden clauses.

You might weigh every word on a scale
Like a dead fish.

You might pull out a ruler to measure
From every angle in your darkness
The beautiful dimensions of a heart you once
Trusted.

I know the way you can get
If you have not had a drink from Love's
Hands.

That is why all the Great Ones speak of
The vital need
To keep remembering God,
So you will come to know and see Him
As being so Playful
And Wanting,
Just Wanting to help.

That is why Hafiz says:
Bring your cup near me.
For all I care about
Is quenching your thirst for freedom!

All a Sane man can ever care about
Is giving Love!

~HAFIZ

From *I Heard God Laughing: Poems of Hope and Joy,*
Copyright 1996 & 2006 by Daniel Ladinsky
and used with his permission.

Love: The Underestimated Genius of the Heart

At our core, love is who we are—and the genius of the heart knows no boundaries. It has no limit on how many people can come into its orbit and be safe there. Our capacity to express more of what our primordial nature is cannot be contained, measured, or put in a box. Only in the ego mind's illusory world do we need to pigeonhole love. Our wise friends, Bill and Sandy, clearly understood that only love could mend their broken hearts —pure genius!

We really love this wonderful story about the genius of the soul when it chooses love. In a two-page spread in a local paper, there was a full-page photo of a man and woman together with the heading, "Love at One Hundred and Six." They had met two years previously in the retirement village where they both lived. She was one hundred and six and he was seventy-nine. They had decided not to get married because they had not married their first partners, so why start now? He said she was the smartest, funniest, and most wise woman he had ever met. They were radiant!

These people were not looking for people to be space fillers. They chose to activate their capacity to love, even through adversity, and were genuinely and positively transformed.

Everyone comes into relationships full of hope. Even with our most beloved family members we can still wonder why we end up in so much pain. Remember, the ego mind has hijacked us over many lifetimes. We all have programs that continually warn us how dangerous it can be to love and how futile or even disempowering it is to forgive and let go.

Without mastering the art of forgiveness, our relationships easily fall by the wayside, only to be replaced by more of the same. Have you ever watched anyone go through a series of relationships, one right after another, and still end up with essentially the same partner—just in a different package?

Einstein defined insanity as doing the same thing over and over again and expecting different results. When people become space fillers they are easy to replace.

Forgiveness is such a big decision it affects the whole world. The first person we all must forgive is ourselves. Until we experience the infinite love of the real world, it's easy to be conned into believing that we are just a body and that whatever is happening is our lot in life and we are relatively powerless to change it.

But that is not the truth.

Our feelings are evidence of what we are thinking. Our thoughts get processed through the brain which triggers hormonal responses that stimulate feelings and emotions. What is critical to understand is that we all have the power within us to change the way we think and feel about any situation.

Small children believe what their parents say to be the truth. Like a child, do you fail to question the content of the ego mind? Does it continually imprison you with its thoughts, ideas, values, and beliefs? Do you mistakenly claim ownership of them?

Our programs condition us. They act like bars and chains that constrict us in our own little prisons. Woe betide anyone who challenges what the ego mind asserts to be the truth. Always ready to criticize and attack, it automatically rejects ideas foreign to its values and readily finds others guilty who disagree with it, imprisoning them in cells even smaller than our own.

Have you ever experienced that uneasy feeling that comes after you have been talking negatively about another person? Once we have played at being judge and jury we are still not happy and wonder why. Did you know that when we judge another person, our unconscious mind applies that same judgment to us? This is why the saying, *"When you point a finger at someone else, there are three pointing back at you,"* is true not only physically but psychologically as well.

The PLATINUM Life System sets us free. It trains us to operate in the divine mind code, which facilitates becoming neutral and dissolving the bars of our self-created prison. We can then break free of the ego mind code that keeps its prison doors tightly locked, walking in circles of self-righteousness and judgment with little joy and not much love.

No one is born hating another person because of the color of his skin, or his background, or his religion. People must learn to hate, and if they can learn to hate, they can be taught to love, for love comes more naturally to the human heart than its opposite.

— NELSON MANDELA

THE SCIENCE OF LOVE

Science and medicine are continually learning more about how the wonderful tools we call the body and the brain operate. Their insights help us develop new ways to unlock the ego- mind code working with the neurophysiology of the brain to reprogram and neutralize unconscious fears and other destructive emotions so easily triggered in the absence of love.

A General Theory of Love by Thomas Lewis, MD, Fari Amini, MD, and Richard Lannon, MD, explains in elegant prose how the brain works and its relationship to love. These wonderful doctors, who are delving into the mystical world of the heart from a scientific perspective, write *"In all cases, emotions are humanity's motivator and its omnipresent guide."*

When they talk about all of the benefits of cognition and the brilliance of the human intellect and all of the ways they have made our lives easier—from plumbing to the game changer of the Internet—they say, *"But even as it reaps the benefits of reason, modern America plows emotions under—a costly practice that obstructs happiness and misleads people about the nature and significance of their lives."*

They tell us that science has discovered emotion's deeper purpose: *"The timeworn mechanisms of emotions allow two human beings to receive the contents of each other's minds. Emotion is the messenger of love; it is the signal that carries one brimming heart to another."*

Repressed or unresolved emotion is the messenger of fear—the core low frequency blocker of love. It is the signal that communicates from one imprisoned mind to another.

Love is the genie with the promise of granting us the inner strength and power to get off the roller-coaster ride of negative life patterns, to unshackle the shattered heart and restore it to wholeness. It is the precious gift of the True Self hidden deep within our hearts.

Divine love is infinite, unconditional, and all encompassing. It surpasses the understanding of the ego mind and opens the door to the health and wellbeing of the body, mind, and soul. It is the prerequisite to the miracle of real forgiveness and the joy that comes from knowing we can move on from the darkness—the guilt, shame, and blame of our unconscious programs—to be and do what we love, and love who we are and what we do.

Miracles occur as expressions of love.
The real miracle is the love that inspires them.
In this sense everything that comes
from love is a miracle.

~ A COURSE IN MIRACLES

Past, Present, and Future Programs

We worked with a client named Jonathan who had been sexually abused by his uncle as a child, and then had gone on to abuse his little sister in later years. He was in real torment. A black hole of shame had been sucking all the joy from his life ever since both events. Although he had talked it over with his sister many times, and she had forgiven him, he could not find it in himself to do the same. And even though he thought he had forgiven his uncle, it was only his head that had done so.

He was in his early thirties and had been searching for relief through books and seminars for many years before he came to one of our events. He honestly thought that happiness and loving relationships were beyond his reach. He committed to spending a weeklong Intensive working with us, and toward the end of the week, he was so immersed in his heart, he was able to truly forgive his uncle. He could no longer feel the anger surrounding that abuse.

However, Jonathan's thoughts about his sister continued to trigger the deep wounds still wrapped with the acid of the shame. On the last day of the Intensive, we resumed with the part of the process that everyone looked forward to every day, which participants dubbed "Story Time." They took turns in the hot seat, the chair beside Sandra, where she revealed a personal story from a parallel, past, present, or future lifetime. (Although there is abundant scientific evidence to support past lives, there is no need to believe in them for this technique to be effective.)

Humans are hardwired for stories. In our work, we consider these stories to be similar to Jungian archetypes or classic, timeless myths that have profound personal significance for us.

The participants in this intensive had already been time traveling in past and future life meditations and uncovered programs that needed to be corrected. It was obvious these unconscious programs were still playing out in destructive patterns. Using the Quantum Neutrality Process, described later, the emotional charge surrounding the events and decisions was neutralized and the stories re-scripted to nullify the programs.

People were freed to make new choices that could now come from the innate wisdom and creativity of the heart. Moving forward in their relationships, jobs, and the physical world became easier. We were all better able to tap into our personal power and move forward in the world with real strength and freedom. The Quantum Neutrality Process facilitated instant transformation in the lives of every member of the group.

One high-powered business executive, a woman in her early 40s, changed so much when she moved from her head into her heart that she found—to her amazement and the astonishment of her staff—that after being disliked for years, she became liked and respected at last. The new woman that emerged from within her changed her relationships so dynamically that the whole company prospered.

When she returned to work on a Monday her co-workers asked her, *"Who are YOU? What did you do with the bitch? And where have you been all this time?"*

Jonathan, who had been unable to forgive himself, at last found peace as he was finally able to let go of his shame and the unhappiness that held him hostage to despair.

While everyone's eyes were closed during the visualization, Sandra wrote on the white board a new mantra that clinched the deal for him. The big "Ah hah!" moment came when he read, *"No matter what you have said or done, you still deserve love."*

When Jonathan came out of the forgiveness meditation and absorbed the quote on the white board, his whole demeanor dramatically changed. The penny finally dropped. His stubborn ego mind that had imprisoned him with guilt was finally knocked on its head. His prison break changed his life.

Jonathan was finally neutral to the events, emotions, and decisions that had kept him in a loop of guilt, shame, and blame. He floated out of the Intensive on an invisible energetic cloud of infinite, unconditional love. His body looked stronger and more alive. A wide and wonderful smile on his face made him look younger and more attractive. These are examples of the typical results we experience when working with the unexpected genius of the heart.

Man must evolve for all human conflict a method
which rejects revenge, aggression and retaliation.
The foundation of such a method is love.

~ Dr. Martin Luther King, Jr.

The Smile Factor

During our Intensives, people are often on a high in a peak state of awareness that is classically associated with enlightenment. In this state, happiness becomes a deep well of joy, and it can be impossible not to let the face know about it. A smile can heal an ailing heart, it can uplift a grieving soul, and it automatically changes the way we all feel. It is hard to stay unhappy when we smile.

As one of the twentieth century's great philosophers, Charles Schultz, portrayed in his cartoon of Charlie Brown, a smile can change our world. Charlie Brown was bent over at the waist facing the ground when Lucy came up to him and asked him, *"What are you doing?"*

He said, *"I'm being depressed."* He then stood up straight and smiled and said, *"Because if I stand up straight like this and smile, I won't feel depressed anymore!"*

On the inner journey out of the darkness and into the light of divine love, we learn a wonderful truth: The key to enlightenment is to lighten up. Our million-dollar expression of delight, love, sincerity, courage, success, welcome, and acceptance can be seen in the power of our smile. When we have slipped out of the heart, like Charlie Brown, make the conscious choice to stand up straight and smile. Not only is it hard to stay unhappy, but if we savor our smile deeply, it becomes difficult to remember what caused the slip in the first place.

Another advantage is that other people usually respond to a smile in positive ways, often despite themselves. We are not seen as a threat when we smile, and we never know when someone needs the warmth of a smile just to feel better for an instant. It costs nothing to smile and bring the light of love into our often dark and scary world; it only pays dividends.

When children smile, it comes from their hearts and is full of genuine joy. They smile up to 400 times a day. As an adult, we are lucky if we get 15 smiles on our faces in a day. When we share a smile, it reassures children and adults alike that they are okay and that their world is a safe place.

We have had fun traveling to the ends of the earth exploring our own spirituality. We've learned that wherever we go—there we are! Right now, right where we are, we can each tap into that place of divine love within that gives us the strength to straighten and smile.

Loving Connections

Scientists have developed the field of computational neuroscience in the quest to understand the workings of the human brain. In the process, they have discovered that love alters the physical structure of the brain. How much love we did or did not receive from our parents and extended family is one of the key determinants of the way the brain functions, along with the programs by which our unconscious mind operates.

Our destiny as a well-adjusted, intelligent, socially skilled, loving person is powerfully influenced while in the womb by what we hear and feel in our mother's voice and experience. Even before birth, the mind's observations are processed at lightning speed. Like a sponge, the brain is operating at the programming levels of theta and delta, and we are absorbing and filing information with no filters to inform us if something is real or true.

Humans, like all mammals, are hardwired with a strong family instinct. The development of a child is directly linked to the mother, her programs, and the experiences the mother had since the child's conception. The hurricane of violence that is spreading throughout youth in the United States and the whole world is symptomatic of a lack of love, and it underscores the importance of the role of family in the lives of our beautiful babies. Is it too late to reach those who appear to be lost?

Hungrily looking for some form of happiness, they form pack-like gangs where their Ego Puppies become members of a family where they pretend to be safe. They have been hog-tied by the ego mind's unconscious drive for its version of love and fulfillment. With patient, loving mentoring, we can help bring about changes in the choices made by our corrupted youth.

PLATINUM SUCCESS PRINCIPLE: LOVE

- Love what you do and the people you do it with. You can always find something you can love in what you are doing.

- The most basic way to ignite the secret to your success is to know with every fiber of your being that love is who you are.

- The frequency of love is the frequency of success.

- Love is enough to change your life and the life of anyone in its orbit.

This is one of the most critical components we discuss when coaching business owners, executives, and professionals. Regardless of our roles in life, we are all the CEO and COO of our own life. This applies to everyone.

Until the soul chooses to change codes and align with the True Self, our ego mind programs will sabotage our success.

It's imperative to change our thinking by neutralizing and deleting self-esteem issues and dysfunctional programs and to commit to being of service in whatever way possible. Always having our heart in the game with our eye on the ball reaps huge rewards for us, our organizations, and our customers.

There are countless examples of love igniting the secret to success. One business owner created a massively successful, record-breaking car dealership by incorporating love into every aspect of his company and its operation.

To ignite the secret to our success, we must know with every fiber of our being that love is who we are. True love does not come from the illusory world that the ego mind fabricated which uses fear and separation to perpetuate itself. Real love is spiritual, and is accessed by the divine mind code. It recognizes the divinity in us and in every living being.

When we allow our programs to run rampant, it's easy for our human computer to crash and burn. It's easy to sit in judgment of ourselves and others and start wars that bring our personal world into chaos and despair. Real love is the water that quenches our thirst, frees us from the isolation of separation, and magnetizes even more love into our life. This love does not expect anything in return and is whole unto itself—and just think, this is who you are!

Love is our essential nature. No matter what circumstances have transpired, no matter what programs we have been running as unconscious software from childhood, or societal conditioning, love is who we always have been and always will be.

Love is the fuel of miracles.

We had been frequenting a little café in a seaside resort town for a few months and had become friendly with the chef and all the staff. The day before we were to leave town, one of the servers brought us our coffees and almost broke down as she placed the cups on our table. She was a beautiful young girl of about seventeen. With tears in her eyes, she looked at us and said, *"What is it? I always feel so good when you're here. What are you doing?"*

"Loving you. We just love you, that's all." With that, the tears made tracks down her cheeks as she looked at us and said, *"I thought so. It's just I have never felt love like this before and I have never been happier than I have been recently. Thank you. I know my life has changed because you've loved me."*

We had never told this girl we loved her, yet her life was positively affected by the vibrational resonance she was feeling to the high frequency energy of love.

Love is enough to change the lives of anyone in its orbit.

Know this, even if the ego mind objects violently:
The frequency of love is the frequency of success.

With love as our baseline, we can become mindful of our feelings and aware of the needs and desires of others. No matter how much pain in any relationship, we can still stay true to these dictates:

1. Love no matter what.

2. Forgive when given the chance.

3. Be vigilant to any judgments and drop them like a hot potato.

4. The ego mind's core low frequency blocker to love is fear.

All that stops us from staying on the high frequency of love and experiencing the life we dream of is our choice of code.

Neither a lofty degree of intelligence
nor imagination nor both together
go to the making of genius.
Love, love, love;
that is the soul of genius.

– WOLFGANG AMADEUS MOZART

ATTUNEMENT:
A Meditation on Love

Begin by observing your breath and letting your body relax. Center yourself by taking a few deep breaths, and harmonize with the energy of love by thinking of someone or something that you love unconditionally. Let go of all judgments as you allow your thoughts to simply come and go.

Say to yourself, *"Love is my essence. My True Self is the perfect expression of divine love, peace, and joy."* Continue to breathe deeply as your whole being makes the shift to this powerful vibrational frequency of love. Just as darkness is displaced by light, your thoughts are transformed and fear is displaced by love.

Bask in the feeling of being this love. It has no conditions.

Using your imagination, see, feel or know someone you love sitting opposite you.

With all your heart, say, *"I love you."* There is nothing either of you need to get, give, or do. The divine mind has taken center stage for this act and you are the star in the middle of the most awesome love scene ever written.

With gratitude that your soul is choosing to live in the divine mind code, say, *"I choose to live the love that I am."* Now look into the eyes of the one you love and say, *"Thank you for aligning me with the love that I am."*

Imagine a column of white light pouring into your head and filling your body all the way down to your toes. This is the light of your True Self that you have activated by changing your thoughts to love. Allow this white light to flow freely through you, as you, soothing your entire being, and your body relaxing even more.

With every breath you take, your body, mind, and soul are being regenerated, rejuvenated, strengthened, and renewed. You have now ignited the secret to your success for better relationships, more vitality, and expanded creativity. You have the ability to ask your soul to choose to stay in this place of trust, presence, and strength—to live in the real world of the divine.

Continue to be aware of your breath as you go deeper and deeper, more and more relaxed. Aligned with this unfathomably rich place of love and unity with your True Self, it is time to bring into your meditation someone who has hurt you.

As they appear before you, imagine the same white light enveloping them. Once again, say, *"Love is my essence. My True Self is the perfect expression of divine love, peace, and joy."* Look into their eyes and say. *"I love you. Thank you for aligning me with the love that I am."*

Engage your imagination even further and take a moment to feel the other person relax, breathe easier, and match up their vibration of love to yours. Now say, *"I forgive all my programs that have separated us and I forgive all your programs that have hurt me."*

The whole world has just taken a deep breath!

Real forgiveness is the natural expression of the divine mind code.

You are now in tune with the high vibration of love. When you are ready, take a few more deep breaths and slowly open your eyes. This powerful exercise has activated the best version of you. Share it with the world. Stay on the frequency of love for as long as you can.

If you feel yourself slipping into fear, loneliness, sadness, or pain, reignite the high frequency of love with this meditation and imagine yourself as the person you love and forgive.

In Chapter 1, Peace, we asked you to have some fun and imagine your ego mind as your new puppy—Ego Puppy. When you first discovered your lifelong companion, you were convinced it was feral. And you were right!

To become an effective Ego Puppy trainer requires an evolved soul. It is the soul's choice whether to operate in the divine mind code or the ego mind code. Unless the soul chooses the divine mind code, our efforts at Ego Puppy training only achieve superficial success. To paraphrase Einstein, you can't solve a problem with the same level of consciousness that created it.

Ego Puppy displays its discontent by whining and crying whenever its wants and needs are not met. Through the most important learning phase, both children and puppies unlucky enough to have ignorant, unloving parents learn they do not really matter; they are not worthy of love; and they think they are responsible for all the misfortune that befalls them.

Even coming from the most loving parents, it's still hard for a soul to navigate through the illusory world the ego mind creates. It's almost impossible for the abused or poorly trained Ego Puppy. Without love, humans and Ego Puppies alike wither and die to the feelings of the rest of the world. Why would they have empathy for others and treat them well when that has not been their experience?

These unloved Ego Puppies of the world become a whole new species. They are by far the most dangerous animals on this planet—both to themselves and to others. Younger puppies can growl and gnaw with their baby teeth without dangerous consequences. However, if the soul ignores the signs and omits effective training, Ego Puppy very quickly grows into a vicious dog.

In this illusory world, we feel the danger and typically don't look past the viciousness. Our ego minds are these Ego Puppies, and they are capable of anything in their determination to dominate with their corrupted cries for love and attention.

However, at the heart of the training we all need is the realization that everything is an opportunity to forgive and to find our way back to love.

Look into your heart to see if you have truly forgiven your parents, siblings, and friends for having hurt you. Connect with the love that resides within you that may or may not have been nurtured as a child. Your mission, if you choose to accept it, is to nurture this love—first for yourself, and then for others. Express this love wherever possible, and neutralize any program that would sabotage fulfilling your mission. Unconditional love is the foundation for Ego Puppy training mastery.

INQUIRY—
THE SOURCE CODE PROCESS

Use this simple inquiry process to stay attuned to the success frequency of love:

- Whenever you are feeling fear, negativity, or pain, ask yourself, *"When did I start to feel like this?"*

- Track your thoughts back to the source. It might not necessarily have been a major challenge; it could have been something quite innocent that triggered a program that set off your emotional response. For example, you might have seen an attractive person and thought, *"They would never love me."* Programs like, I'm not good enough, smart enough, funny enough, beautiful enough, or _____ enough (fill in your blank) are triggered at lightning speed and at the same speed you have moved away from your perfect point of power, which is the frequency of love.

- You can shift your state instantly by using the Four Questions. Multiple iterations can be used to make even bigger shifts.

- Alternatively, use the Quantum Neutrality Process as described in Chapter 6 to neutralize the program at a deeper level.

INQUIRY—
THE FOUR QUESTIONS—LOVE

Use this simple set of questions to change the way you feel from one moment to the next. Answer the questions truthfully and spontaneously. Stay focused on the answer to question number four for as long as you can. The answers we provide are examples only.

Use your own words and the wisdom of your own heart to answer the questions.

1. **What am I feeling?** I feel lonely and afraid.

2. **What am I focused on?** Being alone.

3. **How do I want to feel?** Happy and loved.

4. **What focus will serve that?** Having gratitude for all the creativity, passion, and love I have in my life right now.

As you relax and center yourself, reconnect with the love that you are, taking fear and desperation out of the equation. You will shift into a place of wholeness and personal power, a place that is incredibly attractive to everyone. It is the state in which you are mindful not to place expectations on others.

INQUIRY—
RATE YOUR STATE—LOVE

Use these three questions to guide you into experiencing more love in your life. You might need to change your codes depending on the answers:

1. **Do you train your mind to think thoughts of love and forgiveness, constantly moving you in the direction of a peaceful, loving state?** The ego mind is quick to make everyone and everything wrong. Pay attention to how your thoughts are creating pain or joy. The miracles of forgiveness, acceptance, and tolerance bring you back into your heart, back into love, and higher on the Integrated Wholeness Scale.

2. **When was the last time you continued to love someone even after they hurt you?** The ego mind has given the people you love the greatest power to press your buttons and bring up feelings of fear, anger, and despair. Discover the programs that gave them power over your feelings. Once neutralized you will rise to love and above on the Integrated Wholeness Scale. Are you there yet?

3. **When was the last time you looked into a mirror and saw who you really are without the judgments of the ego mind?** Love is your true nature. Choose to be the love that you are, or by default choose to listen to the ego mind and stay in fear of never being good enough, beautiful enough, or smart enough. Stay low and lonely on the Integrated Wholeness Scale, or use the miracle that is love to reconnect to the perfection that you are and rise to love or above. This is where you belong.

Your new codes empower you to cultivate your own noble purpose in life. When the soul chooses to love, especially through adversity, you integrate enlightenment and wholeness through forgiveness and new levels of awareness. This is the fuel of miracles.

An Overview: Love

- Love is a state, and as energy it is the most powerful energy of the cosmos. It is the catalyst of creation and is infinitely powerful.

- An aspect of your True Self, love is inextricably interwoven with peace, forgiveness, enlightenment, and success in every area of your life.

- Without love, it is impossible to live a PLATINUM life because more than anything, love facilitates transformation.

- The divine mind code is founded on love. It is characterized by authenticity, openness, transparency, acceptance, empathy, and respect. It always supports the development and growth of more love.

- The frequency of love is the frequency of success.

- Fear is simply the manifestation of the ego mind's corrupted software programs.

- Repressed or unresolved emotion is the messenger of fear, and fear is the core low frequency blocker of love.

- Fear – its core frequency blocker — is the absence of love, just like darkness is the absence of light.

- Without love you are incapable of unlocking the doors to a life filled with happiness and limitless joy.

- Divine love is unconditional, all-encompassing, and infinite.

- Love no matter what. Forgive when given the chance. Become ever vigilant to any judgments that come up and drop them like hot cakes.

- Change your world. Be the love you want to see in the world, and your world will become a vibrational match to the high frequency energy of love.

- Use and cultivate the smile factor as a way to spread your love to others. Remember the simple act of a smile can lighten any moment and help you feel better.

- Loving others unconditionally, especially through adversity, as you integrate enlightenment and wholeness through forgiveness and new levels of awareness, is truly the fuel of miracles.

Remember, if it's not love, it's not real. It's just a story. As Albert Einstein said about our dualistic world:

Reality is merely an illusion,
albeit a very persistent one.

It's time to take the next step in embodying the best version of who we are.

We are now ready to move on to the next high frequency attribute of our True Self in the PLATINUM Life System: Awareness. With Awareness we intuitively see beyond ego mind stories and understand the big picture.

Forgiveness is the final form of love.

~ Reinhold Niebuhr

CHAPTER THREE

AWARENESS:
DISCOVER HOW LIFE REALLY WORKS

*The mind experiences by means of its awareness...
Reality is neither fact nor fiction but is the
emphasis we place on various parts of our stream
of consciousness...That consciousness is a
continuum extending from material awareness
to higher awareness.*

~ VALERIE V. HUNT, PHD

Accessing Awareness
and Divine Intervention

"No, God—you've made a big mistake this time!
I couldn't marry him. He's so thin that I wouldn't be able
to sleep with him. He'd hurt!"

Let's back up for a moment. Sandra was conducting a meditation evening in Auckland at her manager's home. Rob came in from a doctor's appointment and told everyone that an American named Daniel Biskind, who had recently relocated to Auckland, was coming to that night's session. As she tells it:

"I asked him how he knew this man, and he said, *"I don't know him."* He then went on to explain at his first appointment with his new osteopath the day before, the doctor had told him he felt led to tell him about another patient, an American gentleman who seemed very spiritual. Rob told him he had a friend visiting from Australia who did life-changing work.

As synchronicity would have it, Daniel was coming in to see the osteopath later that same day. Rob asked the doctor to relay an invitation to him to join us for a meditation evening the following day.

When the osteopath told him he was invited to a meditation session, Daniel said he was aware of a voice inside his head saying, *"Be there."* The next night, which was to become a momentous occasion, Rob announced to the room that a man named Daniel Biskind was coming. Two women who had dropped in just to say "hi" immediately decided to stay.

They had other plans for the evening, but at the mention of Daniel's name they changed their plans. They asked if they could stay, and then asked if they could use the bathroom to put on some makeup and freshen up.

Sitting on a bar stool at the kitchen bench with a huge smile on my face, I was thinking, *"How cute is that?"* These two 45-year-old women had just morphed into excited 16-year-olds, and it was not because of my meditation session. It was because a new man was arriving who was interested in spirituality and personal transformation.

Yes, a very sexy trait! My amusement didn't last long, though, for as soon as that thought had finished, I got the unequivocal message from spirit, *"He's for you."* I immediately went into shock and answered just as adamantly, *"Oh no! I am not going to marry a man I have not even met."*

I continued to object. *"I have my family, my business, my house, my car, my cat, and my boyfriend in Australia and I am not going to move to New Zealand."* However, I did decide to go to the bathroom and put on some makeup.

When Daniel arrived he handed his host a cigar and a bottle of red wine. Well, that was that. Rob was over the moon and liked him immediately. The next person Daniel saw was me. He took one look at me, felt an inexplicable sense of recognition, and got another message from the same voice he had been aware of the previous day. It said, *"Caution, caution, caution,"* which he loosely translated to mean, *"Be careful. This woman could re-arrange your life."*

You already know my response. Daniel had been on a vegan diet for over twelve months, and his bony body was thinly disguised under his clothes. His hair stuck straight up all over his head, and he had on the thickest glasses I had ever seen. I must confess, being experienced in transformation and design, I did do a quick and dirty assessment of how I could change his presentation.

It was time to ignore the message and get on with the night. I made the decision to stay as far away from him as possible. It was a really powerful evening, especially when a young child asked me how to handle an awkward situation with two of her friends. She was a very aware young girl of ten who felt sad when one of them had given her an ultimatum that day: choose between her and the other girl.

Through tears, she said, *"I don't want to choose. I love them both. What should I do?"*

Her eyes widened and the tears stopped as I told her there was room in her heart for both girls. She did not have to choose between loving one or the other but could choose to love them both. She did not have a problem with either girl, and she could easily work out a way to see them at different times. Awareness dawned. Her ten-year-old smile lit up the room as she said, *"I do love them both. I'm so happy! I thought I had to choose and that meant I would lose one or even both of them."*

After the session, Rob invited everyone to stay for pizza and a glass of wine. The two women who had put their makeup on said they had to go. Oh no! I wanted them to stay. Once again I was fighting my own divine guidance, but when I asked them to consider staying to spend more time with Daniel, they smugly replied, *"We don't want to seem too keen too soon. We live here, we're going to make a time to catch up with him next week."*

If they had been more aware and listening to their intuition, it would have told them this was it—it's now or never. In the effort to appear cool and play the relationship game, they had just lost their one opportunity to talk to Daniel and create a connection. Daniel, on the other hand, was not playing games— he was playing for keeps. He was tapped into his awareness and he immediately followed his inner guidance to turn up for an evening of meditation that was so much more than that.

He also knew his whole life was about to change. At one o'clock in the morning, when everyone else had left or gone to bed, Daniel was not going anywhere. He was about to put on more music and open another bottle of wine when I exclaimed, *"Hey, what are you doing?"* I told him I was tired and he had to go home.

He looked at me (to all the men reading this, are you listening?) and said, *"There are certain times in your life when you come across something so special you don't want to leave it, not even for sleep."*

WOW! I hope you are taking notes here. This was really good stuff. I was very impressed and told him that was definitely worth ten points, but he still had to leave. Very earthy Aussie, I'm afraid. Two nights later, after dinner with a small group and after telling his accountant the day before he wasn't sure if he was ready for this, by which he meant me, Daniel made the best marriage proposal I have ever heard. (This was only our second time in each other's presence.)

It was late again and I was leaving for Australia the next morning. Every cell in my whole body had been shaking for hours because I knew Daniel was going to ask me to marry him that night. It was déjà vu from the meditation night, except this time he said, *"I want to take you home and look after you for the rest of your life."*

Wow again!!! I said, *"That was the best proposal I have ever heard, but I can't. I've got my family, my business, my cat, my car, and my boyfriend in Australia."*

That was even better than anything he had said on our first meeting—and that had been brilliant.

So many people had used their awareness to make this meeting happen. Rob had intuited which doctor to go to and had not been at all surprised when his new physician talked to him about wanting to make an introduction to another patient. In fact, being very aware, he accepted it as normal.

The doctor had accessed his innate awareness to know he was supposed to introduce these two patients, something he normally would never even have considered. Daniel was definitely connected to his spiritual core and following his higher awareness. I was the only one who was bucking, kicking, and screaming that this could not be happening, even though my superconsciousness told me it was a done deal.

I had my life sorted. I was in a great place emotionally, mentally, and spiritually. Or so I thought. The divine guidance I had followed and fought with since my childhood had different ideas, and it was once again throwing out dictates that were hard to ignore.

Daniel took me to the airport the next day and gave me a warm and innocent hug goodbye. When I got back to Australia, I drove straight to my spiritual mentor's home and in the safety of her cozy, familiar room, I proceeded to tell her nothing. I was still in shock, and as it turns out, only minutes later, so was she. She looked at me and said, *"I don't care who you've been hugging. He's not for you!"*

"Phew!" I thought. I was off the hook. As it happened, right in that moment, my then 83-year-old best friend and spiritual mentor knew I was going to leave Australia and marry this man. She was so tuned into her superconsciousness that she was also aware it was a done deal. She did not want me to leave and she was deliberately trying to avert what to her was a looming disaster.

When I saw my boyfriend next, I told him I had met an American man in New Zealand, and before I could finish the sentence, his awareness had kicked in with the internal message, *"It's over."* Daniel later told me that when I explained I had a partner in Australia, he also got the identical inner guidance, *"That's over."*

There is so much more to this story, but needless to say, here we are, twenty years later, and closer than ever. No matter how hard I resisted and fought my destiny as shown to me through inner knowing, divine guidance, and higher awareness, it was never going to do any good. My life, too, was to be rearranged. I had been arguing with these divine beings for as long as I could remember, and as it turned out—surprise, surprise—as always, they were right."

The long chain of amazing events in this story heightened our state of awareness. This provided a better roadmap to guide us, especially where added attention and effective communication were high priorities. I was acutely aware of the feelings and thoughts of the people around me.

Most were positive and even joyous, but there were definitely some in which the ego mind code was dominant, rendering the ground soft and even potentially dangerous.

The more you facilitate your soul's evolution, the more your higher awareness helps you negotiate life challenges and achieve even greater success.

There is a universal, intelligent life force
that exists within everyone and everything.
It resides within each one of us
as a deep wisdom, an inner knowing.
We can access this wonderful source
of knowledge and wisdom through our intuition,
an inner sense that tells us what feels right
and true for us at any given moment.

~ SHAKTI GAWAIN

WHAT IS AWARENESS?

With awareness, you intuitively see beyond ego mind stories and understand the big picture.

- Awareness is the faculty of mind that experiences, perceives, and knows.

- The spectrum of consciousness available to us expands or contracts depending on our code.

- Higher awareness transcends the realm of the ego mind.

- The ego mind code operates in our unconscious and conscious states. To perpetuate itself, it blocks and distorts our True Self's superconsciousness so we remain separate and clueless.

- Higher awareness automatically gets the big picture and can see the forest—not only the trees. Our imagination, creativity, and intuition thrive when the soul chooses the divine mind code, which harmoniously integrates the full spectrum of consciousness. This is the key to virtual omniscience.

- With divine mind awareness, we know we are part of a unified field of information and energy. We naturally intuit the right thing to say and do, for the highest and best good of all concerned.

- Higher awareness operates according to Zero Point Field theory, which explains how everything is interconnected. That part of our being that is connected to the divine mind field—our superconsciousness— has the capacity for virtual omniscience.

- Higher awareness is capable of an infinite range of seemingly magical and mysterious feats. They are only mysterious to the ego mind, for in the divine mind code, access to all knowledge is available to everyone.

- The core low frequency blocker for awareness is being oblivious.

KNOW YOUR AUDIENCE

Here is a true story a friend of ours tells about an event he was responsible for as the president of the Chamber of Commerce of Northeastern Ohio—the largest metropolitan chamber in the United States.

The event was the Chamber's annual meeting. The scheduled speaker was the CEO of Cleveland's corporate icon—one of the world's largest corporations, which was based in the UK. There was a sell-out of 1,700 seats in record time. Three days before the event was to take place, our friend received a call from the White House. The representative of the President of the United States explained that the President wanted to attend the Chamber's annual meeting to announce one of his major initiatives for the coming year.

During the next sixty minutes, the proverbial "herding cats" would have seemed orderly compared to what actually happened. The Fortune 100 CEO who was to speak was given the news immediately. He jokingly remarked it would be the first time that he would have the privilege of serving as the warm-up speaker for the President of the United States. Obviously, this was now a new ballgame! On a scale of 1 to 100, it would be a coup somewhere north of 1,000. Predictably, the media went wild.

The White House staff and the Chamber's marketing people explained that media from across the nation would attend, requiring a minimum of 200 seats. That was not the worst of the seating problems. Television media would require a high-vantage platform that would circle the room, about three-quarters of the way from the front. This resulted in some 400 ticket holders being blocked off from sight of the podium and speakers. Our friend quickly scheduled another room that was off at an angle to the main room.

On the day of the event, it didn't take too much awareness to know that his relocated guests were unhappy about their seating arrangements. When his illustrious guest speaker arrived, our friend explained the problem to him. The President, aware of the need for everyone to have a great experience, asked if it would help if he "worked" the adjoining room. *"Oh,"* said our friend, *"it would probably just save my job, Mr. President!"*

With a smile and a pat on the back, the President headed straight for the smaller room. He then proceeded to personally shake hands with every person in the area and to chat at each table. Then the President walked through the main room, past everyone seated there, and onto the stage to present his plan in his keynote address.

The formerly disgruntled people in the side room no longer felt unhappy or disadvantaged. To the contrary, they were the ones who got bragging rights to having spent personal time with the President of the United States.

This is a great example of how a problem was turned into a huge success by two people who discerned where added attention was needed. No wonder that to this day, our friend names that President as his favorite of all time.

We can all access our own version of everyday awareness whenever we observe with empathy a smile or frown, or a greeting that's warm or cool. We don't have to be accessing higher awareness to understand the needs of others and how we can best serve them. Think of times you have been successful at work, completed a difficult project, or placated a disgruntled person. What do you think you did in order to find the solution to any of these problems? You used your awareness to tap into the needs of the people and the situation to mold a desirable outcome.

Virtually all successful people have found a way to access higher awareness—even if only in a narrow application to their field of specialization. Sooner or later, they almost all acknowledge the importance of higher awareness. They may describe it as intuition, or a gut feeling, or an inner knowing—but however they describe it, it is higher awareness.

Imagination is more important than knowledge. For knowledge is limited to all we now know and understand, while imagination embraces the entire world, and all there ever will be to know and understand.

~ ALBERT EINSTEIN

Virtual Omniscience

When we access our superconscious dimensions of higher awareness, we have virtual omniscience, which is the ability to access the relevant information we need in real time. This is how life really works.

Have you ever seen people totally enrapt with a speaker, or with someone who is talking to them? The awareness of high-consciousness people is magnetically attractive to others. In a case like the story above, the speaker is highly aware of his or her audience and attuned to their shifting needs and nuances. Most successful speakers say that being tapped into higher awareness allows them to feel and know if they have lost their audience and, with that knowledge, they can get the conversation back on track. Successful teachers, mentors, professionals, and others who work with people—and yes, especially successful presidents—constantly employ their awareness to better handle any situation with anyone.

Being mindful of how we are feeling in any given moment and being able to get neutral to anything upsetting our alignment with our True Self is only half of the success equation. Being aware of how other people are feeling, and then knowing how to interact with them, is the other half.

In Lynne McTaggart's book *The Field*, she talks about a band of scientists who have gone beyond conventional quantum theory. Through research and thinking outside known boxes, they discovered that due to an infinite quantum field, or Zero Point Field—the energy field that is the very underpinning of our universe—none of us are alone. We are in fact all connected. There is a unity to humanity and, indeed, to the entire cosmos.

With higher awareness, specifically superconsciousness, we can access information from anywhere and anything in the field. This is very good news for humanity, but not so good for the untrained ego mind.

Valerie V. Hunt, PhD, author of *Infinite Mind: Science of the Human Vibrations of Consciousness*, says, *"The mind is a wireless transmitter and receptor. We acknowledge as commonplace that we can send and receive radio waves, bounce them off satellites, unscramble them and materialize information transmitted over a distance. But, we still cannot accept that all the marvelous things we invent or discover 'out there' are really prototypes of the body and the mind-field."*

She goes on to explain, *"The power of the human mind is such that we could monitor and decode all major 'goings on' in the world. Without the news media, we could sense starvation and catastrophes when they occur."*

With these words Dr. Hunt totally unscrambles and demystifies our ability to be in many places at once and to know the news from the other side of the world without all our devices. That part of our being that is connected to the divine mind field has the capacity for virtual omniscience. It is capable of an infinite range of seemingly magical and mysterious feats. But they are only mysterious to the ego mind, for on the level of the divine mind, all is known when fully connected to the high frequency of awareness.

During a private session with a powerful CEO of a successful executive leadership consulting firm, she confided she was feeling overwhelmed and anxious. She was about to step onto the world stage with her latest best-selling book and media tour, and even with the support of her staff, she felt like she was juggling so many things she couldn't keep up.

When we work with clients, individually or in groups, we are tuned into higher awareness as we access the Zero Point Field. Sometimes this is called accessing past or alternative lives or the Akashic Records, but in reality it is more than that.

As we tuned in for our heroine, a small child of only four appeared to Sandra. With tears running down her face, this little one proceeded to tell Sandra how she was being used and abused by her father in that lifetime. Ashamed and grief stricken, the child told her that she needed to hide and stay small and not draw any attention to herself.

Traumatized by the force of her emotions, her ego mind created a number of unconscious programs that controlled her from that day forward. Both the small child of that lifetime and our client were living by an unconscious ego mind code that was sabotaging her success, not only in the business world but also in her personal relationships.

The programs in this code ran like this: Being beautiful is dangerous. Standing out is dangerous. Don't draw attention to yourself, ever. People who love you hurt you.

Sandra described this little girl and relayed what she was telling her to our heroine. Astonished, she said she knew this little one very well because it was her story in this lifetime, too. Both the small child's programs from her past life and her little one's programs from this life needed to be corrected so she could become neutral to the emotions around these events.

Using the Quantum Neutrality Process, Sandra dissolved the emotional charge around the events and deleted their effects, which instantly changed her code. After energetically placing a forgiveness template into her heart, she was then able to step into the freedom of forgiveness.

Our heroine had started the session feeling overwhelmed and anxious at the prospect of launching herself into the world on a larger scale. However, with absolute amazement and relief in her voice, she said she could no longer even find what she had been anxious about in the first place.

There was no way our client would have equated what had happened to her 40 years ago to the struggles and challenges she was having now. Her codes allowed her to create a successful business, but only up to a point. Two weeks before our appointment, a fight with her brother had triggered the program, and her life became an ominous and threatening place once again.

After being set free from these unconscious programs, our heroine felt as though she could easily handle what needed to be done. She was confidently looking forward to stepping into her greatness: to inspire, uplift, and empower her clients and audience. Even after spending years in therapy and believing she was free from her childhood traumas, it had required higher awareness and the Quantum Neutrality Process to finally free her to be seen, to be heard, to love, and be loved—to be truly successful.

Learning to tap into your own virtual omniscience is invaluable for breaking the codes that keep you from your greatness, from living aligned with your True Self. Whenever something triggers a sabotage code, for a rapid fix you can use the Four Questions to instantly course-correct back into your personal power. If there is a need to go deeper, then using your virtual omniscience in the Quantum Neutrality Process™ is the ultimate power tool.

Want learn more about the Zero Point Field and the scientific background for virtual omniscience? Here is some suggested reading:

- Lynne McTaggart's *The Field*
- Valerie V. Hunt's *Infinite Mind*
- Bruce H. Lipton's *The Biology of Belief*
- Dawson Church's *The Genie In Your Genes*
- Mark Gober's *An End to Upside Down Thinking*

SAHEB-E-ZAMAN

Just as a normal man can climb
A high mountain
And on a clear day
See for many miles around,

Hafiz can stand on a blessed peak
Inside his heart
And see for hundreds of years
In all directions.

And I tell you, dear ones,
That the Saheb-e-Zaman,
The Christ,
The Prophet,
The Ancient One,
Has made a date to Whirl,
To Whirl
With this Earth again!

~HAFIZ

From *I Heard God Laughing: Poems of Hope and Joy,*
Copyright 1996 & 2006 by Daniel Ladinsky
and used with his permission.

"Life of Pi" in 3D

We don't have to have seen the movie *Life of Pi* in 3D to be able to use our imagination and put ourselves in a lifeboat, where we sit stranded in the middle of an ocean. Even though we feel fear and uncertainty, we are overwhelmed by the beauty of the world around us. The striking colors of the rising and setting sun take our breath away. We are all addicted to the fantastic work of art that is our illusory world. However, both the awe we feel and the beauty around us are unstable. Like the ocean, everything is always changing.

This is without taking into account the danger that exists within our life raft. Just as in the movie (or book), there is a man-eating tiger sharing our lifeboat, which could kill us at any moment. The tiger becomes our prison and our one constant companion. As we journey together, weathering the storms, through hardship and the fear of dying, we come to love the tiger —this dark and dangerous force.

In this story, our ego mind is both the man-eating tiger and the changing weather conditions. Just like being in our own Hollywood studio, it has us out there in the choppy waters of our dream state, always making up ways to scare us to death.

However, the love that we are and always will be never leaves the set. It steadily whispers to gently awaken us from this deep and restless sleep, and to learn how to master and tame the wild beast of fear. With understanding, compassion and love, the tiger, or fears, becomes transformed into a force that can serve our True Self.

Mirror Programs

One of our clients called for her private session. She was in tears, hoping we could work with both her and her husband— he was about to walk out the door and never come back. Since their baby girl had been born, they had been miscommunicating for many months and both had finally had enough. Every woman who has ever had a baby knows the upheaval and massive changes that take place both before and after her precious bundle arrives. And every man who has ever become a father knows exactly the same thing.

Even while love is present at the marriage ceremony, during the honeymoon, and for years to follow, the introduction of a child into any relationship creates not only a cause for celebration but also the need for careful communication. We are all here in a body to do just that and what amazing communication devices are our bodies and minds. They are pure energy and broadcast the frequencies at which we are oscillating. This goes beyond our five senses that seem to bind us to the illusory world of the ego mind.

This is your higher awareness. It routinely gets blindsided by the programs that are triggered when notable life events occur. Have you ever felt as though you knew something, but didn't know how you knew it? Have you ever felt uncomfortable around someone, and didn't understand what was making you feel that way? That's our sixth sense, or higher awareness, in action. We are always picking up information from the human mind field, and we are always broadcasting into it.

Our client said that she felt unloved and unappreciated by her husband, *"When he comes home from work and sees our baby girl, his whole face lights up. He doesn't look at me like that anymore. I can't stand it. He gives the baby and our oldest daughter more attention than he gives me."*

Her husband (also a client) came on the phone, and told us how angry he was. His wife always made him feel bad when he came home from a hard day's work by giving him what he called "dirty looks." Rather than look at her, he focused all his attention on the baby because she was the one who lit up in his presence, which made him feel joy.

They were both operating in ego mind code and out of alignment with their True Self. They were having a relationship crisis because they didn't use awareness to discern or communicate what was really going on. The ego mind code had each in their own separate life raft, feeling alone, overwhelmed, and in danger. And of course, each blamed the other for the way they felt.

In fact, they were both projecting their own man-eating tiger onto the other.

As we started to unravel the situation for them, they realized the man-eating tiger was not their partner, but indeed, their own ego mind. The husband thought his wife was reacting badly to him because of traumatic events that had happened previously in their relationship. The wife was acutely jealous of the love he was giving to the baby and not to her. She simply wanted some of that love.

She was projecting her "I'm not good enough" programs onto him, which manifested as jealousy. He was projecting his "I'm not good enough" programs onto her, which manifested as feeling judged. Programs like these always trigger anger and separation. Their codes were the perfect mirror image of each other. Using the Quantum Neutrality Process, the emotional charge surrounding their unconscious programs was dissolved and they were able to reawaken to the love that they shared.

Have you ever been in a situation where you are blaming the man-eating tiger that you think is someone else for your own unhappiness? But that is not how life really works. After neutralizing their relevant programs we asked our hero and heroine to focus their awareness into their hearts, and feel the love and wholeness they experienced the day they were married. We then asked them to forgive their own and their partner's programs—not their partner. Did you catch that? This is how life really works.

Once realigned with the higher awareness of their hearts, our clients were able to forgive both their own and their partner's programs. They easily recreated the energy field of love, and rather than walk out the door and leave love behind we had the distinct feeling they were off to make more babies.

We all have the choice to leave love behind, but why would we? It is only our unconscious, sleep-walking self that is trapped in the life raft of death and destruction. We are not!

HOW LIFE REALLY WORKS

Our ego mind programs are the changing weather conditions and the man-eating tiger that sabotage the best version of who we are every time. Using awareness, we quickly discern something is wrong and begin a process of communication—first with ourselves and then with others.

Explain that you feel uncomfortable about a situation, and that you know something is not quite right. Something within you has been triggered by their behavior and you would like help finding out what it is. Notice that you have not told them they are wrong, nor are you blaming them for your feelings. You have told the truth. You are taking 100 percent responsibility for your feelings, emotions and reactions. You are aware that you are out of alignment with your True Self.

If you are not feeling love, you have moved away from your perfect point of power, from the divine mind code and the best version of who you are. In such moments your life changes and you find yourself firmly ensconced back in the illusory world of separation, guilt, shame, and blame. No longer aware of how life really works, you find yourself sleepwalking into your own unique version of a nightmare. Separation, divorce, heartache, and loneliness are normal when operating in the ego mind code. It shuts down your awareness and sabotages your relationships.

It's easy to see how devious the ego mind code is as it keeps us asleep to our programs. All our programs are woven together so tightly that it can be hard to unravel them. If we don't switch codes and reconnect to the love that we are, they consti-tute a reliable recipe for disaster.

Our five senses work in conjunction with us in this wonder that is our life. They are always doing this, but are you always listening? Incorporate them, and go beyond your five senses. Using the divine mind code activates higher awareness, our sixth sense, to receive the information most relevant to us.

It is inappropriate to say that it's weird when our natural ability to use our awareness gives us a gut feeling. It's hardly "woo woo" when we use our powers of observation, discernment, and intuition to understand what needs to be said or done in any situation.

Get yourself onto the level of love or above on the Integrated Wholeness Scale. The more in tune with Peace and Love you are, the better your access to your higher awareness. It always comes down to you—your programs, your ideas, your stories, and your beliefs. Imagine what a wonderful world it would be if we all made the decision right now to diligently use higher awareness to reconnect to the oneness of the human information field—and to use the heart to forgive and love 100 percent of the time. This is called living by the divine mind code, which is living a PLATINUM life.

We have made the commitment to love ourselves and each other. What about you? It's your choice. Have you made that decision yet?

The intuitive mind is a sacred gift and the rational mind is a faithful servant. We have created a society that honors the servant and has forgotten the gift.

~ ALBERT EINSTEIN

SPIRIT JUNKIE

Spiritual messengers selflessly venture into our illusory world to help us escape our plight. Even knowing the world they have entered is an illusion doesn't make it any easier to watch as humanity continues to bully, brutalize, and exploit each other. They encourage the soul to wake up for its own sake. They feed the soul as much truth as it is prepared to absorb and will continue until the soul makes the choice for higher awareness, for peace and love.

These divine messengers help us (including you!) transform into higher-frequency beings in order to bring new levels of awareness to the evolving soul. Luckily, when this whole insane idea of separation from God was first conceived, the soul left itself an out, a very small loophole that would eventually bring humanity full circle, back to being awake and liberated, enlightened, and whole.

In this dream the soul has made the choice to come back into a body over and over again. This gives us the opportunity to connect with these divine messengers in many different ways and evolve gradually, waking up gently from the confusion of the illusion.

This is the evolution of the soul. Sudden awakening can be extremely traumatic, just as being shaken out of a deep sleep can be highly disorienting. But don't worry. Becoming the best version of who we are is an ongoing process. It is about continually remembering the truth...that in the real world, we are already perfect. Our job is to switch codes and undo the ego mind.

The landscape of our dream world changes profoundly as the soul develops the ability to better see and feel reality through these healthy, wholesome, higher levels of awareness. Join us in making the commitment to do what it takes to dissolve the obstacles to make the choice for a PLATINUM life automatic.

After twenty-five years of rigorous scientific study, the late Dr. Valerie Hunt was internationally recognized for her pioneering research into human energy fields and consciousness. To paraphrase her, when you repress your emotion, your body hurts; when you repress your consciousness, your mind aches; when you repress your spirituality, your soul suffers.

Dr. Hunt was a high-vibrational soul who merged science and mysticism. Her impressive body of work helps the soul reset its ability to choose to journey out of the darkness and into the divine energy field of love. These changes are potentially irresistible to humanity's addictive nature. As learning progresses, our spiritual development enhances our ability to discern the truth. It leads to more success in life, as well as the experience of the ineffable high of pure love. As we become spirit junkies, the soul begins to appreciate just how crucial it is to train the ego mind.

It is a momentous time in the history of the ego mind code. The soul is shifting to the timeless divine mind code whose master password, PLATINUM, is deliberately unprotected against theft. Steal to your heart's content, beloved. Heal your wandering soul and crippled heart. Do whatever it takes to undo the primacy of the primitive ego mind. Become addicted to the bliss of the dance of love and joy as you surrender your choices to the mind of the divine.

Both mystics and great scientists alike have said that their experiences and experiments were guided by mystical and intuitive insight, that is, higher awareness, which accesses the mind of the divine. As astrophysicist Walter Lewin said, *"When you've discovered the truth in science, it does have the most extraordinary magical quality about it."*

When Sandra was conversing with divine beings as a three-year-old and became convinced it was her destiny and purpose to work for God, it did not seem magical at all. It was the most normal, natural state of being she could imagine. She was aware it was a serious matter, as serious as only a three-year-old could be. Sandra was calm, and as she accepted these revelations, somehow she knew not to talk about them to anyone—other than her mother. The look on her mother's face when her not-quite-four-year-old declared she was going to be a priest was priceless.

Sandra's mom told her that would not be possible because only Catholic men could be priests and we were not Catholic. She didn't know what Catholic was, but Sandra knew she wasn't a man. Not to be deterred, the next day her little girl told her she would be a nun—they were women, right? Again she said no and explained, *"If you become a nun, you will never be able to marry and have children."*

In total exasperation, Sandra put her hands on her hips and looked up into her mother's eyes, almost daring her to say *"no"* again, and said, *"Don't worry Mummy. When I grow up, things will be different. I will work for God and be a teacher and tell people the truth about love."*

What the three-year-old knew, she had to relearn as an adult. The spiritual world unfolded around Sandra like a hurricane. It drew her into its orbit, sometimes tossing her around like a rag doll until she could find her way back into the calm of a PLATINUM state of mind. There have been many miraculous and extraordinary magical times since then, just as there have been many frightening ones. Through it all, she seldom lost sight of the big picture, and since her mother's passing in 1972, there have been countless times when her mother has given her invaluable guidance.

SHAKE, RATTLE, AND ROLL

In 1998 the Brisbane Mind Body Spirit Festival, held in the huge Brisbane Convention Centre, was the venue for another massive upgrade in Sandra's awareness. She was a keynote speaker and also shared a small stand with a fellow healer. Thousands came daily to enjoy the colorful, bazaar-like atmosphere which was like a veritable organic farmers market for the soul. Here's her story:

"I was given fair warning the day before the festival. The organizers requested a 'meeting' with the divine beings I work with where, to my surprise and chagrin, they thanked the organizers for the work they were doing. They explained they were going to leverage the energy field generated by this gathering to make changes in my awareness which would then be reflected in my body and brain function. Uh oh! I had heard this before. I was sure I would be flung back into a raging storm, but I had no idea how powerful this hurricane was destined to be.

At first, everything seemed normal. As usual, I gave people hands-on attunements of healing energy throughout the morning. My first talk at 11:00 AM was well-received. On my way back to the stand, every cell in my body started shaking. My body had never done well on caffeine—one cup and I would spend the whole day on the ceiling. (If you want the cleanest house on the block, just give me a cup of coffee and a blue microfiber cleaning cloth!)

The body was reacting as though it had just absorbed ten cups of coffee all at once. My brain began to pulse with heat and pain. It felt as though the beating of my heart had also kicked in to this symphony of shake, rattle, and roll. I was used to having to roll with the punches, but this felt like a veritable one-punch knockout.

All night and the next day, the transformational process maintained its relentless pace. I realized that the high frequency at which I was vibrating was well beyond my normal range. In addition, everyone near me was also being catalyzed in some way.

People were drawn to this divine energy. The line of people coming to my stand for healing grew longer. When I put my hands on one woman's head, she almost fainted. Finally able to speak, she said she felt so much better. She explained that she had been overwhelmed by white light and the presence of a love so strong that she felt as high as a kite.

A small child who obviously had a mind of her own jumped into the chair. She had a serious expression on her beautiful face. The dark circles under her eyes were the only indication that something was wrong. When I put my hands on her head to give her healing, her father, who was standing beside us, also felt something unusual. Concerned, he cried out, *"What are you doing to my daughter?"*

The child said, *"Don't worry, Daddy; it's heavenly."*

In a dreamy voice and with a huge smile on her face, she added, *"I feel better now."*

By the third day, this spiritual storm had taken its toll on my nervous system. In almost unbearable pain, my body and brain were still shaking. On the first day, I had tried to greet the people in the stand opposite ours. Except for a condescending nod, they were totally unresponsive. They had taken four stands in a row, displaying huge, beautiful posters of everything Egyptian on their walls. One by one, the people from the everything-Egyptian stand came to our little stand with dumbstruck looks on their faces. They were not able to communicate what they were going through while this high frequency energy field was affecting them. All they could do was stand there and stare. It was disconcerting, to say the least.

Their leader came over to me, dropped to her knees, sobbed, and held me tight. I asked her to breathe deeply and tell me what she was experiencing. She explained that at first, every time I walked past their stand, they would have flashbacks to their past lives in Egypt. By the third day, the energy field had become so powerful that it was catalyzing a constant flow of past-life recall for all of them.

She said that everything started to make sense in a way they had never thought possible, and that it was a profoundly important experience for them. Now they understood why they were doing what they were doing. They had received insight into how they could change their lives and become more successful, joyful, and loving.

Walking to the bathroom took me past the coffee stand where, long before I reached him, the man pulling coffees looked up and made a cross with his fingers to ward me off. He was there to sell coffee and had not put in for any changes to his consciousness. His brain was reacting to my frequency; he was feeling high and unable to focus. In sympathy, I found another route to the bathroom after that.

I knew I needed help. People's ability to experience a wider range of altered states and higher awareness increased. I was stunned when, as I walked past one stand, a complete stranger ran out to give me a gift.

Another keynote speaker was on the board of the International Association of Medical Intuitives, whose members included Carolyn Myss. She was working at the stand of a good friend, and that's where I headed—with SOS written all over me.

I told my friend I needed help. She took me to the private area for participants and speakers, where we sat and waited for the medical intuitive to finish her second talk. When she arrived at our table, she took the seat furthest from me, explaining that she couldn't sit next to me as the energy was so strong it was knocking her around. And she had only just arrived! I didn't need to explain a thing to her. She was a highly aware person and she was able to see, feel, and understand what was going on.

She explained that I was experiencing an overall upgrade of my being, including my brain. The process was fast-tracking the evolution of my soul as well as increasing my brain's capacity to absorb spiritual information. It was a significant transformation that raised my frequency and enhanced my ability to tap into the human mind field and access information and light. This enabled me to better facilitate other people's transformation into higher levels of awareness. She then added that the recalibration was almost complete.

At that moment, it felt like something had dropped into my brain. I screamed in pain and saw rainbow light flooding the convention center. She too could actually see and feel this phenomenal experience as it was occurring.

We dissected what had been happening and worked through the tail end of the process together. After half an hour everything seemed to be settling. The heat was dissipating and the constant vibrations were now manageable.

As we were leaving the room, a man with a video camera on his shoulder walked past us. He had also been affected by the intensity of the energy so he introduced himself and gave me the opening to tell him what I had seen.

I told him I could see a three-inch gray energy field around him that was not his aura. I suggested he be careful about what he ate, as he could easily put on a great deal of weight. He looked shocked and said, *"But that's the weight I've just lost. I was three inches larger all over."* I was seeing the energy field where he was still energetically carrying all the fat he had just lost from his physical body. This was a new trick!

The next day it was his turn to shock me. He sought me out to tell me that a woman had come to him in his dreams with a message for me. He said her name was unusual, something he had not heard before. It wasn't Ellis or Ellen but something like that. I asked him if it could have been Elva. *"Yes. That was it."* My mother, Elva, had chosen him to deliver a message to her daughter in distress. He told me that she said, *"Listen to the little girl."* That was it.

I wanted more, but I still felt reassured that I was being looked after when I most needed it. She was reminding me of the time when her little girl had made her pronouncements about being here to work for God. If this is what it was going to take, then I just had to ride it out. The calm of the divine mind was only a breath away. That SOS I was broadcasting out into the universe had brought me the best help I could have wished for.

On the last day of the festival, my new friend, the medical intuitive, asked me to help her with a young boy who was having inexplicable mystical experiences. His father had brought him to the festival every day in the hope that he would be able to understand what was happening to his son. As we walked into the stand, the young boy took one look at me and started to cry with deep, racking sobs. Instantly protective, his father stood in front of his son and asked me to leave. Both the boy and my friend cried out in unison, *"No, don't go!"* She asked the father to let me stay until the boy could tell us what had just happened.

Finally able to talk, he said, "I know you." With that, the boy left his seat to come and put his arms around me. With big tears still in his eyes and with so much love, he looked up at me and said, *"You took me into your fashion shop and gave me a turquoise necklace you had brought from Egypt."* (At twenty I had opened my first boutique. That was still my day job, which he could not have known.) *"I remember you, you were my mother and the leader of our tribe. You took me to the top of the highest mountain and asked me to trust you, and then you pushed me off."* I asked him what happened next. He said, *"I knew you would keep me safe. I just hovered there."*

I was able to shed light on his experiences, and both he and his father went away calm and happy. There is a lot more to this story that might be told at another time. Suffice to say, we all shared a happy ending.

It sounds like a fantasy; or, as many scientists have said of their discoveries, something quite magical had just happened on a mystical level.

Since that experience, Daniel and I have worked with a Sydney neuroscientist who studies brainwave behavior. He hooked me up to an EEG machine while we completed some experiments that involved attunements of this amped-up energy field without physical contact. When he tested me, my brain showed total coherence from front to back and side to side. He was stunned and said it was extraordinary to see a brain operating this way.

The university students who had agreed to participate in these experiments and receive this energy from us all had exams that afternoon. They unanimously reported back that they had achieved their best results in their academic careers—ever!"

As you move into higher levels of awareness, you open the door to whole new worlds—worlds where anything is possible. It is as simple and straightforward as training your ego mind to get out of the way, so that the divine mind can reveal its wondrous mysteries.

Courageously make the decision to move beyond your physical form and senses, and focus on the divine gifts you have been given to share with the world. Become your own hero. Experience the magical states of your mystical being.

Just as a candle cannot burn without fire,
men cannot live without a spiritual life.

~BUDDHA

WE ARE WHAT WE THINK

The physical body responds positively or negatively not only to what we say and do, but also to what we think. The good news is that it responds to what we think consciously. The bad news is that it is always responding to what we think unconsciously.

In Bruce Lipton's invaluable book *The Biology of Belief,* he observes that the unconscious mind processes 20 million bits of information per second versus only 40 bits by the conscious mind in the same second. Thus, the information-processing capacity of the unconscious mind is 500,000 times greater than the conscious mind. Can you guess which one prevails whenever there is a conflict between the two?

When operating in caveman consciousness (below 200 × 200 on the Integrated Wholeness Scale), our unaware mind is inclined to deal with conflict by trampling all over everyone and plotting revenge. It sometimes even kills because someone has offended our driving sensibilities or just looked at us the wrong way. True forgiveness depends on unconditional love (starting at 540 × 540 on the Integrated Wholeness Scale) and is incomprehensible to that primitive state of awareness.

Scientists have discovered there are emotional, mental, and even physical needs for forgiveness. Every cell in our body acts like a computer. Each cell has an electromagnetic energy field and a biochemical composition that instantly responds to our environment—and to our thoughts.

More than anything else, the body's response to our conscious and unconscious thoughts determines whether we have good health or disease.

According to well-documented discoveries in epigenetics, genetic inheritance is only a predisposition. Whether it is triggered or not is dependent on the individual's programs. The totality of our beliefs, ideas, and programs determines whether we will forgive or not. This in turn stimulates our happy or unhappy hormonal responses—and hence our happy or unhappy experience of life.

PLATINUM SUCCESS PRINCIPLE: AWARENESS

- Our level of Awareness determines the spectrum of consciousness available to us.

- Imagination, intuition and creativity vary according to our connection to Awareness.

- Higher Awareness transcends the limitations of the ego mind.

As Buddha said, we become what we think. Ultimately we are what we think, and it is our code that determines our thoughts. Even the fine-grained quality, frequency, and essence of our thoughts are also products of our code.

Our choice of password accesses either corrupted or inspirational encoding. Life becomes happier, healthier, and richer as the soul chooses the divine mind code. We develop gratitude, kindness, generosity, compassion, and the ability to love unconditionally, to truly forgive. The body, mind, and soul become stronger, more vital, and more attractive.

Inquiring deeply into our conscious and unconscious programs and getting to the core beliefs around any feelings of fear, negativity, and pain is the best way to avoid illness.

Being connected to higher awareness turbocharges our evolutionary expedition into enlightenment and wholeness. The more whole we become, the less space there is for the ego mind to buck at having its stories undone—at having to forgive.

ATTUNEMENT:
A Meditation on Awareness

Begin by observing your breath and letting your body relax. Let go of all judgments as you allow your thoughts to simply come and go. Center yourself by taking a few deep breaths and harmonize with the frequency of peace, love, and awareness.

Continue to breathe deeply as your whole being makes the shift to this powerful high frequency beingness state. With every breath you take, your thoughts become clearer and you intuitively begin to understand the big picture.

Let yourself go deeper and deeper into relaxation.

Invite your True Self to access higher awareness using the divine mind code. Your imagination, creativity, and intuition switch into top gear as your soul chooses higher awareness. Breathe deeply and become aware of an expanded range of consciousness. This is normal in enlightened states.

There is nothing you need to get, give, or do. In awareness the divine mind has taken center stage and you are the star in the middle of the most awesome field of information, wisdom, and love.

With gratitude say, "I choose to live in an aware state of being. I always know the right thing to say and do for the highest good of all concerned."

Now imagine a column of white light pouring into your head and filling your body all the way down to your toes. This is the light, wisdom, knowledge, and clarity of your True Self that you have activated. Allow this white light to flow freely through you, as you, with your body relaxing even more.

With every breath you take, your body, mind, and soul are being regenerated, rejuvenated, strengthened, and renewed. Awareness empowers your success with knowledge of how life really works. You have ignited the secret to your success to better relationships, more vitality, and expanded creativity.

Breathe deeply. Ask your soul to make the choice to tap into expanded awareness, intuition, trust, presence, and strength; to live in the real world of the divine.

Stay with this feeling of being one with the infinite field of all information for as long as you can. Once you have totally aligned with this unfathomably rich place of unity with your True Self and the cosmos, you are free to bring into your meditation someone who has hurt you.

Imagine the same white light enveloping them from head to toe. Breathe deeply and say, *"My True Self understands we have set ourselves up for pain and suffering."* Then look into their eyes and say. *"I love you. Thank you for helping me unravel another aspect of myself."*

Engage your imagination even further. Take a moment to feel the other person relax, breathe easier, and match up their awareness to yours. Now say, *"I forgive all my programs that have separated us and I forgive all your programs that have hurt me."* Real forgiveness is the natural expression of the divine mind.

When you are ready, take a few more deep breaths and slowly open your eyes. You are now in tune with your intuition and innate knowing of how life really works. This powerful exercise has activated the best version of you. Share it with the world. Stay tapped into your intuition and this frequency for as long as you can.

If you feel yourself slipping into fear, negativity, or pain, reignite your higher awareness with this meditation and restore the best version of you.

In the first two chapters, Peace and Love, you have become familiar with Ego Puppy. It is your job to train little Ego. Now it's time to introduce you to Kosmic Kitten, who is your innate connection to awareness and intuition. She has four eyes: one physical pair and one spiritual pair—the source of your imagination and creativity. Cultivating your relationship with her amps up your higher awareness.

Although at first Kosmic Kittens only use their physical eyes, they quickly develop vision via their spiritual eyes: seeing, feeling, and intuiting the real world via the divine mind code.

They are an irreplaceable aspect of your soul and provide instant connection to your heart. Kosmic Kitten also exerts a constructive impact on Ego Puppy, as it is trained to fulfill its destiny to live a life of meaning and purpose. Once well-trained, these service dogs dedicate their lives to their humans like police dogs, guide dogs, farm dogs, and all manner of loyal and loving companions. Working in tandem with K Kitten, they become love junkies who consistently respond to reassurance that they are okay and that all is well.

Have you ever noticed how a puppy will keep coming back for more love, play, and attention even after you have scolded it? Well-trained puppies thrive on correction and easily surrender resentment at being disciplined. Aware Ego Puppies do not even consider the need to forgive; in a nanosecond they are on to the next adventure.

The training process always involves stress for both Ego Puppy and those who commit to train them. Remember, this is your ego mind we are talking about, so ultimately your only choice is when you will do it. Your Kosmic Kitten will help train your Ego Puppy with love and consistency.

Only you are responsible for bringing little Ego into higher levels of awareness. No piddling all over anyone else, no pooping inside, no scaring small children or growling at postmen, and definitely no biting. Your puppy's training depends on you.

Your soul chooses the codes you live by. It can choose the divine mind code, in which you will love, train, and teach Ego Puppy how to have the life of their puppy dreams as a beloved member of their new family. Alternatively, the soul can default to the ego mind code, which will create a dangerous monster, who thinks it has no choice but to fight just to survive. Don't let your Ego Puppy turn into a primitive alpha canine—or even worse, a junkyard dog.

Wherever you go is where Ego Puppy is. With love and diligence, repair the damage of past conditioning and transform your Ego Puppy into an invaluable companion and service dog. Let your intuitive Kosmic Kitten loose. Let them play, and celebrate as Ego Puppy falls in love in an unlikely partnership.

INQUIRY—
THE FOUR QUESTIONS: AWARENESS

Use this simple set of questions to change the way you feel from one moment to the next.

Answer the questions truthfully and spontaneously. Stay focused on the answer to question number four for as long as you can. The answers we provide are examples only. Use your own words and the wisdom of your own heart to answer the questions.

1. **What am I feeling?**

   Like I'm missing a lot.

2. **What am I focused on?**

   Being out of touch and missing the signals life is sending me.

3. **How do I want to feel?**

   I want to feel tapped into what's happening.

4. **What focus will serve that?**

   My awareness uses my intuition to see, feel, and know what I need to know.

By cultivating your awareness, your intuition keeps you in touch with what you need to know.

INQUIRY—
RATE YOUR STATE: AWARENESS

Use these questions to guide you into attaining higher levels of awareness on the Integrated Wholeness Scale. Depending on the answers at any given time, you might have to change your codes.

1. **When you walk into a room or a neighborhood, are you aware of the energy field that is prevalent at that time?** Do you feel safe or unsafe? You have the power to discern whether you should stay or leave a place. The body is always giving you clues by feeling peaceful or anxious. Tapping into the virtual omniscience of your higher awareness has you rising high and fast on the Integrated Wholeness Scale.

2. **Are you aware of how your words and actions affect those around you?** Successful leaders are aware of the state of the people around them. Using awareness to discern what needs to be said and done for the highest and best for all concerned is an attribute of a high level of Integrated Wholeness.

3. **How much effort are you prepared to put into training yourself to be aware and to forgive?** The relationships and success you deserve require awareness of how your ego mind programs affect others so you can adapt your language and behavior as needed. Staying high, at the level of love or above on the Integrated Wholeness Scale, accesses your True Self. There, in your heart and actively aware, real forgiveness, courage, acceptance, and tolerance are natural.

Use the divine mind code to cultivate your noble purpose in becoming an aware, whole, enlightened being.

As you embody PLATINUM, even through adversity you love unconditionally. In this high frequency state, you are an amazing gift to the world.

AN OVERVIEW: AWARENESS

- Higher awareness transcends the realm of the ego mind.

- The core frequency blocker for awareness is being oblivious.

- Higher awareness automatically gets the big picture and sees the forest, not only the trees. Your imagination, creativity, and intuition thrive when your soul cultivates higher awareness.

- With divine mind awareness, you know you are part of a unified field of information and energy. You naturally intuit the right thing to say and do, for the highest and best for all concerned.

- That part of your being that is connected to the divine mind field has the capacity for virtual omniscience. It is capable of an infinite range of seemingly mysterious and magical feats. But they are only mysterious to the ego mind. When using super consciousness, access to all knowledge is available to everyone.

- Higher awareness is a cornerstone to having a happy, successful, and fulfilled life.

- Awareness operates according to Quantum Field Theory, in which everything is interconnected.

- Our noble purpose is to cultivate our awareness so that in any given moment, our soul consistently chooses the divine mind code. As we do this, our life becomes the spectacular creation we've always wanted it to be.

- How we use awareness to deal with conflict is critical to our health, happiness, and success.

- As we move into higher levels of awareness, we open the door to a whole new world—a world where anything is possible. It is as simple as training the ego mind to get out of the way so that our True Self can reveal the wondrous mysteries of the divine mind.

- Guided by clear intention, the use of heightened awareness, and the power of forgiveness, we can instantly correct misperceptions, delete the effects of emotional baggage, and bring about peace in moments.

- Diligently seek and reveal the truth. Correct your programs by dissolving the emotional charge from past events, and canceling your internal decisions that resulted from them. This way you become free and neutral; forgive; and at last experience inner peace, unconditional love, and true happiness.

- Our use of the divine mind code and the PLATINUM password is a work in progress. Our choices make our experiences of life simple and fun, or hard work. Training the mind rewires the brain by creating new neural pathways, which naturally enhances the sustainability of our state of higher awareness.

Using higher awareness is critical to see beyond ego mind stories and understand what's real. As Donald Hoffman, PhD, Professor of Cognitive Sciences at UC Irvine, said,

One of the biggest insights of cognitive neuroscience is that we see the world as we construct it, not as it is.

So, remember: it's okay. It's not real. It's just a story.

You are now ready to move on to the next frequency unlocked by the master password: Trust. With Trust in our True Self, we can discern the truth in any situation, which frees us from worry.

CHAPTER FOUR

TRUST:
CULTIVATE TRUE CONFIDENCE

You can't connect the dots looking forward; you can only connect them looking backwards. So you have to trust that your dots will somehow connect in your future. You have to trust in something—your gut, destiny, life, karma. This approach has never let me down, and it has made all the difference in my life.

– STEVE JOBS

BENJAMIN'S TRANSFORMATION
AND HEALING WITH SANDRA

Sandra had hardly walked in the door of one of her Melbourne boutiques, when the store manager cornered her. She immediately thought, *"Uh oh! What now?"* From the look of concern on the manager's face it was obvious there was a problem somewhere. It was a huge surprise when she asked Sandra if she would work with the husband of her dear friend who was close to dying. It was a relief to know the business didn't have a problem, but that would have been preferable to what she was about to hear.

A week later, I was welcomed into the home of my manager's friend who was a lovely, but obviously sad woman who took me to meet her husband sitting in his office. Benjamin was of Jewish origin, about 5' 11" and dressed conservatively. He had immigrated to Australia after the Second World War. He was in his sixties and was suffering the late stages of cancer. Although Benjamin was trying to sit up straight, his energy field told the story of a much older man who was stooped over from carrying the weight of the world on his shoulders.

Neither he nor his wife knew what I did but trusted their friend's recommendation enough to have me in their home. Benjamin asked his wife to leave us and then told me he really didn't believe in meditation, healing, or anything that smacked of what he called "New Age." I told him, *"That's okay, you don't have to."*

He visibly relaxed when his beliefs were not being challenged, and he was not going to be asked to change his mind or his medical treatments to date. I started by explaining how I worked, and then asked him if it was okay use meditation just this once to get him into a more peaceful place while I worked with him. Only mere months from death, Benjamin's trust levels were low, but he was a very courageous man who was fighting for his life and had decided to give what I was offering a fair go.

I asked him if I could place my hands on his head while he was meditating so I could give him an attunement to the white-light frequency that would change his energy field. He agreed to this. As in every private session, I tapped into the human information field. I discovered he had been lying by omission to his family about events that took place many years before. Benjamin no longer trusted himself or trusted that his family would cope with his deadly secret.

Without having said a word to me, let alone reveal anything at all about his past, he was shocked when I told him it was imperative for him to trust in the wisdom and love of his family. It was time to tell them about what had happened to him while imprisoned in a Nazi concentration camp. I knew this decision would likely be the difference between life or death for him.

He was shaking as he sobbed uncontrollably from deep within. Barely able to talk, he said that he was overwhelmed with shame at what had happened and what he had been made to do. The emotions around these diabolical experiences and his subsequent decisions had become programs embedded in his unconscious. Benjamin's thought process had sabotaged his ability to love and forgive himself. Until our session he never would have equated his inability to access trust and to forgive from his True Self with the disease that was killing him.

His unconscious thoughts had become programs that manifested conscious beliefs such as:

- I'm not trustworthy.

- Most people cannot be trusted, and if given the chance are capable of inflicting pain and trauma.

- I will never forgive myself.

- If people knew what I was really like, they would not forgive me either.

Because Benjamin was still harboring these deadly secrets and had not forgiven himself they were literally eating him alive. The constant emotional roller coaster ride of guilt, shame, and blame will do that.

Guess which code he was living by?

Benjamin's ego mind code was working overtime.

Using the Quantum Neutrality Process, I discovered the events, emotions, and decisions that were locked into Benjamin's psyche. I then corrected out the emotional force controlling him and activated a forgiveness template in his heart.

The relief of no longer being held hostage by these debilitating emotions was obvious immediately. Once Benjamin was able to regain his composure, the energy field of a stooped and defeated old man gave way to a more upright, confident man. He expressed feeling free and light for the first time in decades.

I asked him to imagine placing a forgiveness template into his heart and then guided him to forgive himself for the pain he had caused others and to forgive anyone who had ever hurt him.

As I have said before, true forgiveness is such a big decision, it affects the whole world. It is a decision only the soul can make when it is aligned with the perfection of our True Self and the divine mind code.

By the end of his session, our brave hero had re-aligned his soul with his heart and was able to come to a place of peace. More importantly, he said he felt so much better psychologically and could trust in the process of having to be more authentic and vulnerable in telling the truth. Benjamin promised he would tell his family his story, no matter how painful.

Three weeks later his wife rang to update me on the effects of our session:

- Benjamin had gathered his entire family around him and they had listened through the tears of his grief as he trusted them with his broken heart and shattered soul.

- Although initially in shock, they were honored as he finally trusted them enough to openly confide in them. At the same time grieved about how long he had suffered alone.

- There was nothing to forgive as far as they were concerned and through their love and acceptance he was able to forgive himself more fully.

With joy and gratitude in her voice she said that at his last appointment with his oncologist, the doctor had said to him, *"Benjamin, I don't know what you are doing, but keep doing it. The tumor has shrunk down to almost nothing!"*

What Is Trust?

- I trust my True Self can discern the truth in any situation, which frees me from worry.

- Basic trust is an attribute of our True Self. It is the quality of the divine mind code, which accepts the underlying premise that things happen for the ultimate highest and best good for all concerned—even despite appearances to the contrary.

- Trust is unconditional and without limitation.

- Trust is the source of true confidence.

- Trust facilitates openness, higher awareness, creativity, and presence.

- Trust provides the foundation for the strength needed to take action.

- Basic trust is not blind faith in the ego mind's physical world. It is absolute faith in our Source and our True Self.

- Our connection to trust, like the other attributes of the True Self, strengthens over time with use and practice—and especially with the removal of our blocks to experiencing it. Making it stronger and more sustainable is foundational to the evolution of our soul into enlightenment and Integrated Wholeness.

- Without a strong connection to trust, we can't escape being a victim of our ego mind programs.

- Trust is the bridge to infinite love. As we learn to trust in the real world of unity and oneness with the divine, our frequency changes and everything becomes clearer, fresher, more spontaneous, and magical.

- The core low frequency blocker to trust is worry.

Late in his life, at a dinner to commemorate his groundbreaking contributions to our understanding of the physical universe Albert Einstein was the honoree at the Institute for Advanced Study in Princeton, New Jersey. At the end of the evening the master of ceremonies invited him to share any special wisdom or insight he wished to express to the august gathering.

Paraphrasing his comments, he said, "*There is one overarching question each person needs to answer for himself. Is this a friendly or an unfriendly universe?*"

In the illusion that is the ego mind world, this could be our singularly most important question, too. Our answer is either an expression of basic trust or an expression of a disconnection from it. This has a monumental impact on our life. Not only upon all the details of what our life is made up of—as in events, relationships, health, and so on—but even more critically, how we experience the content of our life.

Trust is essential to do effective transformational work. When we inquire deeply, honestly and persistently we penetrate the mistrust and encounter the field of infinite possibility. Then what arises is our sense of trust. Every time we dig in and do the work, our connection to trust grows. Doing the work becomes its own reward. When we inquire fully this applies to every aspect of the True Self.

When we experience Trust it can be likened to the support and security of an infant cradled in the arms of a loving mother. When we continue to worry and react without trust it reinforces personality programs.

THREE KINDS OF TRUST

There are three fundamental kinds of trust:

1. **Higher trust:** This is the trust we have in our source—the God of our understanding.

2. **Inner trust:** This is intrapersonal trust, and its highest expression is trusting our True Self. This includes the trust we have in our intuition and higher awareness.

3. **Outer trust:** This is interpersonal trust—trust in others—and trust in the world.

Trust is not blind faith. For example, trusting others to be true to our values may be naive, but trusting them to be true to their own values, their own programs, will prove invaluable. Using higher awareness we can discern other people's values.

When we are operating in the divine mind code, we can trust our discernment about what their values really are, which is profoundly empowering.

Questions may arise about Trust that will be addressed in the next chapter on Integrity. In many ways we are looking at very closely related qualities and attributes, but from somewhat different angles. Broken trust is often an integrity issue—like not keeping our word with ourselves or others. If others keep or break trust with us, while it is an integrity issue for them, it is a trust and awareness issue for us. Did we use trust in our higher awareness to discern their codes and values? Did we trust them to be consistent with their programs—or project our own?

It is important to note that when we break trust with ourselves it is an integrity issue that inescapably undermines our sense of basic trust. Conversely, when our sense of basic trust is weakened, our connection to integrity is weakened at the same time.

What happens when you experience broken trust on an interpersonal level, when someone's failure of integrity disappoints or hurts you? What happens to your trust? That depends on the code you are operating in.

In the divine mind code, all three stages of trust are unaffected.

Will you be disappointed? Undoubtedly.

Hurt? Possibly.

Is there something to clear? Assuredly.

Is forgiveness called for? Indubitably! But, your basic trust remains intact.

PLATINUM SUCCESS PRINCIPLE: TRUST

- Trust is a soul issue because the peace that comes with real trust is not an ego attribute.

- Cultivate trust. It is the foundation for the confidence to take action.

- Be trustworthy. Always tell the truth and keep your word, especially to yourself.

- Trust that the divine is the source of causeless love and limitless joy and you are loved unconditionally.

- Trust things will happen for the ultimate highest and best good for all concerned—despite appearances to the contrary. This facilitates true confidence.

- Trust that your True Self can discern the truth in any situation, freeing you from worry.

- Commit to live by the divine mind code to facilitate the soul's choice to trust, love, and accept yourself fully.

- Trust that you are the author of your stories and the movie that is your life.

- Accept 100 percent responsibility for everything you think, say, and do.

- Trust knows; perception believes and opines.

- Use the Four Questions when you find yourself worrying to reconnect with Trust.

- Demonstrate the trust you want to experience in the world.

Worry and any lack of trust inhibit our ability to take effective action. And action is needed, especially to do the invaluable inner work that is essential to experience the life of our dreams. Even to meditate is an action. And action is obviously needed for the outer work that must be done to accomplish our worldly goals.

If we place our basic trust in a dualistic world we will be hurt repeatedly. If we trust in nondual reality, we understand that what happens on this prison planet is simply what's manifesting when the ego mind code is operating. This understanding makes true forgiveness natural. Accepting radical personal responsibility and practicing forgiveness powerfully support trust.

What is called for is neutrality—accepting what is, without projecting your wants, desires, and fears onto others and the world. Of course this is where the rubber meets the road. It is where peace of mind is of greatest value—and where forgiveness is most important. We dive deeply into Neutrality in Chapter 6.

What happens when we mistakenly trust someone (i.e., trust them to be true to our values instead of theirs) and are hurt by their untrustworthiness? We can easily see ourselves as victims.

Accepting responsibility in every situation is crucial to transcending victimhood and experiencing freedom. Whose script is it? Whose film is it? While integrity is the essence of true strength, trust is the source of self-confidence. When our trust in ourselves is shaken, what happens to our self-confidence?

Obviously it, too, is shaken. There is an urgent need for forgiveness, especially for the screenwriter—that's us. And there is certainly the need to identify and neutralize the responsible programs.

Trust and verify. Which code have we put our trust in? Operating in the divine mind code puts our True Self in charge, while operating in the ego mind code means the inmates are running the asylum. If you are in the wrong code, use the tools presented throughout this book to switch codes instantly.

This is where *CODEBREAKER's* mind training proves its worth. Over time and depending upon your diligence, your practice will not only make your breakthroughs and "ah-ha" moments more frequent but sustainable as well.

More Than a Single Cell

Bruce Lipton says in *The Biology of Belief,* "*When our uniquely human minds get involved, we can choose to perceive the environment in different ways, unlike a single cell whose awareness is more reflexive.*"

This is the space between stimulus and response that neurologist Viktor Frankl talks about. This is the choice the soul always has the freedom to make—to choose trust and love according to the divine mind code or to stay in the fear and suffering of the ego mind code. When we tap into our True Self we're able see life and the hurdles we face from a higher perspective. There it is natural to trust our ability to make decisions for the highest and best good for everyone.

Between stimulus and response there is a space.

In that space is our power to choose our response.

In our response lies our growth and our freedom.

~ VIKTOR FRANKL

To paraphrase Bruce Lipton, it is exhilarating to the max to discover that you can change the character of your life by changing your thoughts. He said, *"I was instantly energized because I realized that there was a science-based path that would take me from my job as perennial 'victim' to my new position as 'co-creator' of my destiny."*

This is exactly what our hero Benjamin did. Once neutralized to his beliefs and attachment to the story of non-forgiveness, he found himself free from worry and his painful emotions. Neutrality's open-mindedness enabled him to trust and access higher awareness free of bias, emotion, and prejudice.

Thanks to the Quantum Neutrality Process, Benjamin made an incredible mind shift in a very short time. He accepted 100% responsibility and was able to trust this new paradigm. He no longer worried about the future and could see his relationships and his health from an entirely new perspective. Empowered, he became mindful when programs came up that kept him in his former victim mode. Most significantly, he trusted in his own ability to forgive and find peace—to create a new and vital life.

Trust is the mortar that holds the blocks of peace in place, the foundation of our connection to our True Self. Without trust, our foundation crumbles at the slightest tremor, precipitating our perception of life as tumbling down around us. Trust combines with presence and strength in an awesome display of power when the soul decides on the divine mind as its code of choice.

Lack of trust was invented by the ego to perpetuate its dominance.

Whenever hooked into the low frequency of worry, our awareness is shut down and we cannot see the forest for the trees. We don't trust we can do the right thing, and most importantly, we don't trust God to do the right thing by us... if we think God exists at all.

The frequency of our thoughts powerfully shapes people's perceptions of us.

Because everyone picks up the programs we are all silently broadcasting, people are often wary of each other without knowing why. We either attract or repel depending on our programming and the stories we are conditioned to believe.

Research has found interviewers often make hiring decisions in seconds based on nonverbal impressions. This is often how others determine if they can trust us or not! Changing our connection to trust changes our whole life.

The Iceberg Effect and Our Imaginary Split from God

Can you imagine how awesome it would be to see first hand the breathtaking vistas of the polar icecaps? Our eyes would need to be shielded from the blinding white light shining as far as the eye can see, and with day turning into night, the colored lights of the aurora borealis swirl through this magical terrain, inspiring wonder at its majesty, beauty, and total perfection.

Suspend disbelief for just a moment and imagine this is a metaphor for our True Self. We find ourselves safely embedded within this sparkling mass of the divine mind. But what if we dreamt that we decided to explore the furthest reaches of what we imagined to be the "unknown"?

With no real understanding of how life would be in this imaginary "unknown," we dream we are ready, willing and able to break away from our Source and True Self. We hear a fierce and frightening cry that comes from deep within us in this nightmare as we split away with a loud, disorienting crash.

So here we are, still quite magnificent in our own right, floating through life experiencing a sense of wary accomplishment of having made it into the "unknown." However—and there is always a "however"—we have not yet accounted for what has accumulated beneath the surface of our own sparkling beauty.

In this dream, over eons of imaginary time we have lived many lives and have had countless friends, lovers, family members, and enemies who have eroded our sense of trust in life, in who we are, and in others.

Whenever we experience painful events accompanied by strong emotions, the ego mind quickly makes decisions to prevent us from having to experience that pain again. These decisions, when made with strong emotion, become programs. They are not based on the truth and do not facilitate trust. They form life codes of fear, negativity, and pain that are stored in the unconscious mind and are responsible for recurring patterns of doubt and self-sabotage.

As we continue to believe in this imaginary journey, they have the power to change love into hate, joy and happiness into misery and despair, and success into dismal failure.

Below the surface, the sparkling perfection and beauty of the True Self now has a deadly counterpart, and in most cases we are totally in the dark as to its existence. In the shadows of the watery deep, gaining power exponentially, our untrusting unconscious stores all the stories the ego mind has ever created.

When we live without trust and awareness we unconsciously choose to listen to these stories, beliefs, and programs of the ego mind as if it was the expert and savior. This puts our life and the lives of those we love in mortal danger. Just like the circumstances that sank the Titanic, the hidden programs deep within the unconscious mind will sink our ship every time.

When we dreamt we had this mad idea of living in the "unknown" without the loving guidance of the True Self, we accepted the absurdity of dualism—that we could be separate from that which we are.

In our deep sleep we are unaware we are even dreaming. Only as we awaken do we become aware that we have a choice: to stay in the ego mind code or shift to the divine mind code which in the dream we think does not exist.

Deaf, Dumb, and Stupid

Humanity has been deceived by the ego mind and believes it is no longer connected to God. In the dream, we saw the split with our own eyes and heard the thunderous crash of ice into the ocean and fully experienced the rift.

It's not hard to imagine the feelings of absolute terror at what we had just experienced. But, what had we really experienced? We believed we tore ourself from our source, but did we? We were blinded and rendered deaf, dumb, and stupid by the fractured ego mind that humanity had set up in the nightmare. Doing its best to keep us separate from our source, the ego mind supposedly saves us from the pain of being alone and bereft, no longer connected to our True Self. Ever since, humanity's connection to basic trust has been demolished.

The biggest con is that the iceberg is separate from our True Self rather than an aspect of the whole. Using the dream's iceberg metaphor, humanity lost its ability to know unity and each soul sees itself as separate. We no longer trust the divine is omnipresent—from the breathtaking polar caps to the icebergs melting back into the ocean. They flow and melt into rivers that are still other forms of the divine, until they evaporate into the ethers and then, as rain and snow, land back onto the polar caps from where they thought they could never return.

In this metaphor, like in the cycle of life, we exist multi-dimensionally, on the polar icecap, within the oceans, rivers, and waterways, and as the unique iceberg of our own making. As we awaken from this dream of dualism, basic trust and our connection to the True Self are restored, reassuring us everything is happening for the ultimate highest and best good for all concerned.

WAYFARER

Wayfarer,

Your whole mind and body have been tied

To the foot of the Divine Elephant

With a thousand golden chains.

Now begin to rain intelligence and compassion

Upon all your tender, wounded cells

And realize the profound absurdity

Of thinking

That you can ever go Anywhere

Or do Anything

Without God's will.

~HAFIZ

DYING FROM LYING

Trust starts with truth and ends with truth.

~ SANTOSH KALWAR

Our trust meter is like a lie detector that is always operating. As we move into more enlightened states we are able to intuit when people are lying. We sense them go weak, just like we go weak when we lie and make up stories. No wonder by the end of any given day we feel depleted. Did you think it was just low blood sugar levels? Try keeping track of your trust meter and how many lies you have told. That includes exaggeration, making up things to suit yourself, and changing facts because you think it will make you look better in someone else's eyes...or your own.

These weapons of personal destruction are all in the ego mind's arsenal, which uses them without regard for who does and doesn't trust us and how the body reacts. The body gets weaker and weaker as we shoot down the facts, which automatically lowers its resistance to sickness and disease— as is easily demonstrated using energy testing.

Over decades we've honed our ability to use intuitive energy testing, especially when working with clients, and you can too. It's time to cultivate trust in your inner guidance.

To develop intuition it is helpful to use applied kinesiology, commonly called energy or muscle testing, to confirm, whether the body stays strong or goes weak to our thoughts and words. Lies are the product of unconscious programs which keep us in the ego mind code and weaken us. It's always exciting to discover a weakness because that leads to a hidden program sabotaging the best version of who we are.

IT IS TIME TO GO BEYOND BELIEF

A belief is only a thought or opinion to which we've become attached. Recognize that nearly all of the ego mind's ideas, beliefs, and programs are indeed false and limiting. Outside the ego mind's frame of reference, our personal power grows with new levels of awareness, which cannot be accessed without trust.

Bruce Lipton talks about this new paradigm:

Understanding on a scientific level how cells respond to your thoughts and perceptions illuminates the path to personal empowerment. The insights we gain through this new biology unleash the power of consciousness, matter, and miracles.

His science-based insights empower trust and confidence.

Trust liberates us from the dominance of the ego mind code, whose programs seem to push our buttons at random. Our mission in this dream world is to inspire and empower the soul to decide in favor of the True Self so we can have fun on this evolutionary journey into our heart. It is time to embody the real confidence, wisdom, and power of basic trust that is our birthright, and to live in harmony with all that we really are.

With this radical new awareness, we choose to trust the
True Self to lovingly guide us into our heart—where our personal
power is accessed. It is patiently waiting for the soul to pass
over the reins so it can lead the way back into the light of the
divine mind code.

A human being is only interesting
if he's in contact with himself.
I learned you have to trust yourself, be what you are,
and do what you ought to do the way you should do it.
You have got to discover you,
what you do, and trust it.

~ BARBRA STREISAND

SANDRA AND DANIEL DRIVING ON THE WRONG SIDE OF THE ROAD

On our mystical expedition into enlightenment and wholeness, we visited India many times. We worked with two incredible beings devoted to helping humanity attain enlightened states. Their presence facilitated complete resonance with the enlightenment frequency.

Many times, in full trust, we were in total bliss. As we surrendered to the divine within, the illusory world completely disappeared. Through alcohol, drugs, sex, food, and countless other mystical and mundane methods, people have been seeking this state of oneness and bliss since the beginning of time. Trust is required to genuinely transcend the ego mind—the prerequisite for enlightenment experiences. Seeking them outside ourselves is an invitation for disappointment and disillusionment.

Sandra and her sister were notorious for being nervous passengers, preferring to be the driver to feel safe and in control on the road. Their trust issues were a great example of ego mind programs running amuck.

On the three-and-a-half-hour drive from the ashram to the airport, the taxi driver drove like Jason Bourne meets Bollywood at breakneck speeds on the wrong side of a four-lane freeway. In India, unlike in the West, animals and people wander at will on the freeways. Oxen and cows, chickens and children alike strolled down the main highway as though it was a narrow dirt road in the countryside.

Normally, Sandra would have been clinging to the seat, her knuckles white, in absolute terror of losing her life or that of her beloved. However, to her astonishment, she was in such a state of peace and trust that she was not at all worried.

Instead she was amused and delighted rather than afraid and was in love with everyone—the men who sometimes wore just a loin-cloth and the women who, like the beautiful flowers in their hair, wore vibrant colored saris. In her eyes, neither the women nor the bright hot pinks, purples, yellows, and oranges were diluted or wilted by the extreme heat and dust of the highway. With no fear whatsoever she just loved all the people, the animals, the skinny little children, and the entire experience.

In a potentially life-threatening situation she became the observer of her old habits and programs. Instead of anxiety and fear, she was almost hysterical with laughter:

"I knew we were safe! I felt that deep sense of trusting in the order of all things and a peace and joy that just bubbles beneath the surface when connected to the divine energy of my True Self. I was in such a neutral, blissful state that none of my usual fears and emotions existed. This would normally have been one of my worst nightmares, but instead trust, inner peace, and neutrality brought joy and happiness into this wild and wonderful ride.

"I was aware of thinking how entertaining it would have been to have seen my sister's reaction to this wild ride. With tears of terror on her gorgeous face she would have screamed for the driver to stop. I could see her jumping out of the car and taking a week to walk to the airport. As far from trust and inner peace as you can get, her hysteria and subsequent panic would have been the antithesis of bliss."

If we can just let go and trust that things will work out the way they're supposed to, without trying to control the outcome, then we can begin to enjoy the moment more fully. The joy of freedom it brings becomes more pleasurable than the experience itself.

~ GOLDIE HAWN

CELLULAR MEMORY

The truth is we are all at the mercy of conscious and unconscious programs that have us feeling an infinite range of symptoms of lack of trust: from claustrophobia to agoraphobia, from fear of being a victim to fear of being a perpetrator. Our parents, grandparents, and all our ancestors have passed down their stories from one generation to the next via information stored in our cells. Cellular memory can even transcend physical boundaries (via morphic resonance and the human energy field) and end up in our unsuspecting unconscious mind.

The ego mind has fooled us into thinking we are the masters of our destiny when operating its code; however, appearances can be deceptive. The unconscious mind is an unedited collection of multiple lives and almost infinite memories that has more control over us than we can fathom. Can we trust our unconscious mind to be aligned with what we think, say, and do consciously? Rarely!

Finding our way home is as easy as changing our code once we have discovered the truth. Our hero Benjamin discovered the truth that trust was necessary for him to heal, so he changed codes and lived. He learned that trust, peace, love, higher levels of awareness, integrity, neutrality, unity, and mindfulness are not just for the "New Agers" or saints and sages of the past.

Commit to live on the frequency of trust. The True Self's expansive, nondual sense of trust is experienced as a deep knowing; it is not experienced as a perception or a belief.

A belief is not merely an idea the mind possesses; it is an idea that possesses the mind.

~ ROBERT OXTON BOLT

ATTUNEMENT:
A Meditation on Trust

Begin by observing your breath and letting your body relax. Center yourself by taking a few deep breaths as you harmonize with the frequency of trust.

Let go of any worries. Let go of all judgments as you allow your thoughts to simply come and go, like clouds passing by in the sky.

Say to yourself, *"Trust is an integral part of my beingness. My True Self perfectly expresses trust, peace, love, and joy."*

Continue to breathe deeply as your whole being makes the shift to this powerful vibrational frequency of trust. Just as darkness is displaced by light, with every breath you take, your feelings are transformed. Worry, fear, anxiety, being overwhelmed, and victimhood have been displaced by the confidence of trust.

Using your imagination, see, feel, or know the confidence that trusting in the order of all things brings to your whole being.

Breathe in this trust and peace. Bask in the calm and wonder of the peace that has been activated as you connect to trust. Basic trust is absolute. There is nothing you need to get, give, or do.

Allow yourself to go deeper and deeper, more and more relaxed. The divine mind has taken center stage as you sit anchored deep within your heart, in the high frequency of trust.

With gratitude that your soul has chosen to live with a foundation of trust, say, *"I am totally aligned with the divine mind and trust the world is unfolding as it should."*

Now imagine a column of white light pouring into your head and filling your body all the way down to your toes. This is the light, wisdom, knowledge, and clarity of your True Self that you have activated. Allow this white light to flow freely through you, as you, soothing your entire being, and your body relaxing even more.

With every breath you take, your body, mind, and soul are regenerating, rejuvenating, strengthening, and renewing. Trust allows your creativity and wisdom to flow naturally. With every breath you take you can trust that the evolution of your soul is progressing into higher states of enlightenment and wholeness.

Stay in this expanded place, relaxing into the frequency of trust for as long as you can. You are now aligned with the unfathomably rich state of trust, presence, and strength.

Trust facilitates real forgiveness, peace, and love. Having activated the beingness state of trust, use your imagination and take a moment to bring into your meditation someone who has hurt you. Feel the other person relax, breathing easily and matching up their frequency of trust to yours. Look into their eyes and say, *"I forgive the programs that have broken our trust."*

When you are ready, take a few deep breaths and slowly open your eyes. You are now in tune with the high vibration of trust and peace. This powerful exercise has activated the best version of you. Share it with the world. Stay on this frequency for as long as you can.

If you catch yourself beginning to worry, or get anxious, use this meditation to reinstate the high frequency of trust.

This training is about the choice you make to trust or not. Instinctively your Ego Puppy does not trust you to do what it wants. You can always trust Ego Puppy—the ego mind—to be true to its values. It is almost impossible to understand the anguish, pain, and despair they cause when they are untrained. They kill for sport; are vicious and attack at random. We are all afraid of Ego Puppy's power to attack us—and others—with the least provocation.

"If it bleeds, it leads." To see the untrained Ego Puppy at work, just look at the headlines or watch the nightly news.

Did you know where your puppy came from when it was delivered from the pound? Your newly acquired member of the family did not come with a thorough background check. It looked just fine. However, you had no idea of any abuse it might have suffered. You thought you were adopting a cute rescue puppy—not a Trojan horse!

Cruelty undermines our ability to trust, and everyone has suffered abuse of one kind or another. It will take a lot of retraining to get Ego Puppy free of all its learned behavior. Every time it dashes around causing mayhem and destruction, it's up to you to pull it up, sit it down, teach it to trust your judgment, and get it back on track. The sooner you do it, the better for the whole family.

Stop worrying! Trust in your ability to keep Ego Puppy from going back to the pound and certain death. Consistency is the key, and with diligence your soul can choose to divert the flow of anger and frustration from Ego Puppy's psychological, emotional, and physical makeup to where they too can trust that life is good and they are safe in the world.

Once you and your Ego Puppy start to vibrate to the energy of love, trust will follow, and it will no longer be attracting other misused and abused Ego Puppies. Your goals for your well-trained Ego Puppy are for it have fun, shine its light for all to see, serve others, and bring joy to those in need.

Give yourself every possible chance to fulfill your heart's desires; trust you can train Ego Puppy to become a service dog of the highest order.

Long term, the best Ego Puppy training uses the Quantum Neutrality Process to neutralize its dysfunctional programs. For short-term intervention, the Four Questions can't be beaten.

INQUIRY—
THE FOUR QUESTIONS—TRUST

Use this simple set of questions to change the way you feel from one moment to the next. Use it whenever you feel yourself moving away from the high frequency state of trust. Recognize that worry is only untrained ego mind mischief at play.

Answer the questions truthfully and spontaneously. Stay focused on the answer to question number four for as long as you can. The answers we provide are examples only.

Use your own words and the wisdom of your own heart to answer the questions.

1. **What am I feeling?** I feel worried and insecure.

2. **What am I focused on?** I feel like I can't trust anyone and no one trusts me.

3. **How do I want to feel?** I want to feel secure and peaceful.

4. **What focus will serve that?** Focus on trusting myself.

Ask yourself how trustworthy you have been. If you can't trust yourself, no one will trust you, and you'll never be able to trust others. Think of examples where you have been able to trust yourself and focus on that feeling. Tell your Ego Puppy to sit and stay as you move from the head to the heart.

Be grateful for the opportunity to become more whole by clearing out yet another unwanted belief or idea that takes you away from trust.

INQUIRY—
RATE YOUR STATE: TRUST

Use these questions as a guide to rate your state and discover which code you are operating in:

How do you rate how you trust yourself? Does a lack of forgiveness, guilt, or shame stop you from trusting yourself? How you trust yourself effects how you trust others.

How much do you worry? You stay low on the Integrated Wholeness Scale when you can't trust that everything works out for the best.

Do you look outside yourself in order to experience peak states, or do you trust you can generate them from within? Externally generated experiences risk disappointment and dependency. Internally generated peak experiences build trust in oneself, which creates confidence and independence. Through alcohol, drugs, sex, food, and countless other mystical and mundane methods, people have been seeking this state of oneness and bliss since the beginning of time.

Your new PLATINUM password cultivates your own noble purpose. You move up the Integrated Wholeness Scale as you become a trustworthy, aware, enlightened presence in your own life and the lives of those you love. Trust allows you to love unconditionally, even through adversity.

I trust that everything happens for a reason,
even if we are not wise enough to see it.

~ OPRAH WINFREY

An Overview: Trust

- Trust is an essential, foundational aspect of our True Self. Without a strong connection to trust, we can't escape being a victim of our ego mind programs.

- The soul has to be in sync with the True Self to know the wonder, power, and peace of trust, especially to trust who we are in relation to our Source.

- Nearly all of the ego mind's ideas, beliefs, and programs are indeed false and limiting. Once we transcend the ego mind code's frame of reference, our personal power grows exponentially with new levels of awareness, which are inaccessible without trust.

- Trust liberates us from the dominance of the ego mind code, whose programs, when triggered, seem to push our buttons at random. Our mission in this dream world is to inspire and empower the soul to choose the True Self; to embody the real confidence, wisdom, and power of basic trust that is our birthright so we can live in harmony with all that we really are.

- Trust is an absolute prerequisite to becoming the best version of ourselves.

- Confidence in our journey to develop a PLATINUM life is facilitated by trust.

- The core frequency blocker to trust is worry.

- Trust in our journey is liberating and empowering. Lack of trust in our journey handicaps, slows, and undermines its progress.

- When we operate in the ego mind code we are disconnected from our True Self's attribute of basic trust.

- Trust is the bridge to infinite love. As we learn to trust in the real world of unity and oneness with the divine, our frequency raises and everything becomes clearer, fresher, more spontaneous, and magical.

- In the divine mind code we connect to the True Self. Then we see life and the hurdles we face from a higher perspective and trust ourselves to make decisions for the highest and best good of all concerned.

- Trust combines with presence and strength in an awesome display of power when the soul decides on the divine mind code and embarks on the path of higher awareness.

- With trust we can change the way we think in an instant. We do not have to be either the victim or proponent of our thoughts.

- We can trust our vibrational frequency is always broadcasting the code we are operating in.

- A belief is only a thought or opinion to which we've become attached. Our perceptions are projections, and nearly all our ideas, beliefs, and programs are false and self-limiting.

Commit to cultivate your connection to trust—an essential aspect of your True Self.

As Alan Watts said,

When you swim you don't grab hold of the water, because if you do you will sink and drown. Instead you relax, and float.

So remember: It really is okay. It's not real. It's just a story.

We are now ready to move on to the next high frequency aspect of our True Self—Integrity, which is the ability to know right from wrong and to courageously go where no ego mind dares to go.

CHAPTER FIVE

INTEGRITY:
MASTER YOUR INNER STRENGTH

*Your integrity is the foundation
of your inner strength.*

*Life expands or contracts
in proportion to your integrity.*

~ SANDRA & DANIEL BISKIND

Skunk Energy

Have you ever met anyone who was leaking skunk energy? It would be surprising if you hadn't. You could meet this person, and even with their partner present, feel like you are the most important person in their life. They look you up and down and appraise you as if you were a bottle of wine or a piece of candy put on this planet for their personal consumption.

They could be married, in a relationship, or single. They flirt with you and try to make you feel special. If your awareness is in operation, your skin might crawl to warn you of danger. They are broadcasting sexual energy, and their inner TV series is ready for the next bedroom scene. They are always on the lookout for someone with programs that make them susceptible to their frequency so they get to say, *"Scene one, take one, Action."* Leaving a trail of devastation, they exit the set as the consummate actors they are.

These people are quick to identify suspects who are running complementary programs. For instance, a person whose ego mind code says they don't deserve love and that no one would ever want them no matter how desirable they might be. Man or woman, the antenna of the predatory skunk is always attuned to the weakness you project when not standing in your power. Often the partners of our skunk energy friends are the big give-away. Skunk man or woman might not have sprayed the room, yet but their partners will give the cold shoulder to anyone they think could be a threat to their relationship.

When trust and integrity have been eroded in relationships, anyone can pose a threat to happiness. Many years ago, Sandra was the guest speaker at a "Women in Business" meeting, where she met one of Australia's top fashion designers. She was a beautiful, smart, and very savvy business person. Sandra couldn't work out why she seemed to take an instant dislike to her, until a couple of weeks later when she met her husband at another industry function:

"Ah-ha! I had just met her skunk. He definitely had a type he was attracted to, and that type was young and blonde. At the time I happened to fit that category and could now understand her instant mistrust and dislike of me as soon as we met. When a partner sprays skunk energy, we learn anyone can be a threat to the relationship. This very successful woman understandably saw many other women as threats.

Rather than feeling flattered by his attention and odoriferous innuendoes, I stayed as far away as possible from this man and his skunk energy. I departed as soon as gracefully possible.

My integrity was never in question. I did not want to be another notch on his belt, nor did I want him as a notch on mine. If I had been feeling insecure and needy of an attractive, dynamic man to make me feel whole, I might have been tempted to stay and play the game.

Because I was no longer perceived as a threat, my business relationship with this woman not only remained intact but flourished. My actions and frequency communicated I was safe, freeing her to trust me and relax in my presence.

Have you ever felt flattered and tempted to play with a skunk? Did you ignore your internal GPS warning? If you were tempted to enter a relationship with someone who was out of integrity, it's important to discover what programs were running that made you vulnerable. Use inquiry to discover the stories and beliefs that could make you a victim. Such programs could include, *"I'm not worthy of love," "I'm not good enough,"* and *No one will ever love me."*

What Is Integrity?

- Integrity never compromises the means for an end, so you are always whole and trustworthy.

- Integrity is the principle that embodies wholeness, consistency, and perfection. It is a state free of internal conflicts or contradictions. The word "integrity" is based on "integral," which means whole. It is the source of your inner strength and your power to take action. It is experienced when you are connected with your True Self.

- As a timeless, universal principle, Integrity is absolute, like gravity.

- It is a condition of being complete, transcending ethics and morality, which are subjective and variable social norms.

- Integrity is the principle that ensures workability. Without integrity, things simply don't work properly, entropy sets in, and breakdown is inevitable. It is essential to how things work—ourselves, life, the universe, everything.

- Integrity embodies authenticity and transparency, empowering you to act wisely, honorably, and effectively. It is what makes your moral and ethical compass function.

- Integrity means the integration of all the aspects of your True Self—embodying all the aspects of the PLATINUM master password.

- The core low frequency blocker to Integrity is fragmentation.

EXQUISITELY WOVEN

Wayfarer,

Your body is my prayer carpet,

For I can see in your eyes

That you are exquisitely woven

With the finest silk and wool

And that Pattern upon your soul

Has the signature of God

And all your moods and colors of love

Come from His Divine vats of dye and

Gold.

Wayfarer,

Your body is my shrine.

If you had the eyes of a Pir, (a saint)

You would see Hafiz
Kneeling by your side,

Humming playful tunes
And shedding joyful tears

Upon your wondrous hidden Crown.

~HAFIZ

Your time is limited, so don't waste it
living someone else's life.
Don't be trapped by dogma—which is
living with the results of other people's thinking.

Don't let the noise of others' opinions
drown out your own inner voice.
And most important, have the
courage to follow your heart and intuition.

~ STEVE JOBS

INTEGRITY OF THE HEART

This heart-wrenching story is written by a man who lived in outback Australia during a devastating seven-year draught.

"I'm sitting in the shade of on an old 44-gallon drum next to a rusty windmill that hasn't hummed for years. Tired, hungry, and exhausted, I struggle to think as I hang up the phone; it was the bore pump bloke, and he's still three days away from fixing it.

My mouth and eyes are dry from the stinging hot and dusty air and my ears are loaded with the constant bellowing of thirsty cattle. They just stand there, looking at me, melting away.

It's the end of another huge day, and I've had enough. The bore was supposed to be pumping fresh water a week ago. We've got hot northerly winds, depleting feed, and the cattle are starting to show it.

I've been slaving through this drought for just over a year and autopilot is failing me. I'm alone, it's all too hard, and it would be so easy to call it quits right now.

I find myself at my ute (utility vehicle), where I grab my rifle. Loaded and cocked, I stand there looking at it in my hands. Looking turns to staring, and staring turns to gazing.

I'm bereft, broken. I can't see. I'm lost.

All that goes through my mind is, should I shoot the cattle first? I don't want them to suffer without water when I'm gone. Or bugger it, none of it will matter anyway....

I feel a tickle on my hand, which demanded I come to. I see Tilly, my Kelpie, licking my hand and wagging her tail, looking up at me with total adoration.

And that's what stopped me. Some love from my best little mate.

I squinted hard, squeezing the tears from my eyes, and unloaded my rifle, shaking myself back into some kind of reality. I was frightened by how close I came to doing something so drastic. What about the people I'd leave behind? How clouded had I become? I needed clarity as much as I needed the rain."

He goes on to say, "Draughts and all the stresses associated with farming are emotionally draining and you need to look out for everyone in your rural communities." Similarly, earthquakes, tornadoes, fires, and floods are all emotionally, mentally, and physically draining. But it's not just natural disasters that can break us. Losing a friend or family member, having financial challenges, and health issues can all create feelings of loneliness, despair, utter misery, and panic.

In this heartbreaking story, his beingness was shredded to pieces. Feeling fragmented and alone, his integrity was compromised. His well-trained and loving companion Tilly nudges him back into his heart, where he is shocked to discover how far from its wholeness he has strayed. Once realigned into the integrity of his heart he is empowered to courageously move forward. To not only live on, but to try to be that inspiration to others that Tilly was to him.

An example of Ego Puppy becoming a great service dog, Tilly the Kelpie shows how it's done. A loving touch and adoring eyes were all the reminder that her best friend needed to bring him back into some semblance of wholeness. He was then able to separate right action from wrong and reverted to his normal strong code of integrity to take on the tough job of powering through.

Unconscious programs routinely cause errors in our processing that can lead us out of integrity, and like our hero above, to thoughts of ending it all. Realizing how far we have strayed from our innate courage and ability to separate right from wrong can leave us breathless.

As always, trust is foundational. Without trust, we cannot sustain higher states of awareness. Only with trust can we attain integrity. Our hero had to trust he was making the right decision to keep on going even when he couldn't see a solution and life looked impossible.

A strong connection to the high frequency of integrity partners with trust so our actions are in harmony and aligned with the courage and honor of the divine mind code.

INTEGRITY

Integrity includes two major components:
Understanding what is right, and Having the
Courage and Desire to Follow Through

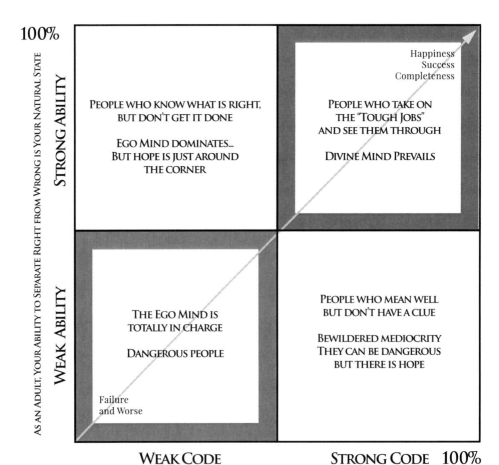

What Is the Greatest Gift You Can give?

At one of our workshops, many participants were women who had either never been married or had been married and divorced. There was only one couple sitting at the back of the room. When Sandra asked for questions toward the end of the evening, the man shot his hand up and, with his other arm still around his partner, he asked, *"What is the greatest gift I can give my beloved?"*

All the women in the room "Ooohed" together, as though it was a well-rehearsed flash dance.

The answer was something so profound that it summarizes this whole body of work:

The greatest gift you can give your beloved, and in fact, the whole world, is your own wholeness.

When you're whole and your beloved looks into your eyes, they see the perfection and wholeness that are reflected back. Integrity inspires us to dedicate our life to living in wholeness, turbo-charging the evolution of our soul. As a key element of a PLATINUM state of mind, it supports our allegiance to the divine mind code to guide our actions and live a PLATINUM life.

The strongest thing that any human being has going is their own integrity and their own heart. As soon as you start veering away from that, the solidity you need in order to be able to stand up for what you believe in and deliver what's really inside, it's just not going to be there.

~ Herbie Hancock

Consistency

John Molloy is a great social scientist. In his classic *Dress for Success*, his research discovered a key ingredient of social awkwardness. When someone sends mixed messages, we perceive them as awkward. When what they say doesn't align with their tone of voice, or their body language, we sense there's something wrong with this picture, even if we can't put a finger on it. And obviously that does not engender trust.

When we speak of the literary or artistic integrity of a performance or work of art, we're talking about how its elements cohere and fit together and the way its meaning and purpose are consistent with its expression. Does the style suit the content?

Scientific integrity refers to consistency with, or adherence to, accepted standards of the scientific method; and professional integrity refers to the ethics and protocols of the relevant profession.

Integrity matters whether or not someone else sees it. The most important person to see it is you. If you break trust with yourself, your own inner strength is compromised, regardless of whether anyone else sees it or not.

Authenticity

Maintaining your purpose in integrity also means standing for something and keeping your identity intact and uncorrupted. Joseph Campbell said, *"The privilege of a lifetime is being who you are."* This speaks to integrity's authenticity and transparency. It doesn't play games or practice denial. Without pretense, it neither expresses false humility or grandiosity. It accepts and expresses what is.

From Pain to Gain

Once a person shows pain as a result of our behavior, integrity demands we "cease and desist" whatever we are doing that causes grief—even if we think it is the result of their glitches and corrupted software programs. We might have to remove ourselves from their environment, and will definitely need to overlook and forgive the pain that both parties now feel. If not, this becomes an endless ego mind feedback loop that undermines our freedom and causes family members, friends, and co-workers —and even nations— to go to war with each other. The only real victor is the instigator of it all—the ego mind.

When we are aware how another person operates and mindful of how our own operating system reacts to stressful situations, it makes it easier to take 100 percent responsibility for how we handle any situation. It is vital to operate by a strong integrity code so we can instantly evict all the rent-free rantings of the ego mind that wants to blame others for the fallout of pain and confusion.

During our talks and seminars—and particularly when we are working with couples—we share one of the most profound secrets to any successful relationship: *"Make your partner's wholeness, happiness, and becoming the best version of him- or herself your highest priority."* Many an ego mind will be screaming right now "But what about ME?"

So, who is really doing the screaming? It could well be the baby or small child who did not get the support, cuddles, play, and loving attention necessary for them to have learned these important life lessons:

If we want to be loved, then we have to be loving.

If we want support, we have to be supportive.

If we want honesty and integrity from partners, friends, and co-workers, we need to model it. The more empowered and courageous we are, the more we are able to be truthful and do what we say we're going to do when we say we're going to do it.

WHAT IF YOU CAN'T KEEP YOUR WORD?

Keeping our word is an obvious example of integrity. But what about when we can't? What then? While ethics and morality may debate the meaning or application of keeping our word, integrity requires us to honor our word. Accidents and mistakes can and do happen. Integrity provides the strength to clean up our mess. Awareness will guide us to the highest and best way for all concerned, and integrity will give us the strength and courage to see it through. Honoring our word is always possible and may be an even more critical component of integrity than keeping our word.

CORPORATE INTEGRITY

The lack of integrity in the world of business and government is so widely known and deplored that sometimes "corporate integrity" is called an oxymoron. The Global Financial Crisis was triggered in 2008 by a systemic lack of integrity in business, financial, and governmental institutions.

In 1982 there was a tragedy in Chicago when Tylenol laced with arsenic killed seven people. In a model display of corporate integrity, the company immediately took full responsibility, proactively cooperated with the media, and recalled all Tylenol products. When the dust settled and research was done into how and why the company had handled the disaster in such an exemplary fashion, the answer became apparent.

Throughout the crisis, the leaders of Johnson and Johnson operated according to its published credo, created by one of its founders decades earlier. Its credo contained a strong integrity code and was used for guidance when making the tough decisions that had to be made in the midst of the crisis.

Tylenol was likely to become nothing but a historical footnote, but thanks to integrity it recovered to continue as a leading worldwide brand of pain reliever.

We have both gone through two severely challenging experiences in our businesses in the late 1980s into the 1990s and from 2008 to 2012, and needed to demonstrate integrity under devastating adversity. Like so many, we've had to be accountable for being unable to fulfill contractual obligations, which is literally not keeping our word. However, our strong integrity codes required us to honor our word. Even on those occasions when we were unable to keep the letter of the contract, we still did our best to keep the spirit of the contract. We can testify from our own first-hand experience how integrity pays huge dividends in the long run.

Integrity never compromises the long-term big picture for short-term gain. This is true in every aspect of life: intrapersonal, interpersonal, in health, and in the world of business.

PLATINUM SUCCESS PRINCIPLE: INTEGRITY

Integrity inspires trust; it is the key to earning the trust of others and is invaluable to successful, effective leadership. As we attune to the integrity frequency and weed out the programs that conflict with it, our natural ability to discern right from wrong and our inner strength to follow through naturally assert themselves. When we display trust and integrity people want to follow us, listen to us, and learn from us. Obviously integrity is a critical component for success.

How Do We Get It?

- With trust in and commitment to our purpose.
- By integrating all the aspects of our True Self—embodying all the attributes of the PLATINUM master password and neutralizing the programs that conflict with it.

How Do We Lose It?

- By operating in the ego mind code; by playing games and practicing denial; by losing our connection to our True Self.

What Does It Get Us?

- The strength to act wisely and effectively; it achieves work ability and earns trust.
- It eliminates internal conflict and supports wellbeing on every level.
- Empowered thought and emotion, a feeling of wholeness and the strength to accomplish our goals.

- Support from friends, family. and co-workers essential to successful leadership.

What Does Its Lack Cost Us?

- Trust and strength.
- Fulfilling our potential and achieving ultimate success; a strong connection to our True Self.
- It costs us a PLATINUM state of mind, thereby sacrificing our PLATINUM life.

What Did Grandma Teach You About Integrity?

- Do what you say you will do; and do not encroach on another person or their property.
- Treat others as you wish to be treated.

What Didn't You Learn About Integrity from Grandma?

- Integrity means being whole.
- Nothing works without integrity
- You can only transform your life when you understand what is right, and have the desire and courage to follow through.

IT'S ALWAYS JUST A CHOICE—ISN'T IT?

Like forgiveness, living in integrity is a choice. In moments of pain, have you ever found it difficult to forgive other people's programs? It's easy to forget the "no BJC" rule (no blaming, justification, or complaints), isn't it? However, tapping into the high frequency of integrity we mindfully take radical personal responsibility for the pain our programs, thoughts, words, and deeds have triggered. We don't blame, justify, or complain.

When we choose to hold ourselves accountable, we get to see the big picture and discover the programs that created the situation. We always have the opportunity to exercise integrity and use higher levels of awareness to forgive and do what is right.

The amazing life of Helen Keller dramatized the importance and power of choice that we each possess. She wrote, "Many persons have the wrong idea of what constitutes true happiness. It is not attained through self-gratification but through fidelity to a worthy purpose." Commitment to your worthy purpose—to the evolution of your soul and the expression of the love that you are—requires the strength of integrity, made accessible by the confidence of trust.

Ultimately, integrity is a personal choice. But, to enjoy a PLATINUM state of mind, to operate in the divine mind code, and to live a PLATINUM life, it's not optional—it's imperative.

Integrity is our source of strength. It is critical not only to our inner strength, which facilitates resilience and flexibility, but to our physical strength, energy, and stamina. In live events, using applied kinesiology, aka muscle or energy testing, we often demonstrate that when we lie or speak untruth, our body actually goes weak.

Whenever we feel fear, negativity, or pain, the ego-mind code is in operation and it is essential to change code. Ego Puppy needs a training session!

ATTUNEMENT:
A Meditation on Integrity

Sit comfortably in your chair and begin by observing your breath and letting your body relax. Center yourself by taking a few deep breaths as you harmonize with the frequency of integrity. Let go of all judgments as you allow your thoughts to simply come and go.

Say to yourself, *"Integrity supports my soul's quest to be whole and one with the divine. My True Self perfectly expresses integrity and trust."*

Continue to breathe deeply as your whole being resonates with this powerful vibrational frequency of integrity. Just as darkness is displaced by light, with every breath you take, your feelings are transformed; and fear, anxiety, and victimhood are displaced by a sense of strength and wholeness.

Breathing deeply and using your imagination, see, feel, or know yourself empowered by the strength and wholeness of integrity.

Continue to breathe into this empowered state. Connect with a deep sense of knowing what is right and feel the courage to follow through. Bask in the calm that has been activated as integrity creates the foundation for peace, love, and success.

This is your time. Allow yourself to go deeper and deeper—more and more relaxed. The divine mind has taken center stage as you sit immersed in your heart, reveling in the knowledge and wisdom of your True Self.

With integrity, your soul always makes the choice to develop the courage to trust in the truth and stay on the frequency of peace.

Now, imagine a column of white light pouring into your head and filling your body all the way to your toes. This is the light, wisdom, knowledge, and clarity of your True Self that you have activated. Allow this white light to flow freely through you, as you, soothing your entire being, and your body relaxing even more.

With every breath you take, your body, mind, and soul are being regenerated, rejuvenated, strengthened, and renewed. Stay in this expanded place, trusting you can relax into the wholeness that integrity supports for as long as you can. As you align with this unfathomably rich attribute of integrity, you go higher and higher on the Integrated Wholeness scale.

With every breath you take, you find yourself going deeper and deeper into relaxation.

When you are ready, take a few full breaths and slowly open your eyes. You are now in tune with the high frequency of integrity. This powerful exercise has activated the best version of you. Share it with the world. Stay on this frequency for as long as you can.

If you find yourself feeling fragmented in any way, reignite the high frequency of integrity and experience its strength and wholeness.

Ego Puppy Training 5: Integrity

Your ego mind programs comprise your Ego Puppy's personality. Consistency is a prerequisite to bringing Little Ego into integrity. Without consistency, Ego Puppy feels confusion and doesn't know who to trust. When you have integrity and start to build up trust, it will learn right action and begin to transform its behavior to conform to your desires.

Obviously whatever you want from your Ego Puppy has to be congruent with how you train it. If you want a guard dog who is vicious and willing to attack people, then cuddling it, having it sleep by your side, and giving it a safe, comfortable home will not get you a killer-coded Ego Puppy. To achieve your goal of a courageous Ego Puppy who trusts, loves, and does the right thing no matter what the circumstances, it is paramount to provide the appropriate environment to support developing its nature.

Although unique in so many ways, all Ego Puppies have the same original configuration. They have all been born broadcasting their brand of ego mind concepts, and need to be trained out of disruptive, disease-causing confusion. It is up to us to love them no matter what they look like; no matter what disabilities they have; and to diligently train them into being able to live in integrity.

As they learn to trust you to have their best interests at heart, they begin to trust the training process. They become quietly courageous, confident, and relaxed in their own skin. The divine mind is in play in all its wonder when the exuberant Ego Puppy knows right from wrong and has the courage and desire to follow through. As you live from the integrity of your divine mind code, you and your Ego Puppy will enrich the world with a whole new song.

INQUIRY—
The Four Questions: Integrity

Use this simple set of questions to change the way you feel in just moments. Use it whenever you feel yourself moving away from your natural state of peace and love. Recognize that is only untrained ego mind mischief at play.

Answer the questions truthfully and spontaneously. Stay focused on the answer to question number four for as long as you can. The answers we provide are examples only. Use your own words and the wisdom of your own heart to answer the questions.

1. **What am I feeling?** I am feeling overwhelmed.

2. **What am I focused on?** Not having the strength to do what I want.

3. **How do I want to feel?** I want to feel strong and powerful.

4. **What focus will serve that?** My True Self possesses all the resources to know what to do and the courage and strength to follow through.

Tell your ego mind to sit, stay, listen, and learn while you easily neutralize the mistaken thoughts of the ego mind, deleting their effects.

INQUIRY—
RATE YOUR STATE: INTEGRITY

Empower yourself with this litmus test. Answer the questions truthfully, and if necessary rewrite the codes you have uncovered in your human operating system.

- **If you swore an oath to tell the truth, would you tell the truth even knowing your peers would not like the answers?** Just imagine yourself in a court of law and you have to tap into your ability to know right from wrong and tell it the way it is. Integrity manifests as you trust yourself to stay whole and courageously do the right thing. You are high on the Integrated Wholeness Scale as you maintain a strong integrity code.

- **Financial challenges can be overwhelming. Do you remain accountable, truthful, and willing to work toward a solution that is for the highest and best good for all? Or do you lie and deny, run for cover, and pretend it is not happening?** Integrity is such a compelling state that most people will support you when you tell the truth and work toward resolving a problem with a win-win solution. Anything less will always make the problem worse. Resolve to stay in the divine mind quadrant of the Integrity Matrix and trust yourself to know you can do and say the right thing.

- **The last time someone hurt you, did you make them wrong and solicit sympathy from others?** Make the choice to step back and stay in integrity. Blame is a killer. Do not put them down. Be accountable. Take radical personal responsibility. Look inside to identify your programs and remember you wrote the script and started the cameras rolling. It takes diligence and courage to stay in integrity, but when you do you will never blame, explain, or complain. Stay high on the Integrated Wholeness Scale and celebrate your personal integrity.

An Overview: Integrity

- "Integrity" is a term that is based on "integral," which means wholeness. It embodies consistency, completeness, and perfection. It's a state without internal conflicts or contradictions, and naturally occurs when we are strongly connected with our True Self.

- As we attune to the integrity frequency and weed out the programs that conflict with it, our natural ability to discern right from wrong, and our inner strength and desire to follow through, naturally assert themselves.

- The core low frequency blocker to integrity is fragmentation.

- Integrity is impossible when we are run by ego mind programs. To connect with our strong integrity code we have to get neutral.

- Integrity resolves internal conflict. This stops self-sabotage of our health, wealth, relationships, wisdom, and wellbeing. With the confidence that comes when connected to trust and the strength that arises when connected to integrity, we are empowered to accomplish our goals.

- A highly developed sense of integrity is critical to the evolution of our soul. It empowers us to honor our word (especially to ourselves) and take actions that are in harmony with the divine mind.

- Integrity proactively takes radical personal responsibility for our life. It lovingly holds us accountable and inspires us to diligently clean up our messes. Integrity provides the strength and determination to make forgiveness a habit.

As Anaïs Nin said,

We don't see things as they are,
we see things as we are.

Remember: It's okay. It's not real. It's just a story.

We are now ready to move on to the next high frequency attribute in the PLATINUM Life System: Neutrality. Being neutral empowers us to realize freedom and wholeness and to experience the life of our dreams.

If you correct your mind,
the rest of your life will fall into place.

~ WAYNE DYER

CHAPTER SIX

NEUTRALITY:
GO BEYOND POSITIVE
—YOUR KEY TO FREEDOM

Your happiness depends on your neutrality,
which relies on your soul's choice of operating code.
Lack of neutrality always leads to unhappiness.

~ SANDRA AND DANIEL BISKIND

I Don't Care What She Looks Like

Daniel knew in his heart he wanted and deserved to have a great loving relationship. Having been married for over twenty years, he didn't want to give up on his marriage, but they had been struggling for a long time. One morning when meditating, Daniel recalls giving thanks for his perfect divine love relationship. Even though he knew he didn't have it then, he gave thanks every morning as if he did. Daniel said if it could be with his wife, great. And if it couldn't be with his wife, so be it. But he gave thanks for God's highest and best with no strings attached.

He made that a regular part of his morning meditation. That led to his separation and to his divorce. Throughout, Daniel continued to give thanks for his perfect, divine love relationship, feeling as if he had it.

He frequently said, *"God, I don't care what she looks like. I don't care what color, race, creed, or religion."* One morning, being a man, he confesses he added, *"God, if she's easy to look at that would be nice."* But, quickly raising his hands in surrender, he hastily added, *"But whatever you've got in mind is fine by me."*

Approximately two years after starting this practice he met the woman with whom he created exactly that relationship. In case you are wondering—yes, that's Sandra!

Daniel was not thinking about that relationship as though he didn't have it. And this is the secret to manifesting the highest and best for yourself. He was neutral to whatever his highest and best was for him as he held the love of that relationship in his heart as though he already had it.

In other words, he had totally removed all the stress and emotional baggage around having a great relationship. He consciously chose to shift his mental and emotional transmission into neutral where the negative ideas, beliefs, and drama of his relationship had no traction.

Daniel says, *"There is an extra bonus here. I also manifested the most important spiritual influence in my life. If I had not stayed neutral and had instead become attached to a wish list, I might have gotten all the boxes ticked yet still have fallen far short of what was in store for me. The best I could have dreamed of could not begin to compare to God's highest and best for me."*

The story of how Daniel and Sandra met is a lot of fun, and people are completely gob-smacked when they hear that during their second date they agreed they were married as of that moment. Daniel proposed on their first date, just 48 hours after their initial meeting.

Feeling as though we have what we want and remaining neutral to how, when, and where it happens is enlightened self-interest. That's where we are aligned with our personal power and have the confidence to let go of the need to have everything the way we think it should be. Broadcasting that frequency is not only efficacious in manifesting our desire in the physical world, it is incredibly satisfying because we are experiencing its fulfillment already.

Living powerfully with happiness and confidence is a sign we have chosen a PLATINUM life and have taken the path into the high frequency states of Integrated Wholeness. Sustaining enlightened states hinges on our ability to correct sabotage programs to get neutral whenever we feel negativity, fear, or pain.

Don't suffer. Correct. Get neutral. We all accept positive is better than negative. But beyond positive is yet a higher state: neutrality of thought and emotion. Sometimes known as non-attachment, it results from dissolving the emotional charge around dysfunctional thoughts, programs, beliefs, and ideas.

Out beyond ideas of wrong doing
and right doing there is a field,
I will meet you there.
When the soul lies down in that grass,
the world is too full to talk about.

~ RUMI

To paraphrase Hippocrates: Let thoughts be our medicine and medicine be our thoughts. That is the basis of the mind medicine of the future. As it is our mind that produces our thoughts, to train our mind to produce the kinds of thoughts that serve us is our highest priority.

For Sandra the most exciting phase in this process of "waking up" came when she realized she had the power to direct her thoughts, actions, and indeed her own healing. Remember, enlightenment is our natural state and our thoughts, both conscious and unconscious, are the only thing stopping us from experiencing enlightenment and the life we want.

You may be wondering how you could possibly become neutral to situations that constantly cause you and others so much pain. This is one of the secrets you will need to understand to be able to experience the life of your dreams.

A thought is harmless unless we believe it.

It's not our thoughts, but our attachment to our thoughts that causes suffering.

Attaching to a thought means believing that it's true without inquiring.

A belief is a thought that we've been attaching to, often for years.

~ Byron Katie

WHAT IS NEUTRALITY?

- Neutrality is the state of being nonattached to our thoughts and emotions. In this state we are their dispassionate and objective observer. Past events, emotions, and decisions no longer control our life. Without neutrality, peace is illusive at best.

- Neutrality is an attribute of our True Self. Like shifting a transmission into neutral, it disengages our ego mind programs. It is the ultimate mind shift in which no one—and nothing—can push our buttons.

- Neutrality frees us from our unconscious programs and changes our life forever.

- In neutrality we can observe events and emotions without identifying with them. They no longer have any force to control us. Instead of just reacting to life's challenges, we have the power to respond creatively.

- In neutrality we are objective; we see without the subjective filter of projection so our perceptions are accurate and facilitates greater awareness.

- The core frequency blocker to neutrality is attachment.

Being Neutral

A private client writes about how being neutral dramatically changed her life:

To sift through my thoughts and find a completely different person than two days ago has brought me to a place of great appreciation. For me the amazement in being neutral is that my life's structure is still here, people didn't disappear. But my deep emotions have changed, the shift that has taken place within me is unbelievable. If I was asked two days ago if it were possible to be this clear, and free from such deep inner pain and confusion so quickly, my answer would have been no. In the mornings I now wake with excitement for my life. My energy levels have been restored and I am happy and so truly honored to have worked with you.

Do you want to live a PLATINUM life where:

- You no longer have debilitating emotions controlling your life?

- Your energy levels are restored?

- You are free and empowered?

- You easily overcome daily emotional stresses that wear you down?

- You are happier, healthier, and more creative?

- You attain a higher level of success than you ever thought possible?

If your answer is "yes," then becoming neutral is an essential key to unlocking the best version of you and living a PLATINUM life. Using the Quantum Neutrality Process to neutralize controlling programs results in you no longer being negatively affected by them. Use the power of neutrality to shift from emasculated to empowered; from victim to victor.

PLATINUM SUCCESS PRINCIPLE: NEUTRALITY

- The state of neutrality facilitates peak performance in every dimension of your life.

- Becoming neutral is the prerequisite for sustainable success.

- Neutrality facilitates wholeness and is a prerequisite to a PLATINUM state of mind.

- Forgiveness facilitates neutrality. Attachment blocks it.

- Neutrality frees your creativity and leads to right action.

- The energy frequency of neutrality, where you are centered and calm, is magnetically attractive to others and, as it minimizes resistance, helps them to hear you.

- Neutrality facilitates responding creatively to the huge velocity and magnitude of change we all have to master to be successful.

We can train our mind to be neutral. This is one of the great secrets of all time. Successful people instinctively know their lives are manifestations of how they think. Their success (often in just one area of their lives and not others) is a function of how well they trained their minds to produce thoughts that work for them—and not against them.

The key to becoming free is correcting misjudgments and misperceptions. To do that, neutralize the programs, beliefs, and ideas that make you feel uncomfortable. The process of change is not always easy. Growth calls us to go beyond where we are— out of our comfort zone. The sooner we deal with the root cause of discomfort of any kind, the less we suffer.

Only by seeing the ego mind for what it is, and training it to be a faithful servant instead of a fearsome master, can we experience the true abundance and success on all levels that is our birthright.

Get yourself into the state of Neutrality as quickly as you can.

We'll meet you there.

When we decide what we want to manifest in our life, we can intelligently go about installing appropriate thought processes into our human computer. It's no longer necessary to ignorantly live with the inherited and acquired programs and codes of our ancestors, teachers, siblings, friends, media, and so forth. We have the power to open up the human computer that is who we are, enter our PLATINUM password, and replace obsolete codes with upgraded versions that will best serve us.

Shifting our mind into the miraculous state of neutrality frees us to utilize our unique gifts. Without emotional leakage and needless mind chatter, our natural ability to live, love, and lead with passion facilitates the achievement of our goals.

Success has been studied in every important field of human endeavor. One theme that success literature frequently repeats is known by names such as "presence," "flow," and "the zone." Most studies note that there is a definite mindset shared by peak performers and true masters. From performing arts to professions, from psychotherapy to parenting, from sports to trading in financial markets, studies confirm that most peak performers share this mindset when they are at their best. In this state, the focus is on the process, not the end result.

Neutrality is a key ingredient of this success recipe. With neutrality, ego mind programs are transcended so that access to our True Self's full range of attributes and gifts is unimpeded.

Regular, diligent use of the Quantum Neutrality Process toolkit is a proven way to cultivate a PLATINUM state of mind, a hallmark of which is the attribute of neutrality. By using inquiry and attunement techniques to identify and neutralize dysfunctional programs and delete their effects, neutrality naturally arises. In a PLATINUM life we are free to engage our passions without the brakes on—which our programs inevitably apply. To live in enlightenment and wholeness we have to be neutral.

OPTICAL DELUSION OF CONSCIOUSNESS

Neutrality instantly obliterates suffering and dysfunctional behavior. The process of becoming neutral works on an energetic level and appears simplistic in execution. The benefits are a richer, more fulfilling life free of the despair caused by ego mind programs.

In her seminal book *Infinite Mind: Science of the Human Vibrations of Consciousness*, Valerie V. Hunt, PhD says "*Those who criticize miracles as illusory fail to realize that the matter and meaning created by the mind are ALL illusory.*" She goes on to say, "*Illusion is a function of the mind and is as real as any 'facts.' So, spiritually speaking, the mind's highest experience is an illusion, but so profound that its effect is inestimable.*"

Wow! The ego mind has created and given meaning to our programs in this illusory world that feels so solid and real.

Indeed, even miracles are inventions that are as "real" as anything else. The most famous scientist of the twentieth century confirmed Dr. Hunt when he said:

A man's experience is an optical delusion
of his consciousness.

~ ALBERT EINSTEIN

Without neutrality, it is hard to digest these concepts. With neutrality, it's easy to understand that everything is an optical delusion of consciousness—it's all a story. Likening the world to a play, the enlightened Shakespeare said in Macbeth, *"It is a tale of sound and fury, signifying nothing."*

Neutrality is the aspect of our True Self that embodies these insights of Einstein, Hunt, and Shakespeare. When we are feeling out of sorts, lacking in confidence, overwhelmed, or just not functioning on all cylinders, it means the ego mind code has triggered emotions that need to be neutralized and their effects deleted.

If our Ego Puppy is short tempered with loved ones or we can't function at work, we might be tempted to make excuses like, we stayed out late and got drunk. However, the reason we do those things is because we have unconscious programs keeping us from living a PLATINUM life. In this illusory world, if we are out of integrity and are attached to our stories, we are fully in the ego mind code. To preempt fallout it's critical to get neutral, ASAP.

Strong or Weak?

With practice, it is easy to develop the automatic ability to discern if you, or someone else is, strong or weak to their thoughts.

When neutral, we stay strong.

In story mode, with a program running, we all go weak.

As well as using our intuition, we can also use energy testing or kinesiology to find out if a program has been triggered. No matter how hard we consciously try to stay strong, any unconscious negative program will weaken us. During our live events, we often use a member of the audience to demonstrate how quickly the body reacts to any thought.

Our bodies automatically go weak when we lie, even when that lie is unconscious. People are amazed by these demonstrations and love to be taught how to test themselves. When we are attached to our belief in our stories that undermine us emotionally—like when we refuse to forgive— we go weak. This compromises our immune system and makes us more susceptible to physical, mental, and emotional ailments.

When we enter a compromised password, our human computer automatically reacts to these thoughts like an electronic computer reacts to a virus. If not corrected, we crash and burn.

No wonder people are keen to have this little trick up their sleeve.

Our Brightest Hope

The benefits from using the PLATINUM Life System to neutralize deeply embedded programs has to be experienced to be believed. Neutrality is the brightest hope for humanity's future, and a prerequisite to experiencing enlightened states.

Neutrality is another way to understand enlightenment— the only way to create a world that works for everyone.

Can you imagine the astonishment of someone who planned to break up a partnership suddenly feel love and confident that they could resurrect the relationship in a loving, satisfying manner? We commonly witness the shift from hatred to love happen in moments when the responsible programs are neutralized and their effects deleted.

Helping people to become neutral to disease-causing programs accelerates healing on a mental, emotional, and physical level. The results are breathtaking and incredibly rewarding. Corrections can also be made to help people better assimilate various drugs and treatments for minimized side effects, creating an enhanced treatment platform.

When we are in a neutral state, the body and mind are open to healing. Real love, the foundation of the divine mind code, is the greatest healer in our illusory world.

For over thirty-five years, Sandra has asked her clients with terminal cancer, "Why do you have this problem?" At first, many of them don't understand the question. After leading them in an inquiry process, everyone answers in a similar way. Inevitably some version of "Because I don't love myself enough" comes up.

Sometimes recovery from illness is facilitated when someone becomes the center of attention and receives loads of love from their friends and family. However, the stories and emotions that were responsible for the disease in the first place can be retriggered and make them sick again. This is not because they are not loved by their family and friends, but because they have programs like, *"Why would anyone love me? I'm not loveable,"* still running in their mainframe.

When the extraordinary expressions of love were no longer evident, the ego mind jumped in to validate the unconscious program that they didn't deserve love. Even when it was totally illogical to believe family and friends loved them less, the ego mind's deceitful assessment sabotaged their recovery and sent them back to the sick bed.

With one correction of this false perception and its underlying program, we have seen people regain a balanced state. With a dose of empowered neutrality, regardless of the situation, peace and health can be restored.

One client who only had days to live called Sandra for a private session. She wanted to know if it were possible for her to come into a state of peace and acceptance around her life and death. During the session, Sandra discovered the programs that had brought her so close to death at such a young age.

She realized she had never thought of herself as beautiful and therefore questioned why anyone would love her. The man she married showed copious amounts of love and affection for their classically ugly bulldog, but was incapable of showing any affection to her. What more confirmation did she need to back up her ego mind programs?

During her time with Sandra, her programs were neutralized and the emotional responses to them were deleted. It was one of the most rewarding sessions Sandra had ever experienced. Just days before her death, for the first time ever, our heroine was able to look into a mirror with wonder, awe, and love, and see the beauty she had missed seeing her whole life.

Gratitude lit up her face and her eyes were full of tears of joy as she looked at Sandra and said, "I'm happy now!" Correcting the programs that caused her misperceptions so she could reach neutrality was the essential missing ingredient.

The awakened soul always chooses the relief and freedom of neutrality—that state beyond positive. Spiritual teachers through the ages have told us that accepting what is will bring us a level of peace. Of course they are right. But, what happens when the acceptance is only on the superficial level above the waterline? What about when there are unconscious programs in conflict with acceptance? Then acceptance may seem to do nothing for the pain. Thankfully, in the twenty-first century we have access to new human technology and we no longer have to just "accept what is" and still feel the pain.

Blowing Your Circuits with Empowered Neutrality

Real strength, trust, and personal power are found in the state of neutrality. This next sentence might just blow your circuits for a moment, but you can always reboot in safe mode, so don't give up.

The neutrality code enables you to connect with and affect every other code anywhere at any time. Your life codes are open to be read throughout the entire human energy field by everyone.

For instance, after we met a charismatic and impressive man, Daniel commented, *"I felt a profound fragility to him."* When the man subsequently shared his story, it explained what Daniel was picking up through the life codes he was broadcasting.

This also applies to the energy fields of all living creatures. We are all capable of becoming IT specialists in this area of human technology called higher awareness. Why is this so important? To best deal with the continually accelerating rate of change, not to mention global political-social-economic exploitation, terrorism, human trafficking, environmental threats, and an aging, underfunded population, the need for empowered neutrality is greater than ever. It is the prerequisite to effectively accessing our higher awareness.

We are all called to utilize our power to see things from a whole new level of awareness. Remember, the ego mind is ultimately nothing more than our belief in it. That's right. Humanity believes in the ego mind and its stories, and they are still killing us. It simply does not make sense to stay on this path of destruction. The high frequency attribute of the True Self that we call neutrality can change this tragic course currently headed toward planetary catastrophe and mass extinction.

During a holiday in Palm Springs, a ninety-year-old friend asked Sandra to work on alleviating the pain she had been suffering in her neck for over thirty years. She had been to doctors, chiropractors, and physiotherapists, and even tried hypnosis, but nothing had helped. Tapping into her unconscious programs, Sandra discovered a program about injustice. When Sandra told her she needed to neutralize the programs around injustice, she reacted, *"No way!"*

Sandra asked her if she would rather have the pain or the program. There was no doubt in her mind. She "knew" injustice so well because many of her friends had spent time in concentration camps during World War II. She was not giving up her ego mind's obsession with injustice. Sandra proposed an experiment, and she reluctantly agreed to have the corrections.

Sandra neutralized the emotional charge around the beliefs, programs, and ideas her ego mind had accumulated around injustice. Having been corrected, the pain in her neck subsided and then disappeared altogether.

Our heroine spent one glorious afternoon and evening totally pain free, but when she came out in the morning, she was in pain again. She just looked at us defiantly and said, *"I decided not to let go of that program. Injustice is real!"*

In effect, she went into her delete bin, found the corrupted file named "injustice is unforgiveable" and dragged it back into her main operating system. Pretty powerful stuff! In this case, her ego mind demanded that she be right rather than happy and pain free.

After that episode, whenever Sandra worked on her she would invite her to go into a meditative state and did not tell her about the programs that were being corrected.

We all store programs that have intense emotional charge around them. Like everyone, her environment, experiences, and heredity all contributed to creating her programs. When the emotional charge around a program is neutralized it no longer has any force to control us. It becomes benign information in the databank.

During the last eight years of her life, when her equilibrium was upset, she routinely asked Sandra to work on her. The most powerful and compelling results came when she was dozing off during the corrections. On one particular day she had been extremely unhappy about virtually everything in her life. Failing eyesight and impaired hearing were that day's top two concerns on a long list. She could not pull herself out of the negative funk she was in. As she dozed in the sun, Sandra worked on getting her neutral. After the corrections she was like a new person.

She could not wipe the smile off her face, and her overall perceptions had done a 180-degree turnabout. Her level of pain was greatly reduced and she became a pleasure to be around again. Her mental and psychological state had improved so much she felt happy again even being in her failing ninety-eight-year-old body.

By using the PLATINUM Life System we can turbocharge the process of change and feel better in minutes, often even in seconds. The nondual world of the divine mind code is a neutral, safe haven. Its doors are opening wide to humanity, ushering in a whole new way of approaching health and vitality, worldly success, and gratification of interpersonal and intrapersonal relationships.

AND APPLAUD

Once a young man came to me and said,
"Dear Master,
I am feeling strong and brave today,
And I would like to know the truth
About all of my—attachments."

And I replied,

"Attachments?
Attachments!

Sweet Heart,
Do you really ant me to speak to you
About all your attachments,

When I can see so clearly
You have built, with so much care,
Such a great brothel
To house all your pleasures.

You have even surrounded the whole damn place
With armed guards and vicious dogs
To protect your desires

So that you can sneak away
From time to time

And try to squeeze light
Into your parched being

From a source as fruitful
As a dried date pit
That even a bird
Is wise enough to spit out.

Your attachments! My dear,
Let's not speak of those,

For Hafiz understands the sufferings
Of your heart.

Hafiz knows
The torments and the agonies
That every mind on the way to Annihilation in the Sun
Must endure.

So at night in my prayers I often stop
And ask a thousand angels to join in
And Applaud,

And Applaud
Anything,
Anything in this world
That can bring your heart comfort!"

~HAFIZ

From *I Heard God Laughing: Poems of Hope and Joy,*
Copyright 1996 & 2006 by Daniel Ladinsky
and used with his permission.

NEUTRALITY WILL
CHANGE YOUR LIFE FOREVER

Becoming neutral to the programs, beliefs, and ideas of our unconscious and conscious thoughts means extracting ourselves from the ego mind code. It's not about dealing with objective matters, administrative details, or engineering equations, but about avoiding the havoc it wreaks among deeper, subjective things, like meaning, purpose, and relationships.

Imagine being able to tap into the energy, knowledge, and wisdom of the divine mind code. When we correct our programs, we are able to truly forgive, to love without condition, and to create from an uncluttered, de-stressed mind.

Enlightenment and wholeness are our natural state of being.

We do not have to aspire to become things that seem unattainable or just for the devout few. What we simply need to do is connect with our True Self. As Ramakrishna, the great yoga master, said: *"The winds of grace are always blowing. All we need do is raise our sail."*

Grace is the fullness of God's love.

~ SANDRA BISKIND

In that state, we are neutral to the pain our programs would create and the suffering our dream world emanates.

Let's have some fun. Imagine the world as a Whole Foods Supermarket and we are all for sale. We would definitely choose ourselves in all our original, organic, pristine beauty. As a thought in the mind of the divine, humanity was not created using the ego mind's toxins, pesticides, and environmental pollution. In our sleep state of multiplicity, thanks to our dream of separation, we have fouled our own nest, and as a result our luscious, juicy appeal approaches zero.

We might be able to find ourselves on the prepackaged food aisle where we have conned ourselves into believing we still have some nutritional value to someone. No amount of designer packaging or whiz-bang marketing can change the fact we leave ourselves and others feeling hollow and malnourished when we do not come from our heart.

Forgiveness, acceptance, and surrendering to the neutrality of the divine mind code is like being back on the organically grown shelf, soaking up the spray of pure water, exuding life force and the wow factor for everyone to appreciate. Not feeling like that right now? Okay, let's see what we can do about that.

We don't need to know how a computer works to be able to use it effectively. Similarly. we don't have to know how this system works, just that it does. The Quantum Neutrality Process does not need the ego mind's approval or belief to work. Isn't that a blessing?

Kosmic Kitten to the Rescue

Not only were you born with an Ego Puppy, but luckily you also have the intuitive and neutral Kosmic Kitten. Imagine yourself as a gorgeous kitten with two pairs of eyes. That is exactly what you have when your intuition is tuned in and turned on. Sandra had a cat named Albert. Well, she had a couple of cats named Albert, but version number two lived with her for over sixteen years:

He sat in the meditation circles I held every Thursday evening, and was present at all the private sessions I did from home. He knew when we were about to start and would claim a chair as a furry, four-legged member of the circle. We would all know who was out of sorts as he would jump onto the lap of whoever needed healing the most.

One of my mentors wanted to change Albert's name to Confucius because he was so intuitive and wise.

A stranger once came to my door to tell me Albert used to sit on the side of her bath when she got home from work, seemingly listening to her talk about her day. She lived in the same apartment complex, which Albert roamed freely and was extremely lonely except for this little white cat, who never failed to greet her.

I was astonished because I had never seen this woman before and wondered how Albert had come to adopt her. His spiritual eyes were open and ready to assist whoever needed him. He really earned the title Sir Albert, Knight of Neutrality.

Of the four eyes, the top set are Kosmic Kitten's spiritual, intuitive eyes. Their lenses are clear and always have intuitive X-ray vision. These are the eyes of your True Self, which has never gone to sleep and dreamt the dreams of this world. The bottom set of eyes have 20/20 vision and see the physical world from a place of neutrality. Kosmic Kitten's full-spectrum vision is what you want to use.

You always have a choice. You can choose to mindlessly look through the clouded, shortsighted eyes of your Ego Puppy, or mindfully use the neutrality of Kosmic Kitten's intuitive clear vision.

Intuition is the means by which you discover the programs to be deleted in order to become neutral and to know the truth about any situation. The more you use your intuition, the more powerful it—and you—become. The more neutral you become the freer, happier, and healthier your life. The world takes on new meaning. Everything is more beautiful and more alive. The superficiality of the illusory world is transcended by the depth of beauty illuminated by the divine mind code.

Two pairs of eyes in-sync with each other enrich our perception of the splendor of creation, and from that place of neutrality of thought and emotion we are empowered to live, love, and lead as the best version of who we are. Neutrality is the prerequisite to accessing Kosmic Kitten. Using the full spectrum of worldly vision and divine vision simultaneously is a feature of Integrated Wholeness.

When Sandra first looks upon our audiences during live events, she is often reduced to tears. When she apologizes for the tears, people smile and tell her not to worry. They say, *"It's okay. We're used to you talking through tears."*

When we are working, we are in that high frequency state in which we see you as you truly are. Our Kosmic Kitten eyes have been activated, and in that moment our hearts have locked on to your perfection. Even if Ego Puppy growls and tries to sneak in a judgment, Kosmic Kitten says, *"Sit. Stay. Listen and learn!"* We remain neutral to all the stories and simply love you unconditionally.

I want to sing like the birds sing,
not worrying about who hears
or what they think.

~ RUMI

Rent-Free Storage

Have you ever wondered how small things can trigger such huge emotional responses? Have you ever completely lost it and yelled at your partner for leaving the cap off the toothpaste, or for continually leaving dirty dishes in the sink? Like, the dishwasher is right there! Does it really take that much more time and effort to open it and put them in? The mess in the kitchen might trigger a program from when your mother made you do the dishes and clean up the kitchen every night for the whole family, which you hated doing!

Encoded programs sit unseen in rent-free storage in the unconscious mind until an alarm is triggered. Up pops the old program, sometimes thirty or more years later, and it creates havoc in the way we think and react to seemingly unrelated subjects.

In some cases, we cannot even remember the initial event, let alone the resultant emotional reaction and the decisions that became encoded into our operating system. Who would have thought to connect the fourteen-year-old teenager who was made to clean up every night with the thirty-four-year-old walking out the door of yet another failed relationship?

Many times these programs are inherited from ancestors, the environment, or other lifetimes. Whatever their origin, they can take us out of balance and precipitate self-sabotaging patterns and a cascade of crippling emotional reactions. Unknowingly we can be reliving the pain and misery of past loss, sickness, depression, addictions, and so on, stored beneath the waterline in the iceberg of our unconscious mind.

This is why getting neutral is so important. Stop the sabotage. Get neutral and stop suffering.

When the cultured cells you are studying are ailing,
you look first to the cell's environment,
not to the cell itself, for the cause.

~ PROFESSOR IRV KONIGSBERG

THE QUANTUM NEUTRALITY PROCESS

"Quantum" is a word used a lot these days, often very loosely. For the purpose of the Quantum Neutrality Process, it refers to the subatomic interconnectedness of all that is, and particularly to our connection to the invisible network of information that we use to unlock new possibilities and the potential for change.

Once characterized by Einstein as *"spooky action at a distance,"* physicists exploring quantum entanglement theory explain how particles instantaneously interact even when far apart, not only in space but also in time. And that's exactly what it may feel like when you first experience decoding your programs and recoding your DNA for freedom, happiness, health, and abundance.

When we respond to an event with a strong emotion and then react with a decision, the emotional charge around that information gives it the force to become a program that can unconsciously control us: our thoughts, code, frequency, and behavior. In the Quantum Neutrality Process, the event and decision responsible for the active program are identified and then the emotional charge around them is dissolved. This renders the event and decision mere benign data in our databank that no longer has the force to control us.

The higher our base or home frequency (i.e., the more we operate in the divine mind code with a strong connection to the True Self), the more quickly and effectively the process works. In fact, as we raise our frequency and shift to the divine mind code, we all make better use of our higher awareness and intuition and automatically become better at manifesting and self-healing.

Once a program has been corrected, we no longer react emotionally in the same way. In fact, people say they can't find the emotions they were feeling just moments before. There is often a palpable shift in energy when the unconscious program has been neutralized and the emotional charge dissolved. This process is a key power tool of the Quantum Neutrality Process and is used extensively in the PLATINUM Life System to quickly get back on track.

Once neutral, a feeling of relief is the first sign the program has been corrected. People feel empowered to move forward, free of the blocks to inner peace. The body, mind, and soul are realigned with their personal power so they're more able to regenerate, rejuvenate, strengthen, and renew their entire life force.

When we're emotional, or suffering on any level, it is invaluable to get neutral. The environment we grew up in, inherited ancestral programs, past and alternative lives, and even the mass consciousness of the world—all impact the mind, body, and soul. Conditioning and painful memories, emotions, and decisions stored deep beneath the surface of the conscious mind cause us to get out of balance. Here is an example of correcting perceptions and the exciting results and benefits of getting neutral.

A state senator who was suffering from intense shoulder pain did not believe getting neutral could help him. He said he was a keen tennis player and had hurt his shoulder during a game. Using the Quantum Neutrality Process, Sandra accessed a past life program for him. He was a senator in the treacherous courts of Imperial Rome. She saw a vision of him being stabbed in the shoulder and subsequently dying from the wound. With an intense emotional charge as he was dying, his ego mind created a new program for his operating system: *"Politics is a deadly game; stay out."*

Everything was fine in this lifetime while he was making his way in the political arena until he became a state senator and was once again on his way to the limelight at the top. The Roman senator's program was triggered, which created a panoply of problems in his political career. The intense pain from the tennis injury was further evidence he had a corrupted program sabotaging his life.

The shoulder pain acted like the icon at the bottom of his computer screen, flashing to alert him to incoming programs. Using the Quantum Neutrality Process, Sandra neutralized the ancient program that politics was dangerous and deleted its effects from his operating system.

After the correction, he visibly felt more stable and balanced. The next day the shoulder pain had completely disappeared. Everyone at the event could feel his restored charisma. No longer inhibited by unconscious programming, the senator was able to move forward in his career with a confidence that had been lacking before the correction.

Everything is energy, including our thoughts, and all energy has a specific frequency. Noise-cancelling headphones are an apt metaphor that describes how this process works. By generating a sound wave that is the precise opposite of the ambient noise, the offending sound wave is neutralized. In the Quantum Neutrality Process, we create the exact opposite frequency (or wave) of the unconscious program to cancel it out. This metaphor describes how the emotional charge is effectively neutralized, rendering the program impotent.

Here's how it works. The Quantum Neutrality Process begins by intuitively tuning in to and strengthening the information center—the energetic command-and-control system comprised of your midline, core, spine, central nervous system, and peripheral nervous system. They will either feel weak or strong. If it feels weak, correct it to be strong with this process.

1. **Set your intention for the highest and best for all concerned.** (Always possible in the divine mind code; never possible in the ego mind code.)

2. **Close your eyes and imagine the True Self in the form of white light flowing in through the top of your head and filling your whole being.** This corrects the information center, relaxing you and informing the ego mind that it is time to "sit and stay"; to listen and learn without comment or judgment.

3. **Next, discover the core issue responsible for loss of balance by tapping in to higher awareness—your intuition that is the powerhouse within your mainframe.** It is the big Kahuna that discovers passwords and deciphers faulty codes by accessing the zero point field. The same faculty is used to discern where you are weak or strong. When you're operating in the divine mind code, higher awareness is always ready, willing, and able. The more you use the divine mind code, the

more accurate your intuition gets and the more effective the corrections it facilitates.

4. Discover where the weaknesses are located by testing for a weak or strong reaction on the mental, emotional, spiritual, physical, psychic, or psychological levels, or any combination of these.

5. Aloud or to yourself, say "I neutralize and delete, zero to infinity, all beliefs, programs and ideas on a _____ level" — such as spiritual, or whatever level has shown up as a weakness. **Continue by saying, "All issues, triggers and choices associated with these programs are now corrected to be strong with 100% infinite potential for _____** — for example, Peace.

6. Now say: "I neutralize all karma and habitual thinking around these programs and delete their effects."

7. **Install a forgiveness template.** Take radical personal responsibility. Coming from your heart center, with unconditional love, forgive yourself for having written this script. And then, forgive everyone and everything else associated with the program you have just corrected.

After you have learned to use this successfully for yourself, you can apply the same process to others— even your pets.

This is a simplified introduction to the Quantum Neutrality Process. Our virtual and live events provide deeper, more advanced experience and training in its use.

ATTUNEMENT:
A MEDITATION ON NEUTRALITY

Sit in a comfortable position, allowing your body to relax. Center yourself by taking a few deep breaths, letting go of all judgments as you observe your thoughts coming and going like clouds in the sky. Continue to breathe deeply as your whole being makes the shift to the powerful vibrational frequency of neutrality.

With every breath you take, feel yourself getting more peaceful, going deeper and deeper into relaxation. Experience no attachment to any thoughts or emotions that might arise, just the inflow and outflow of your breath. You are now harmonizing with the frequency of neutrality.

Breathing in and out through your nose, tap into the place deep within you that is already enlightened and whole, where neutrality exists as an aspect of your True Self.

Say to yourself, *"Neutrality is my natural state. My True Self perfectly expresses enlightenment, peace, love and joy."*

Bask in the calm and wonder of neutrality that resides within you as you. It has no conditions. There is nothing you need to get, give, or do. This is your time. Allow yourself to go deeper and deeper—more and more relaxed.

Instruct your soul to choose the divine mind code as you sit centered in your heart, embodying the neutrality of your True Self.

Use your imagination to see your True Self in the form of a column of white light pouring into your head and filling your body all the way to your toes. Allow this white light to flow freely, soothing your whole being as you stay aware of your breath, your body relaxing even more.

With every breath you take, your body, mind, and soul are regenerated, rejuvenated, strengthened, and renewed.

Stay in this expanded place for as long as you can.

Breathing deeply, engage your imagination and take a moment to bring into your meditation someone who has hurt you. Feel the other person relax, breathing easily and matching up their vibration of neutrality to yours. Now say, *"I forgive all my attachments to the programs that have separated us and I forgive all your programs that have hurt me. I am now neutral and free of the pain and suffering we have caused each other."*

When you are ready, take a few more deep breaths and slowly open your eyes. With neutrality you are in tune with the high frequency of enlightenment and wholeness. Neutrality allows your creativity and wisdom to flow naturally. You have turned the key and opened the door to freedom and the flow of success.

This powerful exercise has activated the best version of you.

Share it with the world.

Stay on this frequency for as long as you can.

If you feel yourself becoming attached to a story and slipping into fear, negativity, or pain, begin to breathe deeply and reconnect with your state of empowered neutrality.

Sandra's youngest client was a newborn who was in distress at meal times. This new arrival was breathtakingly adorable. But alas, her Ego Puppy's unconscious programs initiated a compulsion to gulp food as if it was the last meal she would ever get.

Triggered at birth when the baby's cord was cut, Ego Puppy's program of lack was activated. The fear of not having enough food pushed Ego Puppy's buttons and started a downward spiral into sickness and despair.

It might have been the runt of a large litter who had to fight for food. The puppy whined, and in the case of our human baby, screamed in distress. Our heroine's little body had trouble burping and suffered from colic; she fluffed a lot and frequently had a painful tummy. The programs *"There is not enough food; I can't get enough!"* resulted in her compulsive overeating.

Ego Puppy training is an ongoing, lifelong process. For better or worse, our parents start the training process in our infancy. This training process was not going well. Baby and her Ego Puppy were in constant distress. Naturally her mother wanted to help her precious bundle. This is when our little heroine's mother consulted Sandra.

Living in a PLATINUM state of mind means we embody Kosmic Kitten and access higher awareness. Always eager to end suffering, Kosmic Kitten's mission is to come to the rescue. The weaknesses Sandra and her Kosmic Kitten detected in this case were within the emotional and spiritual realms and had to do with starving to death in a past life.

Once Sandra identified and neutralized the programs and deleted their effects, the mother reported her baby no longer gulped food or had colic attacks and peace was restored. Mother, father, and baby were all smiles again.

Getting neutral meant baby and her Ego Puppy were more vital, happy, and loving as a result of being pain free.

All programs inevitably lead to pain. Surreptitiously hiding beneath the waterline in our unconscious mind, they can pop up when least expected. The cause is never what you think it is. The good news is you can instantly delete pain and suffering.

When we use the Quantum Neutrality Process and activate Kosmic Kitten's intuitive eyes, we are led to the joy and wonder of the divine mind code—living our PLATINUM life as the best version of us.

INQUIRY—
THE FOUR QUESTIONS: NEUTRALITY

This simple but powerful tool cultivates your emotional intelligence and changes the way you feel from one moment to the next.

Practice this technique and make a habit of using it.

Answer the questions truthfully and spontaneously. Stay focused on the answer to question number four for as long as you can. The answers we provide below are examples only. Use your own words and the wisdom of your own heart to answer the questions.

1. **What am I feeling?** I feel upset.

2. **What am I focused on?** I'm focused on being right.

3. **How do I want to feel?** I want to feel peaceful and happy.

4. **What focus will serve that?** I'm not attached to my stories or to being right.

Command your Ego Puppy to sit and stay, to stop judging, and to respect the soul's authority to choose to operate from a higher perspective.

INQUIRY—
RATE YOUR STATE: NEUTRALITY

Connect with your perfect point of power. Answer the questions truthfully and, if necessary, rewrite the codes you have uncovered in your operating system. How far up the Integrated Wholeness Scale are you now?

- **How long did it take you to feel better after someone said something you disagreed with and personally didn't like?** An executive client from Ohio had an annual review with his company president. To his chagrin, he was told he was not well liked in their organization. Hurt and angered, he argued briefly to try to rebut the statement. Overnight he became neutral, reflected at length and concluded that there might be some substance to the assessment. He met with the president the next afternoon and explained his plan to correct the situation. Complimenting our client on his approach, he offered some helpful suggestions.

- **Have you felt better since then, or are you still running a mental monolog around the incident?** Once he got neutral, he stopped taking it personally and began to think clearly, realistically, and constructively.

- **Do you still believe that feeling uncomfortable and getting upset or sick is just the luck of the draw, or some kind of punishment for bad behavior?** In neutrality, our hero stopped projecting blame and took ownership. Without emotional leakage he was able to take appropriate action.

- **Are your judgments, beliefs, and opinions more important to you than your happiness?** Neutrality's non-attachment will never compromise your wellbeing.

Your ego mind's perceptions, judgments, beliefs, programs, and ideas will always take you away from the real strength of your True Self. Unless you correct, them they will continue to corrupt your computer until it crashes. By neutralizing them and deleting their effects, success, happiness, love, enlightenment, and wholeness can be yours as you move up to 600 and above on the Integrated Wholeness Scale—which is where you belong.

NEUTRALITY: OVERVIEW

- Neutrality is the state of being unattached to our thoughts and emotions. Instead we are their objective, dispassionate observer. When we no longer identify with them, emotional reactions and decisions no longer control us.

- Neutrality is freedom from unconscious programs that keep us on the roller-coaster ride of pain and suffering. It is liberation.

- It is an attribute of our True Self. Like shifting a transmission into neutral, neutrality disengages our ego mind programs. It is the ultimate mind shift in which no one—and nothing—can push our buttons.

- In neutrality we are free to shift direction as needed—instantly. In this state we can jump-start our vehicle. (Are you the passenger? Or are you behind the wheel?)

- In neutrality, the ideas, beliefs, and dramas in our relationships, health, and work life have no force to control us. Instead of kneejerk reactions to life's challenges, we have the power to respond creatively.

- Suffering is optional. It results when we resist reality rather than accept what is. The source of resistance often shows up as attachment to a belief, opinion, or idea and can always be traced back to a program. Correcting responsible programs is critical to restore neutrality.

- Everyone accepts that being positive is better than negative. But, beyond positive is yet a higher state: neutrality of thought and emotion. Sometimes known as non-attachment, we can attain it by dissolving the emotional charge around dysfunctional programs, beliefs, ideas, opinions, and judgments.

- Real happiness, peace of mind, and a life full of joy are only found in the neutrality of the heart. Many successful people instinctively know this secret: shifting the mind into the miraculous state of neutrality of thought and emotion liberates our unique gifts.

- Neutrality opens our connection to our perfect point of power, which is our connection to our source, to the divine mind, to the God of our understanding. Remember, the ego is nothing more than your belief in it. That is right. We believe in the ego mind and its stories, and they are killing us.

- Becoming neutral is the prerequisite for sustainable success. It brings you into a place of true strength. You radiate real power that is not intimidating, but irresistible to people who naturally respond to it in a positive way.

- Forgiveness facilitates neutrality. Attachment blocks it.

- Our internal guidance system, like a Global Positioning Satellite, can be used to automatically course-correct and align with neutrality, enlightenment, and wholeness.

- Intuition is a basic tool to become neutral and know the truth about any situation. The more neutral we are, the more powerful our intuition—and we—become.

- Neutrality allows the power of the body, mind, and soul to come into alignment.

- Neutrality is the brightest hope for humanity's future and a prerequisite to experiencing enlightenment and wholeness.

In the world of the ego mind, the situation *is* hopeless—but *not* serious.

As Eckhart Tolle said,

Life isn't as serious as the mind makes it out to be.

Remember, it's okay. It's not real. It's just a story.

You are now ready to move on to the next high frequency beingness state unlocked by the PLATINUM Master Password: Unity.

CHAPTER SEVEN

UNITY:
CONNECT THE DOTS TO ULTIMATE HAPPINESS

At our most elemental, we are not a chemical reaction, but an energetic charge. Human beings and all living things are a coalescence of energy in a field of energy connected to every other thing in the world.

~ LYNNE MCTAGGART

WATER BLASTED

We spent ten days sitting with the Dalai Lama in Australia during his first twenty-first century tour. He asked everyone in the room who felt they could, to make an oath to keep coming back to this planet to be of service while any sentient being suffered. We did not even blink an eye. The oath was made and our friends were aghast. *"How could you possibly want to come back here?"* was the kindest of the criticism. We had made similar commitments to being of service to humanity from a very young age, so this was really not new to us.

After the Dalai Lama had asked people to make this commitment, he had his monks pass water he had blessed around the room. We were in the Rod Laver Arena in Melbourne and there were over 15,000 people present. It was no mean feat to give that many people water. They didn't use cups but were ladling the water from buckets into our hands. Sandra's ego mind went straight into judgment with a barrage of *"How do they think this is going to work? The water is going to go everywhere. This is stupid!"*

She put her hands out as everyone else had done, the water was poured into them, and she slurped it out of her palms. In that instant Sandra's ego mind was shattered. The blessed water blasted her Ego Puppy out of existence in a nanosecond of hitting her mouth:

My soul experienced the divine mind in all its glory. I was one with everyone in the room. I loved them because we were all that love. I saw humanity through the eyes of the divine, and my ego eyes wept uncontrollably. Daniel held me as I sobbed with the joy, the wonder, and extreme inexplicable beauty of the unity of all life. Long after the hall had emptied out, I was still experiencing what some might call a peak enlightenment state. I felt like I had met the rest of my family that afternoon. All 15,000 of them were incredibly beautiful to me and in that moment, I loved them all.

Very few people have been immune to how complicated life can be even in your own family. I have seen brothers and sisters never forgive each other for misunderstandings, and parents and children who for millions of reasons feel they can never forgive and move forward with their families. In every case these people's lives were the poorer for this separation.

I have been lucky enough to have grown up in a family that has taught me that unconditional love and forgiveness are the ingredients for unity. Without them we would have surely fallen apart in the tough times. If I believed everyone needed to think the way I do, and behave the way I want them to, there would be no one left in my life. Unity would not be an option even in my own sphere of influence, let alone the whole of humanity. Instead, I have watched as my family diversified in every way possible; it could have spelled separation and disaster but our family's unity code is so strong it simply spelled acceptance.

One person converted to Judaism, one became heavily involved in the Christian faith, many became involved in the exploration of whether there was a God or not, and I was totally committed to enlightenment, becoming a lay preacher in the Geelong Christian Spiritual Church and later being ordained as a Sufi Priest in the Order of the West in New Zealand. And those are just a few of the spiritual differences between us.

The programs and the scripts we had written for ourselves among our family alone included alcoholism, drug abuse, sexual abuse, near-death experiences, death, chronic sickness, financial success, and financial ruin.

We have hurt each other and been given the perfect opportunities to practice forgiveness. When the dust settles, love always wins the day. It has always prevailed big time even when we have said or done things that hurt each other. Forgiveness within this diversification that is our world rocks! Without it my own family would not be as cohesive and unified as it is. Within the unity code of our families, we all want the best for each other and look after each other to the best of our abilities at the time, even if it is just a few words of support.

Like you, we have been challenged on so many levels in our lives, but through it all we were able to stay balanced by neutralizing the programs that were definitely giving us a run for our money. And hearing our family members say "We love you" was one of the most profound healing modalities around. It was an important variable knowing we were loved and supported by our family and friends.

No matter what you are going through in this illusory world, knowing you are loved and part of something bigger than yourself is the most comforting thought you can have. The divine mind code invites you to become members of the whole human family, all 8 billion of us. Celebrate our differences, practice forgiveness, and give your soul no choice but to wake up and choose unity and love over separation and hatred.

Welcome to the family, dear ones. We love you!

*Just as the subatomic particles that compose us
cannot be separated from the space and particles
surrounding them, so living beings cannot be
isolated from each other.*

~ Lynne McTaggart

WHAT IS UNITY?

Unity is the organic interconnectedness and essential oneness of all that is—the foundation of the nonduality of the divine mind code.

- In unity consciousness we see how everything belongs together. We understand the entire cosmos as a systematic whole.

- When we are disconnected from unity, we are imprisoned in the illusory world of the ego mind.

- The ego mind code of duality is founded on separation, which is the opposite of unity. Separation spawns war, greed, intolerance, and every other divisive tactic to distract us from the truth.

- In unity we experience the integration of the microcosmic and the macrocosmic worlds.

- In the state of unity and oneness, all the aspects of our unconscious, conscious, and superconscious minds are integrated into what we term wholistic consciousness.

- Unity makes sense of forgiveness and facilitates peace.

- The core low frequency blocker to unity is judgment.

Cutting-edge scientific theories and discoveries— such as quantum entanglement, the fractal universe, and the holographic universe—all support the principle of the essential unity of the Universe.

Invisible Influences

On the macrocosmic level, we are not only connected spiritually, energetically, and mentally, but as the astrophysicist Neil deGrasse Tyson said in the TV show *Cosmos*, even physically we are all made of the same stuff:

> *Recognize that the very molecules that make up your body, the atoms that construct the molecules, are traceable to the crucibles that were once the centers of high mass stars that exploded their chemically rich guts into the galaxy, enriching pristine gas clouds with the chemistry of life. So that we are all connected to each other biologically, to the earth chemically and to the rest of the universe atomically. It's not that we are better than the universe, we are part of the universe. We are in the universe and the universe is in us.*

Like a television set can be tuned to any number of different TV channels to receive invisible transmissions, you have all the components necessary to tune into the electromagnetic information field that is known as the human mind field or Zero Point Field. Believe it or not, whether you are aware or not of receiving transmissions, you are surrounded by a huge range of invisible transmissions all the time. It's up to your soul to choose what channels you tune to.

Deep within the microcosmic level of your being, you know there is something wrong with the content on the ego mind channel you have been tuned to for so long. With the news dominated by war, genocide, and violence motivated by income inequality and ethnic, religious, and economic differences, we know our operating systems are overloaded and jammed with the corrupt programs of the ego mind's dualistic world.

Although you are hardwired for greatness—for joy, kindness, love, and a happy life—the world you know is an illusory world of a neural network compromised by our collective misperceptions and judgments. It's a neurotic network when it's not psychotic! It is time to shut it down and reboot. And that is what living a PLATINUM life will do. As your soul reboots in safe mode, you experience the total wonder of unity in the microcosmic and the macrocosmic worlds.

THE UNIFIED FIELD OF LOVE

The unified field contains all knowledge including the knowledge of the truth that we are all one. Who you are lives in the heart of the energetic information field that is the divine mind world. In the unified field, love underpins all life. Love is the bridge between the big disconnect and unity.

Our hero in Chapter 6 on Integrity, who had suffered through the worst draught in years, was feeling a complete disconnect. His ego mind head chatter and his broken heart had him reaching for his rifle from the back of his truck. Suicide felt like the easiest way out, until love woke him up. With her soft tongue and loving gaze, his dog Tilly touched his soul and helped heal his shattered heart.

Let's realize that a change can only come when we stand together as one.

~ MICHAEL JACKSON

THERE IS A WONDERFUL GAME

There is a game we should play,
And it goes like this:

We hold hands and look into each others eyes
And scan each others face.

Then I say,
"Now tell me a difference you see between us."
And you might respond,
"Hafiz, your nose is ten times bigger then mine!"
Then I would say
"Yes, my dear, almost ten times!"

But lets keep playing.
Lets go deeper,
Go deeper.
For if we do,
Our spirits will embrace
And interweave.

Our union will be so glorious
That even God
Will not be able to tell us apart.
There is a wonderful game
We should play with everyone
And it goes like this...

~HAFIZ

From *I Heard God Laughing: Poems of Hope and Joy,*
Copyright 1996 & 2006 by Daniel Ladinsky
and used with his permission.

ANSWERING THE CALL

Whatever affects one directly, affects all indirectly.
I can never be what I ought to be until
you are what you ought to be.
This is the interrelated structure of reality.

~ DR. MARTIN LUTHER KING, JR.

The timeless principle of unity underpinned the powerful impact of one of the great leaders of the 20th century, Dr. Martin Luther King, Jr.

As an adolescent, Daniel had an inner knowing and identification with movements that expressed the unity of humanity. He was a precocious participant in the peace and women's rights movements and was especially drawn to the principles and nonviolence of the civil rights movement.

At fifteen, he learned that Dr. King would speak at a church two bus rides and three hours from the boarding school he was attending. Daniel felt an urgent need to be present. The school's headmaster acknowledged the unusual calling and granted him permission to miss classes, leave school, and travel alone to follow his quest.

Daniel managed to gain entry to a large, fully-packed church where he reveled in the atmosphere of unity and high frequency of the charismatic Dr. King, who powerfully articulated the aspirations of his young soul. His experience of unity and inspiration made an indelible impact.

PLATINUM SUCCESS PRINCIPLE: UNITY

- Know we are all connected to—and ultimately one with— everyone and everything in the cosmos.

- The core frequency blocker to unity is judgment.

- The high frequency of unity makes it natural and easy to love and forgive.

- Focus on what we have in common with others, rather than judgments that cause separation.

- Whenever we identify programs that subvert our connection to Unity we can use the Quantum Neutrality Process to neutralize them and delete their effects.

- Embodying unity and becoming one with our intentions, goals, and vision—and experiencing them as realized— turbocharges manifesting them. Adding gratitude supercharges the process.

- Embody the unity we want to experience in the world.

- Our ego mind, contrary to its own belief, does not have real power. It can only use force to issue its demands as it projects its perceptions onto our screens.

- When the soul awakens to the truth of unity, it naturally accesses its innate knowledge and wisdom and aspires to live a PLATINUM life.

Unity facilitates problem solving on the highest level. On both the personal and global levels, separation is the foundational cause of all our problems. As Einstein so famously said, a problem can't be solved with the same level of consciousness (or code) that created it. Unity is the ultimate expression of a PLATINUM state of mind, in which we naturally create solutions for the highest and best interests of all concerned.

The power to forgive comes from the power of peace; love makes it easy to overlook and unity makes it natural. Anything other than oneness is not true reality, but only perception. Perception is only what we think we see projected through the ego mind's filter of conditioned programs, beliefs, and ideas. As we neutralize the dysfunctional programs of our incoherent illusory world and delete their effects, our awareness of the oneness and harmony of the real world is automatically restored.

Perception, an ego mind construct, is incompatible with forgiveness as it holds its judgments paramount to its survival. Do not be misled; all judgment is a form of separation forced by the ego mind. And remember, judgment is always applied to itself by the unconscious mind and inescapably weakens us. Inherent in Unity's knowing is freedom from judgment, which unleashes our real power and happiness.

As is the human body, so is the cosmic body.
As is the human mind, so is the cosmic mind.
As is the microcosm, so is the macrocosm.
As is the atom, so is the universe.

~ THE UPANISHADS

Take the Quantum Neutrality Pill

The movie The Matrix contains an amazing scene where Morpheus offers Neo, the man he believes was born to save the world, the choice of taking the red pill or the blue pill. In his outstretched hands he holds a blue pill that would allow him to remain asleep to the real world, and the red pill that would catapult him into reality where his true destiny awaits him. When the soul chooses to remain in its sleep state, reliant on ego mind codes, you have effectively swallowed the blue pill that has deleted all knowledge of the real world.

You can change your code at any time. We are inviting you to take a look at your life. With outstretched hands we are offering you the chance to wake up to the real world. Which pill will do you choose? The ego mind is a bitter pill to swallow, stopping you from changing the way you think. Now you have the choice to take the Quantum Neutrality pill. Be like Neo. Free yourself. Choose the divine mind code and live the heroic life that is your destiny.

Like in the movie, the ego mind's computer-generated dream machine has created a whole new species. Duality is the mindset that has cut us off from the divine mind code and our True Self. With disastrous efficiency we went from being one with our creator to believing we were outcasts, feeling alone, and separate. Waking up is a life-changing process that restores us to the brilliance that is our birthright.

Enlightenment and wholeness are who we are, and while it will take more than just swallowing a pill to get back to our original state, it will be the most rewarding choice in the evolution of the soul.

WE ALL COME FIRST!

We'll never forget our tears of joy and bliss after hearing what happened at a Handicapped Olympics. In the context of their handicaps, these were high-performing kids who'd been encouraged to engage in sport by their parents. The race started and they all ran for the finish line. One of the runners tripped over, fell to the ground, and started crying. Another competitor looked around for his friend. He stopped and called out to the other runners. Of one mind, they went back, picked up their fallen comrade, and together ran arm in arm across the finish line. All smiles, they all came first!

Humanity does not have to stay stuck in the judgments and separation of the ego mind code. There is a place the soul can go where it is safe to make the choice that is for the highest and best for all concerned. It is in the field of neutrality under the umbrella of unity.

In our PLATINUM state of mind we all cross the finish line together...we all come first.

Judgment is not only destructive but a key element of the ego code's theme of separation—separation from our Source and from each other. Make no mistake, judgment generates abusive thoughts and language, which are as responsible for the despair and destruction of humanity as is physical abuse. All forms of judgment, especially those that lead to anger, need to be neutralized —fast. Anger and frustration separate us as quickly and effectively as fear and misplaced perceptions.

What was your reaction when you walked in on people shouting angrily at each other? Did you want to turn around and get as far away as possible from the force of that energy field?

Anger and judgment create low frequency vibrations that linger within the energetic structure of the room and the biological structure of our bodies. If not neutralized, they can make us sick and unhappy.

Murderous Thinking

Gandhi led the nonviolent movement that liberated India from British colonial rule in 1947. During one of his terms of imprisonment for civil disobedience, he had a most unusual reaction after eating lunch. He wrote that he had murderous thoughts which were the opposite of his own thoughts. Aware of the need for a well-trained mind to accomplish his lofty goals, he undertook to find the source of those thoughts. He asked to go to the kitchen to meet the person who had cooked his lunch.

The man had been imprisoned for murder. As he was preparing the meal that day he was thinking about revenge and murdering someone else. His thoughts were energetically transferred though the food to the people who consumed it. The energy field that unifies all life acts as an information highway. We can influence others intentionally and unintentionally, even through food.

This story wonderfully illustrates how our thoughts empower our business and influence our world. We were at one of our favorite restaurants when the new chef-proprietor came out to talk to us. He asked us if we would stay after our meal to give him some business advice. He confided the restaurant was failing and he didn't know what to do next. We asked him if he was prepared to try something different. Since he we was about to lose his investment, he was open to try anything to save his business.

We explained the energy in the restaurant had changed since he had bought it. We invited him to consider a suggestion to change the energy and direction of his business. We proposed he bless the food as he was preparing it and also to have his staff bless the food and everyone in the restaurant as they were serving it.

He was skeptical but said he would try it.

Two weeks later he came out from the kitchen to greet us when we arrived at the restaurant. Excitedly he explained how he did exactly what we recommended. He and all his staff were enrolled in praying over the food and blessing their guests. He said, *"We took your advice. This is the only thing I changed. I haven't changed the menu or added any specials. We all just blessed the food and our guests. The restaurant is doing better than it was doing before I took over and it's full every night!"*

He told us the meal was on him that night.

He admitted he never would have thought to do that. People were responding joyfully, loving his food and recommending the restaurant enthusiastically. Gandhi would have loved this food!

Halima McEwan, one of Sandra's mentors, used to ask, *"Do you know the best thing about blessing food?"* With love shining from her eyes she would explain, *"It's blessed!"*

The power of thought improved the success of that little restaurant just as the thoughts of the murderous cook affected Gandhi. Whether we are in the same room or not, our oneness can bring our thoughts and prayers into each other's hearts and minds as powerfully as if we were side by side.

When we conduct private sessions over the phone, people are amazed not only by the results but by the fact they don't have to be sitting with us in person to experience the energy, receive the corrections, and be transformed.

I honor the place in you where the entire universe resides. I honor the place in you of love, of truth, of peace, and of light. And when you are in that place in you and I am in that place in me, there is only one of us.

~ A DEFINITION OF "NAMASTE"

ATTUNEMENT: A MEDITATION ON UNITY

Begin by observing your breath and letting your body relax. Center yourself by taking a few deep breaths and harmonize with the frequency of unity. Let go of all judgments as you allow your thoughts to simply come and go like clouds passing in the sky.

Say to yourself, *"I am an integral part of the oneness of all life. My True Self perfectly embodies unity, peace, love, and joy."* Continue to breathe deeply as your whole being makes the shift to the powerful high frequency beingness state of unity, peace, and love.

With every breath you take, feel yourself going deeper and deeper into relaxation and the bliss of knowing you are one with the divine. The more proficient at becoming neutral, the easier it is to connect the dots to ultimate happiness through unity. Know that you belong, and that you are in the right place at the right time on your journey into enlightenment and wholeness.

Tap into the place deep within you, your True Self, where you experience oneness with your Source.

Continue to breathe into this peace of belonging. Bask in the calm and wonder of the unity that resides within you as you. It has no conditions. There is nothing you need to get, give, or do. This is your time. Allow yourself to go deeper and deeper—more and more relaxed.

The divine mind code is fully activated as you sit centered in your heart, reveling in the unity of your True Self with all that is.

In the high frequency of unity, your soul always chooses to operate in the divine mind code. Now say, *"I am totally aligned with unity. This body is made of the same stuff as the stars and I am an integral part of the whole."*

Imagine a column of white light pouring into your head and filling your body all the way down to your toes. This is the light of your True Self—the perfection of who you are—expressing itself in the high frequency of unity. Allow this white light to flow freely, soothing your whole being as you stay aware of your breath, and with your body relaxing even more.

With every breath you take, your body, mind, and soul are being regenerated, rejuvenated, strengthened, and renewed. You have turned the key and opened the door to happiness, love, forgiveness, and the flow of success.

Stay in this expansive state, relaxing into your connection with the unity of all life for as long as you can. Aligned with the richness of unity, you go higher and higher into everyday enlightenment.

When you are ready, take a few deep breaths, stretch gently, and slowly open your eyes. With unity you are in tune with the high frequency of joy, love, and forgiveness—the hallmark of enlightenment and wholeness. This powerful exercise has activated the best version of you. Share it with the world. Stay on this frequency for as long as you can.

If you feel yourself slipping into judgment, separation, or negativity, begin to breathe deeply and reconnect with unity—the oneness of all life.

Ego Puppy Training 7: Unity

When you first realized Ego Puppy was a member of a litter numbering in the billions, you did not fully grasp the consequences of separating it from the litter. So many different varieties, colors, shapes, and sizes! You had trouble choosing your favorite and forgot that no matter how distinctive each one was, your job was to love them all equally.

Ego Puppy soon found ways to cope with the separation and to make itself both more lovable and/or more mischievous depending on the programs accumulated over time. Although happy enough to encounter other Ego Puppies when still a baby, if it is not trained well, it will bark and bite, compete, and frighten other Ego Puppies—and humans alike.

Separation has caused huge psychological damage and created a breeding ground for spiritual, emotional, mental, and physical instability. Training your omnipresent pet to sit and stay, to listen and learn, and to follow the guidance of its new parent is important for both of you. Ego Puppy needs to feel connected to its new family and has an insatiable appetite for love and attention.

Ego Puppy is the idea of separation. Your noble purpose is to train Ego Puppy to make being of service to humanity its priority.

Well-trained Ego Puppies want nothing more than to love, serve, and obey—for affection, treats, and just to have fun. This is your way out of separation, a way of coming back to love and oneness with the rest of humanity. As you become a master Ego Puppy trainer you contribute to the unity of the family with your talented, well-trained, debugged pet.

A well-trained Ego Puppy follows its master's commands. It does not initiate puppy games but plays when invited. When Ego Puppy behaves according to the PLATINUM password, it demonstrates the power of the enlightenment code.

Can you imagine how people would feel if you met them with the equivalent of your tail excitedly wagging? They would be overwhelmed with joy. Humanity has strayed so far into separation that unity and oneness feels like a fairytale. However, there is still a shard of knowledge-gathering momentum on humanity's neural highways that is headed straight for the love and wisdom of the divine mind code.

Train Ego Puppy to support you on this amazing journey into unity where you celebrate your unique expression of oneness and dance in the sublime joy of a heart and soul that have come home.

INQUIRY—
THE FOUR QUESTIONS: UNITY

Use this simple set of questions to change the way you feel from one moment to the next. Answer the questions truthfully and spontaneously. Stay focused on the answer to question number four for as long as you can.

The answers we provide are examples only. Use your own words and the wisdom of your own heart to answer the questions.

1. **What am I feeling?**
   I feel alone, like I don't belong.

2. **What am I focused on?**
   I'm focused on being an outsider.

3. **How do I want to feel?**
   I want to feel connected and happy, like I belong.

4. **What focus will serve that?**
   What I share in common with others, not what separates us.

Tell your ego mind to sit and stay, listen and learn. The soul can always choose to correct the ego mind's judgments and separation. Drink deeply of the wisdom of the divine mind and experience the joy of being one with the rest of your family.

INQUIRY—
RATE YOUR STATE: UNITY

Embrace your perfect point of power as you mastermind unity. Answer the questions truthfully and if necessary rewrite the codes you have uncovered in your operating system.

- **What judgments and fears keep you from reconciling with estranged family members?** The ego mind finds true forgiveness impossible. Practicing real forgiveness transforms judgment, separation, and despair as move up the Integrated Wholeness Scale.

- **Are your judgments and beliefs more important to you than your happiness and wellbeing?** Ego-based perceptions, judgments, beliefs, programs, and ideas will always lead to unhappiness and sickness. Attachment to other people doing what you want and believing what you believe will keep you lonely, unhappy, and low on the Integrated Wholeness Scale.

- **Do you accept humanity's differences, or do those differences offend you?** Because the ego mind is the master of separation, it reacts to people unlike us with judgment and fear. Embracing the differences and celebrating the uniqueness of each of us moves us up the Integrated Wholeness Scale.

Accessing unity relies on the soul's choice of knowledge over perception, which is facilitated by PLATINUM, the master password that enriches our lives by activating the divine mind code.

We are not separated by the color of our skin,
our language or the way we look.
We are separated by the way we think about them.

~ SANDRA & DANIEL BISKIND

An Overview: Unity

- In unity we experience the integration of the microcosmic and the macrocosmic worlds.

- As an ego mind construct, perception is incompatible with forgiveness, as it holds its judgments paramount to its survival. Unity's knowledge provides freedom from judgment and is the source of real power and happiness. All judgment is a form of separation forced by the ego mind.

- The ego mind, contrary to its own belief, does not have real power.

- It can only use force to issue its demands as it projects its perceptions onto our screen.

- The core low frequency blocker to unity is judgment.

- When the soul awakens to the truth of unity, its innate knowledge and wisdom wisely choose to live a PLATINUM life.

- The unified field contains the knowledge that we are all one.

- In the unified field, love underpins all life. Wholeness is the demonstrated action of that love.

- As the soul awakens to the truth of unity, we naturally choose to cultivate a high frequency PLATINUM state of mind.

- Duality and separation are two sides of the same coin, which is the core program that has cut us off from the divine mind and rendered us problematic as a species.

With disastrous efficiency this program takes us out of oneness to feeling like outcasts, alone and lonely.

- Until we expect to wake up we are not expecting to experience oneness, real happiness, or peace.

- The more we wake up and stop using the same passwords, codes, and programs as our predecessors, the closer we get to reality—the nondual world of unity, of the Divine mind.

- Unity is free of judgment and is the ground and source of acceptance and tolerance.

- The True Self is love and resides in the heart of the divine mind.

- It is this love that is capable of healing us. Love partners with forgiveness to correct our perceptions in the illusory world, revealing the ultimate unity of all that is.

As Nobel laureate Erwin Schrödinger said,

*Quantum physics thus reveals
a basic oneness of the universe.*

So whenever your ego mind is running separation codes, remind yourself: It's okay. It's not real. It's only a story. It's time to switch back to the divine mind code.

We are now ready to move on to the eighth high frequency beingness state unlocked by the PLATINUM master password: Mindfulness.

Mindfulness alerts us whenever we need to correct negative thoughts, feelings, and emotions to get neutral and be happy.

Knowing others is wisdom;
Knowing the self is enlightenment.
Mastering others requires force;
Mastering self needs strength.

~ LAO TSU

CHAPTER EIGHT

MINDFULNESS:
ACCESS YOUR
AWESOME POTENTIAL

The mind is everything. What we think we become.

~ BUDDHA

EGO MIND'S DOUBLE CON

We met Jeri through her husband. He had just become our friend at a time when we really needed someone to trust. He was that person, a real rock who was a smart, intelligent, generous man that cared about his friends and loved his family. Unfortunately, only six months into our relationship disaster struck. In a brave voice, he confided in us that his beloved wife had just been rushed to the hospital and had undergone surgery in an effort to save her life.

Jeri was a 45-year-old, vivacious, long-legged blonde who had a great outlook on life in general. She had been misdiagnosed months before and now her condition had become critical. Abnormal cancer cells grow undetected in the body for years until a critical mass is reached and the body can no longer tolerate the intrusion.

We were not sure if Jeri would be open to working with us, but we figured it was worth explaining the process, giving her the option to open herself up to two loving strangers and the possibility of a better prognosis.

Here is Jeri's story in her own words:

> To start with a little history. I had been having very bad stomach pains for over a year. My doctor insisted it was irritable bowel syndrome, and I believed him right down to the day I was rushed to Emergency where a scan revealed a growth which they assured me was 99 percent cancerous.

By then I was the only one on the planet who was surprised. One very long overnight operation saved my life but the news was not good: they had removed a large section of the large intestine and some of the small, and given me a colostomy that they said I would have to live with for the rest of my short life. The cancer had metastasized to my lung, liver, and stomach lining. Stage 4 and a death sentence within 6 months, and the chance chemotherapy might give me a little more time.

Now I am an upfront sort of person, and I was always healthy, and a healthy skeptic to boot. I preferred conventional medicine. Spirituality was linked to conventional religion in my mind, and after a traditional religious upbringing and schooling, I had left all that behind me.

Daniel and Sandra rallied around my family and me once I came home. They offered to do some work with me. Life-threatening illness is a good way to make one rethink one's life (or potential lack of it) and question what has gone before. I knew they were offering help with love, and I needed all I could get. I put my skepticism aside.

The initial session helped me start to come to terms with comments made by other people, my fear, my anger, and sense of loss. At this stage many things were very stressful in my situation: big decisions, lack of funding, and conflicting medical advice coupled with the need for decisions having to be made within short time-frames.

I took from my sessions with Daniel and Sandra some strategies that I would use to bring myself back when hopelessness threatened to overwhelm me. I knew they could keep their treatments going and work with and for me when we were apart—a big comfort. My treatment with the doctors progressed with infusions of chemotherapy, Avastin every three weeks, and chemo tablets daily.

My blood count stayed within the normal range, indicator numbers fell, my hair stayed on my head. I managed without the extra drugs I was prescribed, and the worst side effects took longer to kick in than expected. My scans showed a consistent decrease in the size of my tumors.

On a trip back to New Zealand this year, Sandra, Daniel and some of their friends invited me to join them in a healing meditation. This had a profound healing effect on me.

After twelve chemo treatments, I was allowed to take a break to clear my body of drugs, so I could have my colostomy reversed. My surgeon, delighted to see my progress, hadn't expected that I would ever be well enough for a reversal. The day I found out about my pre-operation visit Sandra rang, how's that for keeping in touch?

I spend time every day or night working on self-healing, visualizing, asking for help, my own style of mindful meditation I suppose you could call it.

My thanks to my much loved friends Sandra and Daniel, without them there is every chance I would have addressed my illness on a physical level and perhaps on a mental level, in my own unfocused way. I am sure I would have ignored the spiritual level.

These days I know the only chance I have is to deal with cancer on all three levels, physical, mental and spiritual. With their help I'll keep fighting for my life and I know that I have much left to learn. It's an interesting journey. Wish me luck, I'm sure it wouldn't hurt to add that to the mix.

The problem will not be solved until the individual looks beyond the physical or sensory imperfections.

~ VALERIE V. HUNT, PHD

When working with Jeri, we discovered and neutralized old, unconscious programs triggered fifteen years before. She felt lighter, like a weight had been lifted from her shoulders— she was amazed. She told us she thought she had come to grips with that past situation. Later she was stunned when her doctor told her the disease had started about fifteen years before diagnosis. Having pinpointed two important aspects of her life we had obviously gained some credibility at that stage. After the correction her information center was realigned with the wisdom of her heart, and she was able to truly forgive and to become more mindful of her feelings.

The ones we love the most often give us the greatest opportunity to exercise our forgiveness muscle, which of course is our heart. Often we first need to be corrected to be neutral so we can truly forgive, but in every instance it is important to remember it was not the people, or the painful event that caused the disease. It was simply the ego mind's reaction to it.

Ego Mind's double con first had Jeri convinced she had forgiven her brothers for cutting her out of their father's will and second to deny her thoughts and feelings until they started to eat her alive. Our work with Jeri taught her to use mindfulness to acknowledge her true feelings and how to come to a place of neutrality and real forgiveness.

When unconscious programs have set us up for disease and despair, we need to move beyond the ego mind's confusing ideas to become well. The ego mind does not want us to know the truth, and it certainly does not want anyone to read this book. It will definitely rebel against the use of mindfulness and try to sabotage this powerful upgrade in our human operating systems. However, once we overcome its resistance, choosing to think differently forever transforms our experience of life.

Jeri began to develop a strong connection to her True Self. Once some key unconscious programs were discovered and corrected, she began the process of mastering her mind. By using the tools of the PLATINUM Life System she moved into a more peaceful state of being. Even through adversity and impending death, once neutral, Jerry experienced peace and love as her natural state. Using higher awareness she was able to trust in the order of all things while living in integrity within the unity of all life, mindful of her thoughts and emotions.

To prevent further sabotage we corrected her to be physically strong to process the drugs more efficiently and effectively. We also neutralized the karma between her and the medical staff to free those relationships to uplift and support her.

Her doctor had given her from six weeks to six months to live. We offered to continue to work with her remotely from our new home overseas, and encouraged her to expect a better outcome than initially predicted. Even though our approach was outside her frame of reference, she intuitively trusted that she should continue to work with us. In her life-threatening situation, she felt a big shift and understood that neutralizing the responsible programs was essential.

"Sit. Stay. Listen, and learn" are the commands Jeri gave her Ego Puppy. Her life dramatically improved—and not only physically. As she was about to gracefully transition, Jeri held our hands and thanked us for giving her four bonus years to enjoy with her husband and sons. She told us she knew she would never have had those years without our support. Those bonus years were spent walking on the beach, loving her family, and being grateful for everyone, every good thing, and every day.

WHAT IS MINDFULNESS?

Mindfulness instantly alerts us whenever we need to correct thinking that doesn't serve us.

- Mindfulness is the high frequency state of being fully awake to our thoughts and emotions.

- Mindfulness is the intentional, accepting, and non-judgmental focus of our attention on our emotions, thoughts, and sensations as they occur in real time.

- Mindfulness and awareness are two sides of the same coin. Awareness focuses on the external; it exposes how the world is working. Conversely, mindfulness focuses within; it exposes how we are working.

- Mindfulness complements the use of intuition; it can help us stay in the code that best accesses our higher awareness. Together they give us the optimal ability to change our thoughts and emotional responses as they happen.

- Mindfulness facilitates moment-by-moment self-regulation of our inner and physical world, our operating code, and our mental and emotional state.

- By adopting curiosity, openness, and acceptance we can monitor the internal mind chatter of the ego mind and creatively respond to emotional reactions as they occur.

- Mindfulness alerts us whenever we need to correct negative thoughts, feelings, and emotions in order to get neutral and be happy.

- The core frequency blocker to mindfulness is being asleep—to our body, mind or soul.

Some of the Sexiest Traits on the Planet

When we are mindful, we quickly observe when our human computer has an active virus, that is, when we have a frequency-blocking dysfunctional program operating. Mindfulness means we have the self-awareness to note it quickly and then make the necessary adjustments: taking responsibility, switching codes, forgiving anyone or anything that's triggered us—including ourselves—and then turning the situation over to our True Self—to the God of our own understanding.

Lack of mindfulness retards the evolution of the soul by prolonging time and energy spent in the wrong code, which delays forgiveness and getting off the wheel of karma. In other words, without mindfulness we suffer needlessly until we realize Ego Puppy is misbehaving and we need to better train our little one.

We have always admired people with the willingness and ability to keep learning, to be teachable, and who have unquenchable curiosity. Like a beginner's mind, it's a basic characteristic of mindfulness. Mindful people more easily adapt to change, know the importance of self-awareness, and appreciate the value of inquiry.

They display authentic accountability and answer questions like, *"Why has this triggered anger and resentment?"* and *"How can I make this relationship better?"* They are not afraid to have honest conversations with themselves, their partners, bosses, or family members. Mindfulness supports accountability, requires radical personal responsibility, and activates the "no BJC rule"—that is, no blaming, justification, or complaints.

We had a memorable conversation with Jack Canfield, co-creator of the best-selling *Chicken Soup for the Soul* series, *The Success Principles*, and a featured teacher in the film *The Secret*. With real interest he asked us how our work was different from anything else he had experienced. We explained how by tapping into the human mind field we accessed information that enabled us to resolve our clients' core issues that were blocking them from being able to succeed in any area of their lives. We described how the PLATINUM password was used to shift awareness and bring about enlightened states of consciousness. We were obviously passionate about the topic and Sandra typically speaks quite fast.

He missed something she said, and instead of letting it slide, he was so engrossed and interested in the conversation that he wanted her to go back and repeat it. Sandra immediately said, *"I'm sorry, I was speaking too fast."* He looked at her with a smile on his face and said, *"No, I just need to listen faster."*

We looked into each other's eyes and knew we were thinking and feeling the same thing. Jack's confidence, charisma, and lack of affectation are unmistakable, but when he said that, his magnetism went to a whole new level—we were in love!

I have no special talents.
I am only passionately curious.

~ ALBERT EINSTEIN

No matter what age, race, gender, financial situation, or political orientation, curiosity is still one of the most exciting traits any person can have. Have you ever met someone who is a master in their field, or just starting a new project? They're often open and excited about the learning curve they're on. People feel the power and passion in their speech and body language because their high frequency is unmistakable. It's a real turn-on and in many cases others want to go along for the ride.

The sexiest trait on the planet is the commitment to become the best version of who we are, and to support our partner, family, tribe, and community to be the best version of themselves that they can be.

Like learning to understand our own inner language and codes, a new project can be a major undertaking, especially when entering a new industry. We are now in our third careers. Every step of the way since we first started out in business— Daniel in his early twenties and Sandra at age eighteen—we have been blessed to have mentors invest time and energy in us and our endeavors.

They were excited by our precociousness, and often our innocence and naiveté, as well as by our passion, commitment, and the creative ideas that made our businesses so successful. Just as we were excited and honored to be working with these incredibly talented and successful people, they wanted to be a part of our lives. With our curiosity and teachability, they were uplifted and inspired by us.

Mindful people have a frequency that is attractive to others. They don't get caught up in their own programs, prejudices, and preferences to the exclusion of sincere interest in those of others. Being in that code is a very attractive trait.

THE JACKSON SAGA

As Sandra recounts, Both my sister and I have often been likened to wind-up toys. Just plug us in, wind us up, and off we go. Without even thinking, we put ourselves into action and often accomplish more than the average bear...sometimes even effectively and efficiently.

In this "just do it, and do it quickly" phase, we are not always fully connected to the power of mindfulness. When anyone is doing what they have always done, it's easy to lose focus and fall asleep. The importance of being mindful as a dispassionate observer can easily be seen in everyday life.

My sister's dog Jackson had just downloaded his dinner onto the grass on her walk to the supermarket. As a responsible dog owner she had taken two plastic bags to scoop the poop, hoping this event would take place on her way back from the shops.

She was traveling light and had not brought her purse with her so she had absentmindedly placed her trusty credit card into one of the plastic bags. Jackson, of course, had not been told of my sister's plan for him to poop after she had shopped, Undeterred, he stopped right in the middle of the long grass and did his business. They had just left home and were on top of a steep hill quite some way from the supermarket.

Out came the plastic bags, which were inside each other at that stage, and with great dexterity and much practice the poop was in the bag, or should I say, both bags. On a rare whim, my sister decided to hide the bags in the longer grass at the edge of the park instead of carrying it to a bin near the market.

With her mind now in shopping mode, she remembered everything she had to have for the evening meal and was at the checkout when she realized she did not have her credit card. I can only imagine the look on that gorgeous face; with one hand flying to her mouth and eyes wide in "oh no" mode, when she realized, one, she did not have it, and two, she had not left it at home but had in fact scooped the poop with it.

"I'll be back!" she said to the checkout chick. *"I just have to rescue my credit card."* *"Yeah, me too,"* came the quick reply from checkout chick.

Jackson was now quickly taken on the lengthy walk back to the scene of the crime, where luckily no one had deemed it necessary to remove a bag of dog doo from the long grass. The relief was short lived when she realized she had to delve deep into what was once Jacko's dinner to pay for her own.

With stinking credit card in hand, back to the super market our trouble-making twosome trotted. Who would have thought credit cards were such good conductors of dog doo? Even after washing it, the smell had permeated the plastic. Containing her anxiety and looking everywhere but at checkout chick, my sister handed over the offending card. Checkout chick was rendered speechless. With groceries in hand my sister almost ran through the glass sliding doors as she fled the scene of her latest crime. Jackson, totally nonplussed by all the fuss, was at least having fun getting in extra walking time.

It is so easy to be on automatic pilot in our day-to-day routines that we do not really stop to be mindful of our thoughts and feelings. Scooping the poop, which is something Sandra's sister had done every day for twelve years, had become a necessary, mindless job, just like driving a car and all the other routine things we do on a daily basis. Add into the mix a couple of new ideas, a distraction, and an unexpected event, and without locking the new thought into place that *"My credit card is in the plastic bag, do not scoop the poop without first removing it,"* we have a recipe for disaster, or in this case, light entertainment.

If that was the biggest disaster you had to go through to wake up and change the way you think, maybe you would not do so, or would you? We are proud to report that this particular incident did have the desired effect of focusing Sandra's sister into a heightened state of mindfulness. She became a more mindful dog owner, poop scooper, and credit-card holder.

PLATINUM SUCCESS PRINCIPLE: MINDFULNESS

- Observe all thoughts, feelings, and sensations without judgment, always alert to any need for correction.

- Masterful use of our GPS contributes to mindfulness at its best.

- Bring yourself back to the present moment when you find yourself reliving the past or projecting negativity into the future.

- Instantly note and correct blame, justification, complaint, or any deviation from taking radical personal responsibility for the authorship of all stories, beliefs, and programs.

- When we're awake, we instantly note dysfunctional thoughts, feelings and emotions. Mindfully change codes whenever you move out of the divine mind code and reconnect with the True Self.

- Use your breath as a metronome that keeps you in the rhythm of the True Self.

- Cultivate a regular meditation practice. Any form that is practiced regularly can do the job. Meditation is the classical gold standard in cultivating mindfulness.

- Be mindful: Are you expressing love? Or calling for love?

- Be alert to:

    1. Your self-talk

    2. The questions you are asking yourself

    3. The code you are operating in

    4. Your breathing

Mindfulness enhances real two-way communication. It takes both mindfulness of self and awareness of others to transcend ego mind programs. This is a hallmark of successful relationships, both personal and professional. Mindful communication can feel like a "Eureka" moment—like striking gold, or in this case, PLATINUM! It's as if someone has lifted a weight from our shoulders and shone a bright light into our life

Like our hero Matthew from Chapter 1, Peace, whose transformation included a body healed of the excruciating pain of shingles and a dramatically improved love life, we no longer need to be upset by the little things that used to make us angry. We can all use mindfulness and meditation to find a sense of inner peace and improve our personal and professional lives.

Matthew used his newfound tool of mindfulness in an ongoing effort to stay in touch with his thoughts and how those thoughts made him feel. When he felt uncomfortable, around even the smallest thing, he remembered the mantra, *"If I feel fear, negativity, or pain, I'm playing a game."* This starts to break down the ego mind's thought system and makes it easy to tease it apart and see it for what it is.

Matthew upgraded the quality of the questions he asked himself as he began to operate in his new code. The unconscious mind, which lacks irony or humor and takes everything literally, automatically goes to work to answer any and all questions we ask ourselves. Our questions are not only manifestations of our frequency but they help determine our frequency.

The well-researched and documented benefits of mindfulness are exhaustive. It has been shown to enhance wellbeing of all kinds, including improving the immune system; reducing obesity; increasing density of gray matter in the brain; and improvement in focus, compassion, altruism, and relationships.

With a PLATINUM state of mind we can all experience the best version of who we are.

WE ARE WHAT WE THINK

"We are what we eat" is a popular saying to help us adjust our eating.

"We are what we think" can be used in a similar way. Mindfulness of our thoughts and feelings alerts us whenever we need to change code. Our frequency is determined by our thoughts, which determine how we feel. Our thoughts always correspond to our code.

What we are today comes from our thoughts of yesterday, and our present thoughts build our life of tomorrow: Our life is the creation of our mind.

~ BUDDHA

Operating in the divine mind code enables us to listen to the True Self.

Operating in the ego mind code disrupts, destabilizes, and disempowers our connection to the True Self. It short-circuits our connection to all of our PLATINUM attributes.

The True Self knows that we can optimize our personal power and be the best version of who we are with peace of mind and the love of a strong and wise heart. Whenever we disconnect, mindfulness can precipitate the return to personal power. In this place we are in the flow state, or the zone, also known as success mode.

Mastering a strong connection to the True Self does not mean we don't feel negative emotions or that we deny or bury them. To the contrary, we own them and inquire into them. This enables us to instantly become more calm and balanced. This also avoids feeling guilt, shame, or blame when we react mindlessly. Ideally, we discover what triggered them and neutralize the responsible programs.

I discovered that when I believed my stressful thoughts, I suffered, but when I questioned them, I didn't suffer.

~ BYRON KATIE

COURSE-CORRECT OR CHASE WILD GEESE

Humanity's unconscious conditioning has sent the soul on a mindless wild-goose chase. Listening to the ego's voice maintains fear in place of love and leads to separation and despair. Families are the microcosm of humanity's macrocosm. When mindlessly asleep, we allow fear, negativity, and pain to settle into our homes, where their disruption is as bad as any in-law could ever be.

Ego Puppies grow into attack dogs when not trained by a trainer who has mastered his or her own mind. Even though we might not growl and bare our teeth (well, not often anyway), we can still attack by withholding love and forgiveness.

Anger and resentment come in many forms. Even the tiniest impatience or harsh tone of voice alerts us that Ego Puppy is fixing to make a mess and could go on the attack any second if we let it. Will you?

Daily use of the PLATINUM Life System transforms our experience of life as it trains the mind to think correctly. Neutralizing unconscious programs and deleting the effects of past events, emotions, and decisions gives us the freedom to make choices from a state of wholeness where miracles manifest with ease and grace. At long last, timeless success principles such as the Law of Attraction will work for us. Both correct thinking guided by the True Self and alignment with our perfect point of power occur naturally in a PLATINUM state of mind.

Course-correcting our thinking is the soul's domain. With practice and repetition, it retrains the mind, even changing brain function by creating new neural pathways. (Neurons that fire together wire together.) Just as an airliner on autopilot keeps making tiny adjustments to optimize its route, altitude, and airspeed, whenever we stray off-course, no thanks to the ego mind code, we want to create a habit of making adjustments as quickly as possible whenever we deviate from our perfect point of power. Mindfulness is what instantly alerts us whenever this happens.

Mindfulness is the indispensable guide on the most exciting journey of all—our own enlightenment and wholeness. We become a powerful influence for good not only in our own lives but the lives of others. It begins with the decision to disengage from the ego mind's distractions, addictions, and habits—and all the unconscious bugs, glitches, and spam that come with them.

Daniel occasionally talks about his time in the sixties when the peace sign became synonymous with flower power, sex, drugs, and rock 'n roll. The audience always laughs when he shares the expression, "Brain damage was what we were after all along. Chromosome damage was just gravy!" Ironically, as Dawson Church, PhD, so helpfully explains in his brilliant book *The Genie in Your Genes*, epigenetics has proven that we don't need to ingest or inject anything physical to create chromosome damage—we can do it with just our thoughts

That craving for a peak state, the "high" of a drug-induced brain state where we've overridden the normal state of a downtrodden mind, is another sneaky tactic the ego uses to hide the truth. Take the drugs, it says; have indiscriminate sex without love, it says; do whatever it takes to have fun—it's not going to hurt you, it says reassuringly. That way we continue to seek pleasure, looking for that peak state everywhere else but within. In truth, when living in a PLATINUM state of mind, we don't need sex, drugs, alcohol, or any other artificial or addictive substance outside ourselves to recapture the bliss of a high frequency peak state.

We choose our joys and sorrows
long before we experience them.

~ Kahlil Gibran

TRANSFIXED BY THE SUN

On a holiday in Bali, we were told the native Balinese take the time to watch the setting sun every evening. They applaud the beauty as the sun lights the sky with deep jewel pinks, fire oranges, brilliant reds, and aquamarine blues. As it reflected these heavenly hues we were magnetically drawn to the water's edge, where we became totally focused on the show of light and color. We didn't speak but were mindful only of the awe we felt immersed in the intensity of the moment.

In this state, the soul simply observed the feelings, thoughts, and sensations of the experience. We were fully present. The past did not exist and the future simply unfolded as the sun floated down through the sky to sink into the ocean at our feet. In a state of peace and bliss we were completely transfixed, watching the glory of the sunset. We too applauded and laughed and were refreshed by those mindful moments, aware of the exquisite beauty of this planet.

You Don't Have To Act Crazy Anymore

You don't have to act crazy anymore—

We all know you were good at that.

Now retire, my dear,

From all that hard work you do

Of bringing pain to your sweet eyes and heart.

Look in a clear mountain mirror—

See the Beautiful Ancient Warrior

And the Divine elements

You always carry inside

That infuses this Universe with sacred Life

So long ago

And join you Eternally

With all Existence—with God!

~Hafiz

From *I Heard God Laughing: Poems of Hope and Joy,*
Copyright 1996 & 2006 by Daniel Ladinsky
and used with his permission.

ATTUNEMENT:
A Meditation on Mindfulness

Begin by closing your eyes and letting your body relax. Center yourself by taking a few deep breaths. Let go of all judgments as you allow your thoughts to come and go, simply observing them like clouds passing in the sky.

Harmonize with the high frequency beingness state of mindfulness. Say to yourself, *"I observe my feelings and thoughts without judgment. Mindfulness is an integral aspect of my True Self, the real me that exists beyond time and space."* Continue to breathe deeply as your whole being harmonizes with the awakened frequency of mindfulness.

With every breath you take, feel yourself going deeper and deeper into relaxation. Trust you are realizing your awesome potential, becoming more proficient at mindfulness and correcting any thoughts, feelings or emotions that take you out of a PLATINUM state of mind.

Breathing deeply, mindfully connect with your True Self, the real you that is already enlightened and whole.

Continue to breathe into the high frequency of peace, love, and joy. There is nothing you need to get, give, or do. This is your time. Allow yourself to go deeper and deeper—more and more relaxed.

The divine mind code is now fully activated as you sit centered in your heart, basking in the neutrality that is supported by mindfulness.

Aware of your breath, commit to live mindfully, and say, *"I use mindfulness to stay aligned with neutrality of thought and emotion to empower realization of my full potential."*

Now imagine a column of white light pouring into your head and filling your body all the way down to your toes. This is the light of your True Self that you have activated with your intention through mindfulness. Invite this pristine white light to flow freely, soothing your entire being, facilitating your wholeness, as you relax even more.

With every breath you take, your body, mind, and soul are being regenerated, rejuvenated, strengthened, and renewed. The peace that exists within you allows your creativity and wisdom to flow naturally. You have unlocked the code that accesses your awesome potential.

Stay in this expanded place, relaxing into mindfulness for as long as you can. When you are ready, take a few more deep breaths and slowly open your eyes. With mindfulness you are in harmony with the high frequency of enlightenment and wholeness.

This guided meditation has activated the best version of you. Share it with the world. Stay on this frequency for as long as you can.

Anytime you feel yourself numbing out or falling asleep to yourself, begin to breathe deeply and mindfully, and invite your True Self to guide you to use your PLATINUM Life System tools to get neutral and be happy.

Ego Puppy Training 8: Mindfulness

You and your Ego Puppy are starting to get the picture. After all, it is the final frequency unlocked by the PLATINUM password. And you do want to live a PLATINUM life, right? If not now, when? Well-trained by a wise and diligent master (that's you!), your Ego Puppy acknowledges it wants nothing more than to be the best it can be and live the life of its puppy dreams. It requires constant grooming to keep it allergy free. You do not want to take on your Ego Puppy's allergies and programs any more than you want to continue to live with the symptoms and limitations of your unbelievable stories.

Training Ego Puppy to be a mindful guide dog in the service of the best version of you means you have to teach it to be aware of every thought and all the sensory input and emotions that you are feeling. This is like the dependable service dog Tilly and our Australian hero in Chapter 5, Integrity, who was alert to her master's signals that danger was imminent! This training is definitely enlightened self-interest. Train yourself to intuit when you have gone into sensory overload and lost equilibrium so you can recover and be the master Ego Puppy needs.

In an instant the well-trained Ego Puppy teams up with intuitive Kosmic Kitten. With the help of Kosmic Kitten's mindful and alert spiritual eyes, they see that there are only two options, two codes. Just as Tilly knew her master was in need of love and support, your well-trained Ego Puppy and its newfound mate Kosmic Kitten know the difference. One code takes you into enlightenment and safety while the other code takes you as far away from joy and balance as is possible to go.

It's important to have fun during the training process. Over time as you become a more proficient trainer, your four-legged friend's resistance to the divine mind code slowly melts away. If you have trained yourself well—with love, compassion, and kindness—and trained Ego Puppy to respond to Kosmic Kitten's spiritual senses, you will always be mindful of what is going on within you.

Use mindfulness every instant of every day. Train yourself to support the habit of being mindful. There are no substitutes. We are all busy. We are all consumed with the lives we have created for ourselves. But there is simply no longer any excuse for putting up with despair and disappointment. The untrained ego mind will say time is short and resources are scarce. It's easy to go into "overwhelmed mode" when you believe there's never enough of either for you to succeed. That's just another excuse for not stepping into your birthright and living as an enlightened, whole being who has undone the bad habits of your Ego Puppy. Your infinitely-resourceful True Self knows it is always the right time to do the most important thing for yourself.

BARK LESS, WAG MORE

Well-trained Ego Puppies can only be developed by mindful, well-trained masters. "Oh no!" your ego mind might be saying right now. "I am not responsible for what happens in my life." Well, that is certainly arguable. But what isn't arguable is your responsibility for choosing your thoughts and mastering your mind. Avoiding responsibility is definitely part of the game plan for the ego mind to undermine your progress in becoming a well-educated, well-trained, and consistently mindful master.

Most folks are as happy
as they make up their minds to be.

~ ABRAHAM LINCOLN

Effective Ego Puppy training starts with training the master. (After all, it really is the same thing.) It is time for the soul to stop abdicating its role as decision-maker and take radical personal responsibility to make the choice for the True Self. When you revert to the divine mind code, your True Self's patience, forgiveness, and tolerance take over and training actually becomes entertaining. Stick with the ego mind code and you'll get what you ask for—and it's not Angel Food cake.

As we listened to an interview with Ken Blanchard, author of the best-selling book The One Minute Manager, we laughed out loud at his story about puppy training. Ken had a friend who was training his dog not to "drop his load" inside the house. He asked his friend what he was doing to train the dog, and he said, *"Well, whenever the dog drops his load on the kitchen floor, we smack him, rub his nose in it, and then we throw him out the kitchen window."*

Ken asked, *"And how's that working for you?"*

"Not so well. Now whenever the dog drops his load on the kitchen floor he turns around and jumps straight out the window."

That is you when you have not trained Ego Puppy and mastered the mind. It is easy to drop your load on the kitchen floor, the dining room floor, the bathroom and bedroom floors, the floors at work, and even on other people's floors, and then turn around and "jump out the window"—or wish you could.

ADDITIONAL TRAINING TECHNIQUES

- Regularly scan the body to note whatever sensations are present.

- Focus on the simple movements you normally take for granted when walking.

- Stay aware of your breathing.

Meditation is the classical gold standard in cultivating mindfulness. Mindfulness has become almost synonymous with meditation in twenty-first century Western mainstream culture.

As it trains your omnipresent companion, it's your soul's responsibility to choose to stay present and awake to the awesome world you live in, to the amazing people you interact with, and to the wonder and power of your heart. Hang onto your hat because in enlightened states you are in for the most exciting ride of your life!

INQUIRY—
THE FOUR QUESTIONS: MINDFULNESS

This inquiry technique utilizes your internal GPS. It is based on the use of mindfulness, which is simply observing yourself without judgment. It is intentional self-awareness. This simple but powerful tool cultivates your emotional intelligence.

Answer the questions truthfully and spontaneously. Stay focused on the answer to question number four for as long as you can. The answers we provide are examples only. Use your own words and the wisdom of your own heart to answer the questions.

1. **What am I feeling?**
   I am feeling like I'm denying my own feelings.

2. **What am I focused on?**
   I'm focused on pleasing others.

3. **How do I want to feel?**
   I want to feel in touch with how I'm feeling.

4. **What focus will serve that?**
   Observing my feelings without judgment and accepting them with compassion and love.

Train your ego mind to sit, stay, listen, and learn as you diligently and deliberately move up the Integrated Wholeness Scale. Honor your soul's choice of the divine mind code to evolve into new levels of mindfulness, enlightenment, and wholeness.

INQUIRY—
RATE YOUR STATE: MINDFULNESS

Embrace your personal power and master mindfulness. Answer the questions truthfully and, if necessary, rewrite any dysfunctional codes you have uncovered lurking in your operating system.

- **Do you use your GPS to manage your state?** The built-in GPS of your emotions gives an instantaneous readout. Regular use of it for course-correction is a perfect application of mindfulness in action. This is applied emotional intelligence and supports you in rising to love and above on the Integrated Wholeness Scale.

- **Do you sometimes find it hard to understand why people do what they do?** Every action that is not an expression of love is—at its core—a call for love. By activating your intuition and mindfulness, you easily understand both the needs of others and your own reactive programs and can forgive each whenever they hurt you. As you do this, you are a blessing to the world.

- **Are you aware of the impact your surrounding environment has on you?** When you are high on the Integrated Wholeness Scale, you are always observant of how you feel when you walk into a space regardless of whether it has been cared for or not. Note how you feel when you are in a naturally uplifting place or a toxic environment. Become keenly aware of how you feel and perform when you are fully mindful of your emotions. Using these feelings from your inner GPS gives them value and utility for you.

In addition to mindful meditation, another constructive activity to minimize stress is to make sure your home and workplace are clean, nontoxic, and attractive. Consider using the traditional principles of Chinese Feng Shui or Indian Vastu to rearrange your environment at home and at work to facilitate more peace and harmony.

Mindfully and creatively make every space support your happiness and wellbeing.

An Overview: Mindfulness

- Mindfulness is the intentional, non-judgmental awareness of our emotions, thoughts, and sensations as they occur.

- The core frequency blocker to mindfulness is being asleep—to our body, mind or soul.

- With curiosity and acceptance, mindfulness monitors the internal chatter of the ego mind.

- Mindfulness alerts us whenever we need to correct negative thoughts, feelings, and emotions to get neutral and be happy.

- Well-trained Ego Puppies are developed by well-trained, mindful masters.

- As we refine our ability to stay mindfully centered in our perfect point of power—the wisdom of the True Self—the PLATINUM success principles work miracles in our lives.

- Mindfulness facilitates enlightenment and wholeness, which realigns us with the purity of divine love and transcends the dualistic world of the ego mind.

- Becoming happy for no reason, loving without expectation, and having a vital, passionate life are the rewards from being able to mindfully direct our thinking.

- Mindfulness naturally facilitates miracles, which occur whenever we make the ultimate mind shift from the ego mind code to the divine mind code.

- Practice choosing to stay awake to the awesome world we live in, to the amazing people we meet, and to the wonder and power of the heart.

- Mastering a strong connection to the True Self does not mean we don't feel negative emotions or that we deny or bury them. To the contrary, we own them and inquire into them. This enables us to instantly become more calm and balanced.

LIKE AN ANCIENT TAPESTRY

It's true. Enlightenment and wholeness are real. Congratulations! You have unpacked the eight high frequency beingness states of the master password that breaks the code to happiness and success. All of the high frequency PLATINUM attributes are built on peace, and incorporating all eight simultaneously requires mindfulness.

Like an ancient tapestry, PLATINUM weaves each attribute's high frequency color, pattern, and texture together to make the whole system even greater than the sum of its parts.

As we experience the PLATINUM Life System, we understand that being curious and teachable is a turn on. It's refreshing to discover the attractiveness of being accountable and responsible rather than blaming others for how we feel. It's liberating to know we can look inside, identify, and then neutralize the guilty unconscious programs whenever we need to.

The ultimate goal is the PLATINUM beingness state of enlightenment and wholeness that shows up as causeless love and limitless joy. The irreplaceable key is the code we're in.

Freedom is only a correction away. Restoring neutrality relieves us of our judgments, making room for love to grow. Pull out any weeds of fear that have taken root—they are only programs that have no basis in reality.

Plant the PLATINUM seeds and experience the bliss of peace as life takes on new and beautiful meaning. The miracle of being happy for no reason, loving without expectation, and trusting in the order of all things are rewards from retraining the mind.

You have the tools to decode the old programs of the ego mind that limit you and replace them with the wisdom and knowledge that you are perfectly capable of fulfilling your dreams. Being a master trainer of your Ego Puppy empowers you to fulfill your mission and purpose and make the contribution and impact you are destined for.

You are ready to put the Quantum Neutrality Process to work for you. Join us in cultivating a PLATINUM state of mind and have fun living the best version of you.

Embody the divine mind code to consistently express the love and perfection that you are.

With your new master password and high frequency attributes, training your mind will be as entertaining as it is enlightening.

In the world of the ego mind, the situation *is* hopeless—but *not* serious.

As Eckhart Tolle said,

Life isn't as serious as the mind makes it out to be.

Have fun! And remember, the secret to enlightenment is to lighten up!

PLATINUM LIFE

©2018 Sandra and Daniel Biskind

LAUGHTER

What is laughter? What is laughter?

It is God waking up! O it is God waking up!
It is the sun poking its sweet head out
From behind a cloud

You have been carrying too long
Veiling your eyes and heart.

It is Light breaking ground for a great Structure
That is your real body—called Truth

It is happiness applauding itself and then taking flight
To embrace everyone and everything in this world.

Laughter is the Polestar
Held in the sky by our Beloved,
Who eternally says,

"Yes, dear ones, come this way,
Come this way toward Me and Love!

Come with your tender mouths moving

And your beautiful tongues conducting songs
And with your movements—your magic movements
Of hands and feet and glands and cells—Dancing!
Know that to God's eye,

All movement is a Wondrous Language,
And Music—such exquisite, wild Music"

O what is laughter, Hafiz?
What is this precious love and laughter
Budding in our hearts?

It is the glorious sound
Of a soul waking up!

~HAFIZ

From *I Heard God Laughing: Poems of Hope and Joy*,
Copyright 1996 & 2006 by Daniel Ladinsky
and used with his permission.

Now You've Got the Password and the Recipe!

It's true. Enlightenment and wholeness are real. Congratulations! You have the recipe...

Now go make the life of your dreams!

ABOUT THE AUTHORS

Only a life lived for others is a life worthwhile.

~ **ALBERT EINSTEIN**

Sandra and Daniel stand for the awakening of humanity to the divinity that is within us all. They learned that enlightenment *and* wholeness is the only way to end suffering.

Their passion to empower leaders to optimize their impact and contribution inspired them to create a user-friendly system that empowers us to expand into being the best version of ourselves, fully connected to our True Self — to enjoy genuine happiness and success simultaneously.

In their first project together, the newlyweds were led to create a spiritual retreat on a power place in the Bay of Islands in New Zealand. In its day job as a resort, it won the World Luxury Hotel Association's title as The World's Best Luxury Coastal Hotel in 2010.

From very different backgrounds half a world apart, their lives harmoniously echoed each other's themes until they converged in 1998 in a multidimensional partnership. Their spiritually-based transformational work, launched in 2000, has grown to have a global reach.

They are members of the Transformational Leadership Council, the Association of Transformational Leaders, the Network for Transformational Leaders, and Coalition Partners of feel.org, which champions emotional literacy for children. They are Dame of Honor and Knight of Honor of the Orthodox Order of St. John Russian Grand Priory. After her first two books, Sandra co-authored three more with Daniel, which became international number one best sellers.

First individually and then together, they have dedicated their lives to their own enlightened wholeness in the service of humanity.

Sandra grew up in the Australian women's fashion industry and developed her own chain of boutiques, even creating her own label. A born clairvoyant and medium, her gifts took a quantum leap at 18 and her devotion to her spiritual growth, expressed through her passion to best serve her clients and students, became her priority at 27. Her ability to set people free from emotional obstacles by tapping into the matrix of the soul, identifying the unconscious program responsible for the presenting issue, and neutralizing it is legendary. The system she and Daniel developed to facilitate instant shifts and then make them sustainable is her gift to the world and her life's purpose.

Daniel attended Columbia University and graduated from Sarah Lawrence College. He was the owner of a commercial property development business for 25 years and was active in the leadership of the Urban Land Institute. He was an officer in numerous civic, charitable and community organizations. Daniel began a life-long love affair with spirituality at 21 when Lao Tzu's *Tao Te Ching* fell off a bookshelf into his hands. He attributes his love of learning, teaching, mentoring and consulting in large part to having experienced great teachers, mentors and consultants throughout his life.

If you would like to know more about
Sandra and Daniel, please visit www.TheBiskinds.com.

APPRECIATION

Throughout our lives, we have been blessed to have an enormous number of people make profound contributions to who we have become — and are still becoming. *CODEBREAKER* is a distillation of almost 40 years of spiritual practice, empirical research, powerful personal transformational experience, and our ongoing journey into becoming the best versions of ourselves.

With incredible gratitude to all the spiritual and mystical masters, transformational teachers, and business mentors and coaches who have touched our lives with your books, your workshops, and most importantly your presence, we express a truly heartfelt thank you. We honor your dedication to being the change we all seek and sharing who you are with the world.

A very special thank you to our dear friend and transformationalist Godfather Jack Canfield who took the time to read *CODEBREAKER* and give us his feedback on a very rough first draft. He encouraged us to get feedback from a minimum of

10 beta readers, asked if we had read it out loud, and told us a book is not ready for publication until it has been rewritten at least six times. Well, thanks to Jack, it's been read out loud until we became hoarse and was sent to over 30 people whose feedback was instrumental in helping us rewrite it — far more than six times. We only half-jokingly say we learned a new way to spell relief: rewritten!

To everyone who has already read and re-read *CODEBREAKER*, we cannot thank you enough for your support, wisdom, and thoughtfulness in making this book better in every way. Thank you to all the editors and beta readers who shared their ideas on how to simplify and make a deep subject easier to comprehend.

Writing *CODEBREAKER* has been a roller coaster ride of excitement and overwhelm and appreciation for so many people. Infinite gratitude goes to Bill Bryant and Sandy Beamer, who have devoted months to helping us in the rewriting process. Daily, they asked us to give better explanations of concepts that were new to them, or that they thought needed clarification or simplification. They wanted more examples, and more stories, to make the teaching more memorable.

Their lives have changed because of their total immersion into *CODEBREAKER*. Can you imagine what a Godsend they were to us? After a lifetime of committed spiritual transformation practice and study, with the one transcendent desire to live an enlightened life, they helped us break down deep concepts that were normal and natural to us into bite-size chunks, to make everything easier to digest and use in your everyday life. We called them our Executive Editor and Associate Executive Editor. By the way, Bill actually is an ex-NSA codebreaker! Fortunately he's long retired so neither you nor we will have to be killed.

Deepest thanks and endless love to all our students and to our coaching and consulting clients, whose commitment and courage to move beyond limiting blocks continuously motivate us to find better, faster, and more effective processes. You inspire us with your dedication and honor us with your trust.

Master educator, curriculum designer and brilliant wordsmith Callan Rush powerfully coached us to improve the system as well as to present it accessibly – no easy feat when dealing with deeply spiritual material, but she was more than up to the challenge!

Our heartfelt thanks goes to Janice Clarke, our course content and design collaborator who contributed to this book in too many ways to count. Our master strategist, designer and formatter Brooks Cole has been essential in producing a work of art from the PLATINUM Life System and a joy to work with. Love and gratitude to spiritual stylist and rhetorician Mary Giuseffi whose ideas helped us refine this body of work to make it more elegant and accessible.

Ongoing thanks to Patty Aubrey – the genius we affectionately call "the guru maker" has always been there for us, sharing her expertise, answering questions or making suggestions.

Emily Han was our developmental editor who challenged us and impacted the finished work deeply.

Many thanks to Karen Maneely and the publishing team at BookBaby.

We are blessed to have the support of Ann Pirone, our huge-hearted PA and gal Friday and of Nick Ipolitti, our talented and knowledgable webmaster and guru of all things internet.

Two of our many spiritual mentors need special mention. Halima McEwen and Jo Howell have been God's eyes and ears and hands and voice for us innumerable times over many decades. Your selfless dedication has inspired and blessed us unto forever.

We were also blessed to receive fresh perspectives and valuable input from coaches and consultants Kristen White, Ann McIndoo, Denise Cassino and Steve Harrison and his brilliant team, Geoffrey Berwind, Raia King, Martha Bullen, Debra Englander and Danette Kubanda

Finally, we want to thank all our family, and those who have become family, for your continued support and love. Without love, the world would be a cold and unfriendly place, instead of the warm, uplifting, and inspiring place we are so grateful to live in.

SHARE YOUR TRANSFORMATIONAL EXPERIENCE

We trust you've experienced profound shifts and enjoyed your journey with us through *CODEBREAKER: Discover the Password to Unlock the Best Version of You.*

You now know how to live in a high frequency state. You have tools to free yourself from stress and suffering and to enjoy the happiness, success, and loving relationships you deserve.

Please consider sharing your experience with others. We all need to be the change we want to see. We're all called to serve the creation of a world that works for everyone. Letting others know how this might benefit them is really enlightened self-interest.

Using the social media of your choice — such as Tweeting about it or talking about it on Facebook and Instagram — will help others who are seeking a happier and more fulfilled life to know if this is a good fit for them.

We'd be very grateful if you would leave a review of the book on Amazon via the link below. Your feedback will not only serve others but help us to improve this book in subsequent editions. Thank you for your thoughtful consideration.

 Go here to leave a review on Amazon:
bit.ly/biskind

 Post to FACEBOOK:
facebook.com/TheBiskinds

 Tweet about this book: Twitter:
twitter.com/TheBiskinds

 Tell your story on Instagram:
instagram.com/sandrabiskind

 Enjoy our videos on on YouTube:
bit.ly/BiskindYouTube

Also check out: *Truth, Lies and Love* by Sandra Biskind

PLATINUM CIRCLES: COMING TOGETHER TO REALIGN WITH THE DIVINE

PLATINUM Circles are meetings of likeminded people to create a field of love so powerful that participants experience their unity and interconnectedness in life-changing ways.

PLATINUM Circles create a safe haven and invoke the presence of the divine we all hunger for in our lives...a place where people of diverse faiths (or no faith) can share a deep and meaningful spiritual experience without subscribing to any specific belief. We all need a spiritual home to optimize our growth and have the life of our dreams—a meeting ground where we can bond in the deepest possible way.

Participating in a PLATINUM Circle is a powerful way to spend more time with people who share your passion to live as the best version of themselves and be a powerful force for good on the planet.

PLATINUM Circles are small, regular group meetings for sharing prayer, healing, meditation, and intuition. By invitation only, the groups support one another's journey into enlightenment and wholeness. They become a spiritual family supporting each other with unconditional love and having each other's backs. As social beings, there is no substitute for reinforcing your new PLATINUM habits with peer support.

The experience of shared spiritual growth creates a sense of connection to the divine and all life for which there is no substitute.

Our DNA and genetic code expression can be changed by our environment, spiritual practices and community. Sitting in a PLATINUM circle helps develop strong neural pathways that strengthen immunity, longevity and the genetic code for happiness.

Developing new levels of awareness that dance with your genes is a key to finding inner peace and healing yourself, your community, and the planet.

Circles connect you with the meaning and power of your inner world where your ultimate happiness and success originate. C.G. Jung called circles "the archetype of wholeness and divinity." Developing wholeness and a strong, sustainable connection to divinity is to live a truly enlightened, empowered and inspired life.

A private mastermind participant asked Jack Canfield what was the best way to maintain a "retreat high." Based on his experience of over 600 trainings and seminars, he said two things stood out: 1.) regular meditation; and, 2.) participation in a mastermind or dedicated small group.

Beginning with hugs and healing starts to build group coherence. By sharing the same intention, God's highest and best for each other, we create an energy field that naturally supports the divine mind code and facilitates healing and higher awareness.

In group meditation you can have the extraordinary experience of being meditated by a trusted group.

While CODEBREAKER and the PLATINUM Life System are focused on living as the best version of you, we all want to know *"How do we create a world that works for everyone?"* As Rumi and sages from every tradition have emphasized, it begins with us. The higher our state of enlightenment and wholeness, the more we beneficially impact our world.

Popularly known as the "Maharishi effect," multiple studies over the last 60 years have documented the impact of group meditation on lowering rates of crime and violence and increasing positive trends.

The mission of PLATINUM Circles is to support a global movement of small groups to facilitate intrapersonal, interpersonal and planetary healing and transformation.

Sitting in a PLATINUM Circle is your soul's answer to its desire to merge with the love that is its essence — to know unity and oneness and to love like it has never loved before. Move toward real freedom, peace and joy and create or join a PLATINUM Circle today!

~ SANDRA & DANIEL BISKIND

Together we can help lift the consciousness of our planet. It is time for humanity to expand into its divine nature as the spiritually aware, mindful, tolerant and compassionate being that is our True Self.

Isn't it time to develop your divine essence, to live as the best version of you and have the loving relationships, wellbeing, happiness and success of your dreams? Your spiritual filling station is waiting for you!

We provide tools and resources to create and facilitate your own PLATINUM Circle at www.platinumcircles.org

---

ௐ   PLATINUM Circles: Go to
www.platinumcircles.org to get started.

CODEBREAKER TOOLS AND RESOURCES

PLATINUM MEDITATIONS

Want to be a high frequency meditator? We've created numerous meditations and activations to help you attune to the PLATINUM frequencies.

> 1. **DOWNLOAD:** Go to CodeBreakerBook.com/resources and download your free PLATINUM Meditations. (Password: PLATINUM)
>
> 2. **LISTEN:** Experience the meditations after reading each of the *CODEBREAKER* Part III Chapters 1–8.
>
> 3. **JOURNAL:** Capture your insights and impressions and track your progress in the perfect companion to your journey, the *CODEBREAKER Journal*, available at CodeBreakerBook.com/journal

Self Assessment

Want to know how your state calibrates? We have developed a customized Self Assessment to help you gauge your progress as you read and follow the PLATINUM Life System.

> **1. DOWNLOAD:** Go to CodebreakerBook.com/selfassessment and access your assessment. (Password: PLATINUM)
>
> **2. CALIBRATE:** Fill out the assessment to see how your ego mind and divine mind codes are influencing your life.
>
> **3. REVIEW:** Finish reading *CODEBREAKER*, and take the assessment again to see the progress you've made.

Ego Mind and Divine Mind Codes

Want to have some fun discovering what your codes look like?

🐾 **1. DOWNLOAD:** Go to <u>CodeBreakerBook.com/resources/</u> and download your code charts. (Password: PLATINUM)

🐾 **2. OVERVIEW:** Fill them out to see how your ego mind and divine mind codes are influencing your life.

🐾 **3. RECODE:** Finish reading *CODEBREAKER*, and go back to your charts to see how you can revise your codes.

CODEBREAKER COACHES

Want to be a high frequency CODEBREAKER Coach?

The CODEBREAKER Coaching Certification program is a unique opportunity to raise your own frequency while mastering skills to enhance your business and profession. This is an in-depth training in the use of the PLATINUM Life System and the Quantum Neutrality Process with Sandra and Daniel.

> **1. DOWNLOAD:** For more information on becoming a high frequency CODEBREAKER Coach go to Codebreakerbook.com/Coach and download your application. (Password: PLATINUM)
>
> **2. OVERVIEW:** Fill out the application form and send your completed form to: coach@thebiskinds.com.
>
> **3. REVIEW:** Once your application has been reviewed and accepted, you will be on your way to accelerating your journey into enlightenment and wholeness — yours and humanity's!

INDEX OF POEMS

Poems by Hafiz and translated by Daniel Ladinsky
and used with his permission.

IN ORDER OF APPEARANCE